Edmund Quincy, Josiah Quincy

Speeches delivered in the Congress of the United States

By Josiah Quincy, member of the House of representatives for the Suffolk district of

Massachusetts, 1805-1813

Edmund Quincy, Josiah Quincy

Speeches delivered in the Congress of the United States
By Josiah Quincy, member of the House of representatives for the Suffolk district of Massachusetts, 1805-1813

ISBN/EAN: 9783337185466

Printed in Europe, USA, Canada, Australia, Japan

Cover: Foto ©Suzi / pixelio.de

More available books at **www.hansebooks.com**

CONGRESSIONAL SPEECHES

OF

J O S I A H   Q U I N C Y.

1805–1813.

SPEECHES

DELIVERED IN THE

CONGRESS OF THE UNITED STATES:

BY JOSIAH QUINCY,

MEMBER OF THE HOUSE OF REPRESENTATIVES FOR THE SUFFOLK
DISTRICT OF MASSACHUSETTS,

1805–1813.

EDITED BY HIS SON,

EDMUND QUINCY,

FELLOW OF THE AMERICAN ACADEMY OF ARTS AND SCIENCES; MEMBER OF THE AMERICAN
PHILOSOPHICAL SOCIETY HELD AT PHILADELPHIA, AND OF THE HISTORICAL
SOCIETIES OF MASSACHUSETTS AND NEW HAMPSHIRE.

BOSTON:

LITTLE, BROWN, AND COMPANY.

1874.

PREFACE.

Seven years ago, — September, 1867, — I published a Life of my father, which had a reception from the public of the most gratifying description, far beyond my warmest hopes. Five editions were disposed of in the course of two years, and the demand has not yet entirely ceased. This success I attribute chiefly to the interest felt in my father by the many eminent and useful men in all parts of the country who gratefully remembered his influence .on their characters while President of the University, as well as by the newer generation who learned to know and admire him from the active part he took in the political agitations which went before the Civil War, and the Emancipation which it compelled. It was, however, my opinion then, as it is now, that his permanent repntation, after the generation that knew him personally shall have passed away, and his claim to a modest place in the history of his country, rest rather upon his action on the wider scene of national politics at Washington, at a most interesting and critical period of our affairs. I therefore made liberal extracts from his Congressional Speeches as an integral and vital portion of his life, and I have reason to think that these were regarded by the best of my readers as adding largely to the interest of the book. My own opinion being thus re-enforced, I venture to offer to the public this collection of his Congressional Speeches in full, hoping that it may be regarded as an illustration, not without value, of the spirit and temper of the times when they were uttered.

The passage of history to which my father's Congressional career belongs, lies at that precise distance from the present day which makes its facts indistinct to the minds of all of our contemporaries, excepting the daily dwindling number whose memories go back to those times. It is too remote for the memory of the mass of living men, and not remote enough to tempt the hand of the philosophic historian. The period, however, from the inauguration of Washington to that of Monroe, will be found full of materials for brilliant treatment by the American historian whom we yet wait for. Party spirit has never been so fierce and malignant, passions and opinions have never clashed so furiously, equally honest and patriotic men have never differed more bitterly or more sincerely, than in those far-off days. The old ideas encountered the new ideas, and the collision shook civil society to the centre. Great men, too, were called for, and appeared upon the scene, whose figures are now but indistinctly discerned through the mists of time, but who will yet be displayed in their just proportions by the light to be thrown upon them by genius. John Jay, Alexander Hamilton, Fisher

Ames, William Pinkney, Samuel Dexter, Timothy
Pickering, James A. Bayard, will again become
the household words they were three quarters of a
century ago. The germs of the union of the Democratic party and the Slave Oligarchy, which gave
the nation over into the hands of the Slave Power
for more than half a century, to be rescued only at
the fearful cost of the Civil War, will there be
detected and displayed. And the mischiefs of a
doctrinaire statesmanship were never better shown
than in the miseries inflicted upon the whole
country, but especially upon the Northern Atlantic
States, by the reduction to legislation of the
political reveries of an *idéologue* like Mr. Jefferson,
in the Embargo and the Non-Intercourse and the
War of 1812, in which these measures naturally
culminated, though unforeseen and undesired by
their author. It is observable that the interest
and importance of the portion of our national history with which these speeches of Mr. Quincy have
to do, were more fully understood and set forth by
the London " Spectator," and " Pall Mall Gazette,"
and the Paris " Revue des Deux Mondes," all of
which journals had able and elaborate articles on his
Life, than by some American periodicals, which
inclined to regard it as an obscure and insignificant
chapter in our annals. When the historian of the
future shall come to treat of those events, the
public utterances of public men will be among his
best materials for that revivification of the passions
and opinions of the men of the time which forms
the living spirit of history. I trust that this collec-

tion will then be considered as neither useless nor
unimportant as expressing the thoughts and emo-
tions which made up the inner life of no inconsiderable portion of the American people.

As to the merit of these Speeches as specimens
of parliamentary oratory, it is not for me to speak.
Whatever may be their force and skill, critically
considered, be the same less or more, I know that
they are most characteristic of the man, and very ex-
pressive of the sentiments and feelings of the noble
Federal party to which he belonged, and which at
one time he led. I should hardly, however, have
presumed to collect them in this permanent form
had I not been encouraged to do so by the judgments of men to which my own must bow, and
which more than confirmed any estimation I might
have put upon them myself. Among these encouraging counsellors I may be permitted to name
my valued friends, the late Senator Sumner, and
Mr. Motley, the historian of the Dutch Republic,
both of whom held opinions as to my father's rank
among parliamentary orators which I shall not venture to repeat, and which I cannot but consider as
heightened in some degree by their reverential affection for his person. But, all allowances made,
enough of encouragement remains, given by judges
so eminent, to make it the less presumptuous in me
to hope for a favorable reception for this collection
from the small but enlightened class who care for
matters of the sort. One thing I may be permitted to say of these Speeches of my father.
They *are* his Speeches, as they came from his mind

and from his lips without amendment or correction of mine. Some very eminent orators of our time have carefully revised and altered their speeches, or left them to the correction of their friends, years after they were delivered. Thus, doubtless, admirable literary performances have been secured to us, but they are not the speeches as they were uttered by the speakers in the heat of debate, characteristic of the men and of the times, and perhaps rather smell of the lamp than savor of the Senate-house. My father never cared enough about the matter to do any thing of the kind, and I consider it the part both of filial duty and of good taste to present his speeches to the public of to-day as they were addressed to the public of seventy years since. I feel that any attempt of mine to improve his style would only impair its force and injure its characteristic qualities. I have confined myself, therefore, as editor, to the correction of obvious errors of the press, or of the imperfect reporting of those times, and I have thus endeavored to print these Speeches as nearly as possible as he spoke them.

I have ventured to prefix to each Speech a short introduction explaining the political circumstances under which it was delivered. I judged that some elucidation of the kind would be useful to readers who are not familiar with the history of those times. I have made them as brief as is consistent with this object.

DEDHAM, MASSACHUSETTS,
November 1st, 1874.

b

CONTENTS.

SPEECH

ON THE BILL FOR FORTIFYING THE PORTS AND HARBORS OF THE UNITED STATES.

APRIL 15, 1806.

1

SPEECH

ON THE BILL FOR FORTIFYING THE PORTS AND HARBORS OF THE UNITED STATES.

April 15, 1806.

————

[The state of affairs, domestic and foreign, at the beginning of 1806 was briefly this. Of the sympathies and antipathies of the Federal and Democratic parties in relation to France and England, I have given some account in the preface to this volume. For the quarter of a century, from the beginning of the French Revolution to the battle of Waterloo, the hopes, the fears, the passions, and the politics of the United States were indissolubly connected with those of Europe. We were, during those years, in continual danger of being drawn into the wars which, with brief intervals of truce, occupied the nations of Europe. It was against this peril that the warning voice of Washington was raised in his Farewell Address when he admonished his countrymen to beware of "entangling alliances" with foreign powers. These were no superfluous words of caution, and it is likely that it was our poverty rather than our will that restrained us from taking a part, most disastrous to ourselves, on one side or the other of those fateful conflicts, according as sympathy with France or with England had the ascendant in the public opinion of the time.

Previous to 1805, these wars had indeed been of direct benefit to the United States. Being the only neutral power of any maritime importance, the carrying-trade was almost entirely in American hands. All the colonial productions of France and

Holland and of Spain, since her alliance with France, were first brought to some American port and thence reshipped to the respective mother countries. The American ship-owners, thus having the advantage of double freights, carried on an immensely profitable business; and large fortunes, as they were esteemed in those simple days, were made in it. The English government at last discerned that this system gave France the benefit of the trade of her own colonies and those of her allies almost as fully as in time of peace. So the Courts of Admiralty revised the old doctrines of International Law, and confiscated several American cargoes on the ground that our flag was used as the cover of a fraudulent transaction, the property having never really belonged to the American merchant, having been landed in the neutral port merely for reshipment to a hostile one.

These decisions, destroying as they did a most lucrative trade, created great dissatisfaction; and they were the beginning of those unfriendly relations between the two countries which finally culminated in the War of 1812. And, although the neutrality of the United States was vitally beneficial to France and Spain, they could not resist the temptation our rich merchant-vessels offered to their cruisers, which often seized them on small pretexts, or none at all, and thus gave rise to the French and Spanish claims of our later history. Besides these complications, we were in a condition of very dubious friendship with Spain, which had then some remains of her former pride and power. In 1803 Bonaparte sold Louisiana to the United States under circumstances which colored our whole history for two generations, and of which we shall give an account by and by. Spain had ceded back to France, in 1800, this territory which she had received from that power, in 1762, in compensation for her losses in the war which ended in the conquest of Canada. Whatever motives induced this action, it was certainly without the expectation that this territory would be almost immediately handed over to a growing republic conterminous with her other North American possessions. Had she been strong enough it might even have been made a *casus belli*. As it was, she protested energetically against the treaty of 1803; actually occupied posts within our undoubted boundaries; and her minister, Irujo, treated President Jefferson with insolent contempt.

Our foreign relations being in this queasy condition, when a slight and unforeseen contingency might bring a fleet upon our coasts and into the harbors of our cities, it seemed as if some kind of preparation should be made against such a possibility. Mr. Jefferson did not deny this, and he urged the necessity of preparation against possible hostilities. But, in his morbid fear of spending money, he limited his suggestion to the equipping of gun-boats to lie in wait for the enemy and issue from their ambush on his approach, and to a classification of the militia, by which, on the approach of danger, the younger men should forsake the plough and the work-bench and rush to the rescue. The Federalists, and especially those representing the commercial States, thought these precautions quite insufficient. As the commerce of the country furnished almost the entire support of the government, and had provided the fifteen millions required for the purchase of Louisiana and the two millions for that of Florida, they deemed it but reasonable that a moderate proportion of the money they supplied should be spent in the fortification of the Atlantic cities. During the seventeen years of our national existence, only seven hundred and twenty-four thousand dollars had been spent for the fortification of the nine chief commercial cities!' By the bill, during the discussion of which the following speech was delivered, one hundred and fifty thousand dollars was appropriated for the defence of New York, and a motion to substitute five hundred thousand was treated with contempt and received only twenty-seven votes. All propositions to increase the amount, or to leave a blank sum to be used at the discretion of the President, were laughed to scorn. — ED.]

MR. CHAIRMAN, — Gentlemen seem disposed to treat this subject lightly, and to indulge themselves in pleasantries, on a question very serious to the commercial cities and to the interest of those who inhabit them. It may be sport to you, gentlemen, but it is death to us. However well disposed a majority of this House may be to treat this bill ludicrously, it will fill great and influential portions of this nation with very different sentiments. Men, who have all that human nature holds dear — friends, fortunes, and families — concentrated in one single spot on the sea-coast, and that spot exposed every moment to be plundered and desolated, will not highly relish or prize at an extreme value, the wit or the levity, with which this House seems inclined to treat the dangers which threaten them; and which are sources to them of great and just apprehensions. I do not rise, Mr. Chairman, merely to support the motion made by the gentleman from New York. It is not the fortification of this or that particular city which I mean to advocate. I should have preferred a general appropriation, leaving it to the discretion of the executive to apply it to those ports and harbors which are either most exposed or most important. And if, by any thing that shall occur in the course of the discussion, the House shall be induced to change what at present seems to be its disposition, I hope the augmented appropriation will be made in that form. It is to the general duty which is incumbent upon this legislature to protect the commercial cities, that I would call its attention. This duty is so plain and imperious, that, in my opinion, an awful weight of responsibility rests upon this House. Every class and collection of citizens have a right to claim from government that species of protection which their situation requires, in proportion to their exposure, and to the greatness of the stake which society has in their safety. Our obligation to protect the commercial cities does not result from the particular exigency which at present impends over our nation, but from the nature of those cities. The duty is permanent and ought to be fulfilled by a permanent system. A regular course of annual appropriations may in a very few years put all our capital cities in a state of reasonable security, and, at no very distant period of time, without any additional imposition on the people, give every city on our coast an adequate defence. It is in this light that I consider the question now before the committee to be important. Not that any sum which may be inserted will be immediately sufficient for all the objects for which we have to provide. But that any augmentation of the appropriation will be a pledge to the nation of the disposition of this House to commence a system of defence for our cities : any evidence of which will give just satisfaction to great masses of your citizens, as an appearance of a want of it will fill them with no less discontent and dismay. In this point of view I ask the indulgence of the committee to a few observations on the importance of fortifications, their utility and practicability.

As to the importance of the objects for which we ask a defence, it seems to me either not understood or not realized. Almost all who have spoken on the subject have dwelt chiefly, if not altogether, on the amount of revenue drawn from the commercial cities; as if their value was to be appreciated, and our duty to defend them measured, by the annual produce they yield. This, it is true, makes a natural part of the estimate of their worth, but, as I apprehend, by no means the most important. Their situation, the number of the inhabitants, the great portion of the active and fixed capital of society which they contain, are, in a national view, standards much more just and more elevated by which to ascertain their value and our obligations. I ask, sir, what is the amount of the capital of this nation which is invested in the single city of New York? The annual product it yields to our revenue is three millions of dollars. Now suppose the average of import duties is only ten per cent *ad valorem* (a sum certainly below the real average), the annual amount of capital deposited in imports is then thirty millions of dollars. The amount of value in exports cannot be estimated at less than twenty millions. If to these be added the capital of its banks, the amount of stock always on hand, that of its shipping and other personal property, — all of which no one can rate below another fifty millions, — the result is that there is in annual deposit, within the city of New York alone, one hundred millions of the active capital of this nation. I know how far this is below the real estimate, but I state this sum that no one may hesitate to admit my position. I ask, then, what is it worth to insure this sum against the risk of an invasion, not on calculations on the great national scale, but on a mere insurance-office arithmetic? I have been told that to insure that city against such a risk, for one single year of war with any of the great maritime nations of Europe, would be worth five per cent. That is the insurance for a single year of war would repay the expense of fortifications, even should they cost five millions of dollars. But, suppose this calculation extravagant, can any one doubt that such an insurance in time of peace, against the double risk of war and of attack in case of war, is worth one-half per cent? Even at this premium, six years of insurance in time of peace would repay the expenditure of three millions, — a sum more than adequate to the defence of that city. In making this statement, I would not be understood to pretend or to propose such an appropriation : it is not asked. My object is to call gentlemen to consider what is the market worth of security, and that they may not deem the moneys they apply to these objects — as they seem willing to deem them — absolutely thrown away. This great mass of the national wealth, thus concentrated on the bank of one of the most exposed harbors in the world, is liable to the insult and depredation of the most despicable force. Two seventy-four gun-ships may, at this moment, lay that city under contribution or in ashes with impunity. They might make it the interest of the inhabitants of that city to pay an amount equal to the whole annual revenue we derive from it, rather than to submit to the hazard and miseries of bombardment and conflagration. For in such case the mere destruction of property is but an item in the account of anticipated misfortune. The shock to credit ; the universal stagnation of business ; the terror spread through every class, age, and sex ; the thousands who have no refuge in the country, but must take the fate, and be buried under the ruins, of their city, — all these circumstances would enter into consideration, and make the pecuniary sacrifice, however great, appear trifling in comparison. I have used the city of New York only by way of example. The same observations are applicable to every other commercial city in the United States in proportion to its magnitude and the

nature of its situation. Two seventy-fours might sweep
the coast from Savannah to Portland, and levy an
amount equal to the whole annual revenue of the
United States. It would be better for any city voluntarily to pay a contribution equal to its proportion of
that amount, rather than to take the alternative of that
destruction to which, on refusal, it would be obliged to
submit. Is such a state of things as this a light and
trifling concern ? Are such portions of the wealth of
the community to be left exposed to the caprice of
every plunderer ; and are propositions to protect them
to be treated with contempt or ridicule ? Can any duty
be more solemn or imperious than that which has for its
object a rational degree of security for those ports in
the United States which are beyond all others exposed
to hostile attack, at the same time that they comprise,
within the smallest possible compass, immense masses
of the national wealth and population ?

The importance, then, of the objects to be defended
will be admitted. But the utility of fortifications, as a
means of defence, and their practicability in certain
ports and harbors, are denied. With respect to the general utility of fortifications, I ask, by whom is it denied ?
By men interested in that species of defence ? By the
inhabitants of cities ? By those the necessity of whose
situation has turned their attention to the nature of
fortifications and their efficacy ? No, sir : these men
solicit them. They are anxious for nothing so much.
They tell you, the safety of all they hold dear, — their
wives, their children, their fortunes, and lives are staked
upon your decision. They do not so much as ask fortifications as a favor : they claim them as a right. They

demand them. Who are they, then, that deny their utility? Why, men from the interior. Men who in one breath tell you they know nothing about the subject, and in the next pass judgment against the adoption of any measures of defence. It is true, sir, to men who inhabit the White Hills of New Hampshire, or the Blue Ridge of Virginia, nothing can appear more absolutely useless than appropriations for the defence of the sea-coast. In this, as in all other cases, men reason very coolly and philosophically concerning dangers to which they are not themselves subject. All men, for the most part, bear with wonderful composure the misfortunes of other people. And, if called to contribute to their relief, they are sure to find, in the cold suggestions of economy, apologies enough for failure in their social duties. The best criterion of the utility of fortifications is the practice and experience of other nations. Now, I ask, was there ever a nation which did not defend its great commercial deposits, by either land fortifications or sea batteries? All history does not exhibit such an instance. Are we wiser, then, than all other nations; or are we less exposed than they? Are we alone to escape the common lot of humanity? Can we expect to be rich, and not tempt the spirit of avarice? To be defenceless amid armed pirates, and in no danger of robbery or insult? I ask again, sir, how is the inutility of fortifications proved? Suppose, for the sake of argument, it should be admitted — which, however, I deny — that they cannot be erected in sufficient force to defeat very great armaments; yet is it nothing to prevent the piratical attempts of single ships? Is it nothing to deter an invader? Nothing even to delay an attack? Is it worth nothing to have the chance of crippling an assailant? The only argument I have heard urged against the utility of fortifications is, that the whole coast cannot be fortified ; so that, protect as strongly as you will particular points, the invader will land somewhere else. Sir, this is the very object of fortifications. No man ever thought of building a Chinese wall along all the indentations of our shore, from the St. Mary's to the St. Croix. The true object of fortifications is to oblige your enemies to land : it is to keep them at arm's length. If they cannot reach your cities with their batteries, and would attack, they must come on shore. They are then only a land force, and our militia will find no difficulty in giving a good account of them. The only remaining arguments in the possession of this House, against the utility of fortifications, are the opinions of various gentlemen, delivered on this floor; and that of the secretary at war, as stated in his report. As to the former, they certainly do not merit a serious refutation, because no gentleman who has spoken has pretended to a practical or even theoretical knowledge of the subject; but, on the contrary, most, if not all of them, have candidly confessed their ignorance. It is of more importance to consider the opinion of the secretary at war. That part of his report which relates to the harbor of New York contains his general opinion against the practicability of defending such a harbor by land batteries, and two facts in support of that opinion. Now, as to the general opinion of the secretary, I am willing to allow it whatever weight any gentleman may choose to attach to it ; but certainly it ought not to be conclusive in an affair of such immense importance; especially when it is contradicted by the tenor of the applications on your table, and by the opinions of other individuals of as high military and scientific reputation as the secretary. Much less does this his opinion claim from us an implicit confidence; since the only two facts he has chosen to adduce are very far from being a sufficient basis for the broad opinion he has built on them. The first fact is one which occurred in the harbor of New York in 1776. A British ship of forty guns passed the batteries on the Hudson, under circumstances favorable to the effect of the batteries, and sustained "a tremendous fire" without being sensibly "incommoded." Allowing this fact its full force, it can weigh but little against the utility or practicability of fortifications. That was the second year of the war. Our batteries were erected on a sudden emergency. Our artillerists had probably little experience. Will it be pretended that the batteries this nation, in its present state of affluence and experience can erect, will not exceed, both in location and power, those which at that time protected the Hudson? Besides, to draw from a particular instance a general conclusion is contrary to all rules of just logic. Various circumstances, altogether accidental, might have occurred to have produced that result, which might never occur again. If this instance be a good argument against the validity of land fortifications, there is an equally strong argument in the history of our revolution against the fashionable mode of defence by gun-boats. I take the fact only from verbal information; and, if I am incorrect, there are gentlemen on this floor who can set me right. During the war, a

British frigate of forty-four guns, called the " Roebuck,"
took ground in the Delaware ; and though we had gun-
boats *quantum sufficit*, who pelted her to their hearts' content, during one whole tide, she received no manner of
injury, at least none of any importance.   If I have this
fact correctly, it is just as strong against the efficacy of
gun-boats as that produced by the secretary is against
land batteries.   One word here concerning this mode of
defence by gun-boats, which seems to concentrate all
the naval affections of our rulers, and to have on freight
all their military hopes.   It is not denied that these are
weapons of considerable effect ; or that in certain situations they are useful ; or that, in aid of other and heavier
batteries, they may not sometimes be important.   It is
only when they become the favorites, to the total exclusion of more powerful modes of defence, and draw
away to the less power appropriations which are wanting for the greater, that the system which upholds
them becomes an object of contempt or of dread.
Nowadays, sir, put what you will into the crucible, —
whether it be seventy-fours, or frigates, or land batteries,
— the result is the same : after due sweltering in the legislative furnace, there comes out nothing but gun-boats.
I ask if our cities are attacked by any maritime nation,
will it not be by line-of-battle ships ; and who ever
heard that a line-of-battle ship was defeated by gun-
boats ?   I do not pretend to be learned in these matters ;
but, as far as I have been able to gain information, it is,
that when there is any thing of a heavy sea, even such
as is often in the harbor of New York, gun-boats are of
very little efficacy.   It is true, in case of a calm, if they
can get their object at rest they have a great advantage ;

that is, if you can get the bird to stand still until you
can put salt upon its tail, you can catch the bird. But
the worst of it is, that it is too cunning for that. The
ship of the line chooses its own time for the attack, and
will always select that which is least favorable to its
adversary.

But to return to the report of the secretary at war.
The next fact it states is the battle of Copenhagen.
Now if this be adduced merely as an evidence of a particular instance of the inefficacy of land batteries, I do
not think it important enough to take the time to
examine. The true question is not whether New York
can be defended in a particular way, but whether it is
capable of defence at all, by combining land with float-
ing batteries. In this point of view, the instance
adduced by the secretary is perhaps the most memora-
ble on record, and the one, of all others, in which those
who advocate a defence of our commercial cities ought
to exult as in an incontrovertible evidence of the truth
of their system. What was the fact? One of the best
appointed naval armaments of the most powerful maritime nation in the world, under her most favored and
fortunate commander, was sent to attack Copenhagen.
The Danes were taken by surprise. Every thing,
apparently, was in favor of the assailant and against
those who acted on the defensive. To fifteen line-of-
battle ships, the Danes had nothing to oppose but their
land and harbor batteries, fortifications, and block ships.
And what was the result? Why that, after a most
bloody and well-contested battle, the British first asked
a truce. To this day the Danes claim the victory.
Olfort Fischer, the Danish commander, in his official

statement of the battle, declares that, before the flag
of truce was offered, two of the British ships of the
line had struck their colors, and that for some time their
whole line was so weakened that it fired only single
guns. Intelligent Europeans assert, and even candid
Englishmen will allow, that, if ever Nelson was beaten,
it was on that occasion. But suppose all this to be
erroneous. Suppose that Nelson obtained a real victory,
does it thence result that the fortifications and the
block ships with which Copenhagen was defended were
useless? By no means. Still that battle is an illustrious and irrefragable instance of their utility. It is a
fact on record, worth a million theories, in favor of the
efficacy of a harbor defence against a maritime force.
Sir, the end for which those batteries were erected is
attained. Copenhagen is defended. The storm which
would have desolated the city has spent its force on the
artificial shield. Let gentlemen calculate the probable
cost of those batteries, and suppose by expending a
similar sum in the harbor of New York, that city might
be defended as Copenhagen was and from a like danger.
Is there a man that can hesitate as to the wisdom of
such an expenditure? Sir, the city of Copenhagen on
that day was preserved from a devastation which the
cost of twenty such batteries would not have repaired.
I conclude, then, that our commercial cities can be
defended, even the most exposed of them: land batteries combined with harbor batteries are equal to the
object. To this question of practicability, concerning
which so much is said, I humbly conceive this not
the place where it ought to be decided. It belongs
to the executive. That is the proper department to

examine into it. Our duty is to make the appropriations, to show at least a disposition to defend. If New York cannot be defended, is it the same case with Charleston, Savannah, or Norfolk? Shall we leave the whole defenceless, because a particular part is vulnerable? Sir, let us confess the truth. The limit of our power to defend is not in the nature of the cities, but in our disposition to appropriate. Not in the inefficacy of land or harbor batteries, but in our insensibility to the danger of the commercial cities and unwillingness to make the pecuniary sacrifices their protection requires. On all sides we are met with the objection, "Where are the means?" "How is the public debt to be discharged, if we incur such an expense?" Mr. Chairman, none of these difficulties are insurmountable, when southern land is to be purchased, or when our new territories on the Missouri and Red River are to be explored, or when Indian titles in the western country are to be extinguished. We have paid within these two years fifteen millions of dollars for Louisiana, and have sent off two millions more to purchase the Floridas. I ask on what principle can either of these purchases be made palatable to the people of the United States? Do they want more land or wider dominions? On neither of these considerations would they for one moment have submitted to either purchase. It was because the possession of the Mississippi through its whole course was essential to the security and happiness of our brethren beyond the mountains, that the purchase of Louisiana was sanctioned by public opinion, and if ever that of the Floridas receives the acquiescence of the people, it will only be from the conviction

2

that the possession of those countries is necessary for
the tranquillity of our southern frontier. All this we
have done for the security of the south and west: we
now ask for reciprocity; grant us something for the
security of the north and east. Let not the people see
that all the incomes proceed from one quarter of the
Union, and all the expenditures are made in another.
Let them not learn from experience, that the ball of
favoritism and that of empire is travelling south and
west. I ask, what are the Floridas, or what is Louisiana, in comparison with the single city of New York?
This city alone is worth forty Louisianas. Yet when
Louisiana was purchased, did the increase of the public
debt prevent the bargain? Or, later, was the question
of "means" an obstacle to the appropriation for the
Floridas? The seventeen millions of dollars thus expended for the security of the south would have put
every commercial city of the United States into a complete state of defence. I do not, Mr. Chairman, introduce the purchase of Louisiana and the Floridas in this
connection lightly, or without antecedent reflection: I
would hold up to this house a mirror in which it may
contemplate itself and see its own features. It is
impossible not to remark that the sympathies of the
majority of this legislature do not extend to the sea-
coast. But whatever will meliorate the condition of
the interior excites all its sensibilities and awakens all
its anxieties. Look at this moment on your table:
there are now no less than four, I believe five, Indian
treaties which have been ratified the present session,
the appropriations for which occasion no alarm about
the public faith or the public purse. It is worth our

while to notice the particulars. By these treaties the
United States agree to pay : —

First, cash down	$37,600
Next, the following annuities : —	
$1,600 for ten years	16,000
$12,000 for eight years	96,000
$11,000 for ten years	110,000
	$259,600

In addition to which we are to pay other annuities,
amounting to $4,000 for ever. These last cannot be
estimated at less in any market than $50,000, but
which I rate only at   40,000

$300,000

Besides which, our appropriation for the Indian department and for the support of the civil government
of Louisiana, and our other south-western territory,
exceed   150,000

$150,000

Thus in this single session we shall have appropriated
four hundred and fifty thousand dollars, for the security
and protection of the south-west. But for our ports
and harbors, an appropriation of one hundred and fifty
thousand dollars for the mere repair of old fortifications
is thought to be an enormous expenditure. Even this
is violently opposed. But any additional sum to begin
new works is not only hopeless, but cannot even be
named without exciting a smile of contempt.

Now let us look at the other side of the account. It
will be found, by the report on your table, that the
nine capital cities of the Union — Portland, Portsmouth.

Boston, Newport, New York, Philadelphia, Baltimore, Norfolk, and Charleston — have had expended in fortifications for their defence, since the establishment of the federal government, only seven hundred and twenty-four thousand dollars! That is to say, your appropriations in one session, for the security and comfort of the south-west, is more than half the whole amount expended during sixteen years for the security of all these great commercial cities, which contain two or three hundred thousand inhabitants, and which paid into your treasury the last year upwards of nine millions of dollars! It is impossible that this state of things should not be understood and realized by the people of these States; and that at no very distant period. It requires only some actual suffering, some real misfortune, resulting from your ill-timed parsimony or misplaced affections, to rouse a spirit in the commercial States which will shake this Union to its foundation. Of all times those will be the most dreadful and the most to be deprecated by every real lover of his country, when the party passions shall run parallel to local interests. Whenever any great section of the Union shall deem itself neglected, and the opinion becomes general among the people that they are either sacrificed or abandoned, that they have not any, or not their just, weight in the national scale, a series of struggles must commence, which will terminate either in redress or in convulsions. Events of this kind are not to be prevented by common-place declamation about submission to the will of the majority. A real reciprocity must exist. Intelligent men must see and feel that a regard, proportionate to their real interest at stake in the society, is entertained for them by their rulers. With such perception and experience your Union is a bond of adamant which nothing can break. Without them, I will not say it will be dissolved, but this I will say, — it cannot be happy, even if it should be lasting.

It is impossible to form a just estimate of our obligations to defend the commercial cities, without having a right idea of the nature and importance of commerce to the eastern States, and attaining a just apprehension of its influence over every class of citizens in that quarter of the Union. From what has fallen from various gentlemen in the House, it is very apparent that they do not appreciate either its nature, its power, or the duties which result from our relation to those who are engaged in that pursuit. The gentleman from Virginia (Mr. J. Randolph) told us the other day, that "the United States was a great land animal, a great mammoth, which ought to cleave to the land, and not wade out into the ocean to fight the shark." Sir, the figure is very happy so far as relates to that quarter of the Union with which that gentleman is chiefly conversant. Of the southern States, the mammoth is a correct type. But I ask, sir, suppose the mammoth has made a league with the cod, and that the cod, enterprising, active, and skilful, spreads himself over every ocean, and brings back the tribute of all climes to the feet of the mammoth; suppose he thereby enables the unwieldy animal to stretch his huge limbs upon cotton, or to rub his fat sides along his tobacco plantations, without paying the tithe of a hair, — in such case, is it wise, is it honorable, is it politic, for that mammoth, because by mere beef and bone he outweighs the cod in the political scale, to refuse a portion of that revenue which the industry of the cod annually produces, to defend him in his natural element; if not against the great leviathan of the deep, at least against the petty pikes which prowl on the ocean; and if not in the whole course of his adventurous progress, at least in his native bays and harbors, where his hopes and wealth are deposited and where his species congregate?

Other gentlemen have shown an equal want of a just apprehension of the nature and effects of commerce. Some think any of its great channels can be impeded or cut off without important injury. Others that it is a matter of so much indifference that we can very well do without it. The gentleman from Pennsylvania (Mr. Smilie) told us some days since, " that for his part he wished that at the time of our Revolution there had been no commerce." That honorable gentleman, I presume, is enamoured with Arcadian scenes, with happy valleys. Like a hero of pastoral romance at the head of some murmuring stream, with his crook by his side, his sheep feeding around, far from the temptations, unseduced by the luxuries of commerce, he would

> . . . " sport with Amaryllis in the shade,
> Or with the tangles of Neæra's hair."

I will not deny that these are pleasant scenes. Doubtless they are well suited to the innocence, the purity, and the amiable unobtrusive simplicity of that gentleman's mind and manners. But he must not expect that all men can be measured by his elevated standard, or be made to relish these sublime pleasures. Thousands and ten thousands in that part of the country I would

represent have no notion of rural felicity, or of the tran-
quil joys of the country. They love a life of activity,
of enterprise, and hazard. They would rather see a
boat-hook than all the crooks in the world ; and as for
sheep, they never desire to see any thing more of them
than just enough upon their deck to give them fresh
meat once a week in a voyage. Concerning the land of
which the gentleman from Virginia (Mr. J. Randolph),
and the one from North Carolina (Mr. Macon), think
so much, they think very little. It is in fact to them
only a shelter from the storm ; a perch on which they
build their aerie and hide their mate and their young,
while they skim the surface or hunt in the deep. The
laws of society and the views of enlightened politicians
ought to have reference, not to any ideal, theoretic state
of human perfection, but to the equal protection and
encouragement of every species of honorable industry.
I know it has been said by way of apology for not doing
any thing more in defence of commerce, that it already
was indebted for its prosperity to our laws and regulations. The gentleman from Virginia (Mr. J. Randolph) told us expressly " that the votes of southern
men had given us our drawbacks and discriminating
duties," whence he would conclude that our commerce
and navigation had nothing more to ask at their hands.
The honorable speaker, too, referred the prosperous condition of our commerce to the adoption of the Constitution and to the provisions established under it. I am
the last man in the world to deny the happy influence
of that instrument in meliorating the condition of this
nation. But our commercial prosperity is owing much
more to accident and nature, and much less to law, than

we are apt to imagine or are willing to allow. Every
year we get together on this floor to consult concerning
the public good. The state of commerce makes a capital object in all our deliberations. We have our committee of commerce and manufactures, and a great part
of every session is exhausted in discussing their provisions, limitations, and restrictions, until at last we slide
into the belief that commerce is of our creation ; that it
has its root in the statute book ; that its sap is drawn
from our parchment, and that it spreads and flourishes
under the direct heat of the legislative ray. But what
is the fact ? Look into your laws. What are they ?
Nine-tenths — I should speak nearer the truth should I
say ninety-nine-hundredths of them — are nothing more
than means by which you secure your share of the
products of commerce ; they constitute the machinery
by which you pluck its Hesperian fruit, and have nothing to do with the root that supports it, or with the
native vigor which exudes into this rich luxuriance.
Sir, the true tap-root of commerce is found in the
nature and character of the people who carry it on.
They and their ancestors for nearly two centuries have
been engaged in it. The industry of every class of men
in the eastern States has reference to its condition, and
is affected by it. Why then treat it as a small concern;
as an affair only of traders and of merchants? Why
intimate that agriculture can flourish without it ? when,
in fact, the interests of these two branches of industry
are so intimately connected that the slightest affection
of the one is instantly communicated to the other. I
know very well that there is a great difference between
the relations of commerce and agriculture in the south-

ern and in the eastern States. And this is one of the chief causes of that diversity of sentiment which prevails among those who dwell in these different parts of the Union. In the southern States there are comparatively few, if any, who depend on commerce altogether for subsistence. Whatever affects commercial prosperity produces no general distress or discontent, Perhaps insurance or freight may advance a little in consequence of its embarrassment. Perhaps one or other of their great staples may find not so ready or so high a market. But these inconveniences throw none out of employment or out of bread. Very different is the state of things in the eastern States. There commerce is not merely as the honorable speaker called it, " a waggon, a mode of conveyance of product to the consumer ; " it is more, infinitely more : it establishes within the country an immense fund of internal consumption. All its dependants, merchants, tradesmen, mechanics, seamen, and laborers of every class and description, look to it, either for that profit which makes a great portion of their happiness, or for that employment on which their subsistence depends.

The state of agriculture is adapted, and has been for centuries, to the supply of the wants of this internal consumption. The farmer is bound to commerce by a thousand intimate ties which, while it is in its ordinary state of prosperity, he neither sees nor realizes. But let the current stop and the course of business stagnate in consequence of any violent affection to commerce, the effect is felt as much, and in some cases more, by those who inhabit the mountains, as by those who dwell on the sea-coast. The country is associated with the city

in one common distress, not merely through sympathy
but by an actual perception of a union in misfortune.
It is this indissoluble community of interest between
agriculture and commerce, which pervades the eastern
portion of the United States, that makes our treatment
of the commercial interest one of the most delicate, as
well as important questions that can be brought before
this legislature. That interest is not of a nature long
to be neglected with impunity. Its powers, when once
brought into action by the necessity of self-defence,
cannot but be irresistible in this nation. Sir, two-fifths
of your whole white population are commercial; or,
which is the same thing as to its political effect, have
their happiness so dependent upon its prosperity that
they cannot fail to act in concert when the object is to
crush those who oppress or those who are willing to
destroy it. Of the five millions which now constitute
the white population of these States, two millions are
north and east of New Jersey. This great mass is naturally and indissolubly connected with commerce. To
this is to be added the like interest, and that of no
inconsiderable weight, which exists in the middle and
southern States. Are these powerful influences to be
forgotten or despised? Are such portions of the Union
to be told that they are not to be defended, neither on the
ocean nor yet on the land? Will they — ought they —
to submit to a system which, at the same time that it
extracts from their industry the whole national revenue,
neither protects it abroad nor at home? It needs no
spirit of prophecy to say they will not. It is no breach of
any duty to say they ought not. No power on earth can
prevent a party from growing up in these States in sup-

port of the rights of commerce to a sea and land protection. The state of things which must necessarily follow is of all others to be deprecated. As I have said before, when party passions run parallel to local interests of great power and extent, nothing can prevent national convulsions ; all the consequences of which can neither be numbered nor measured.

Mr. Chairman, I do not introduce this idea to threaten or terrify. I speak I hope to wise men, — to men of experience and of acquaintance with human nature, both in history and by observation. Is it possible to content great, intelligent, and influential portions of your citizens by any thing short of a real attention to their interests, in some degree proportionate to their magnitude and nature ? When this is not the case, can any political union be either happy or lasting ? Now is the time to give a pledge to the commercial interests that they may be assured of protection, let whatever influence predominate in the legislature. A great majority of this house are from States not connected intimately with commerce. Show, then, those which are, that you feel for them as brothers ; that you are willing to give them a due share of the national revenue for their protection. Show an enlightened and fair reciprocity. Be superior to any exclusive regard to local interest. On such principles this Union, so desirable and so justly dear to us all, will continue and be cherished by every member of the compact. But let a narrow, selfish, local, sectional policy prevail, and struggles will commence, which will terminate, through irritations and animosities, in either a change of the system of government or in its dissolution.

SPEECH

ON THE BILL FOR AUTHORIZING THE PRESIDENT TO
SUSPEND THE EMBARGO UNDER CERTAIN CIR-
CUMSTANCES.

APRIL, 1808.

SPEECH

ON THE BILL FOR AUTHORIZING THE PRESIDENT TO SUSPEND THE EMBARGO UNDER CERTAIN CIRCUMSTANCES.

APRIL, 1808.

[SEVENTY years ago commerce was the chief occupation of the sea-bound States, giving wealth to the capitalists and employment to the masses. The course of England and France had done much to cripple the operations of trade; but it was left for the government of the United States to give it its *coup de grâce*. The governing, or Democratic party, with Mr. Jefferson at its head, entertained very extravagant notions as to the importance of American commerce to Europe, and especially to England. Mr. Jefferson thought he saw in commerce the means of carrying on a war with England, at the expense only of ruining the mercantile class and the multitude dependent upon it for support. In these ideas an act forbidding the importation of certain articles from England, including the principal objects of commerce, had been passed in 1806, known as the Non-importation Act. But the final blow was held back until the December of the next year, when the famous embargo was laid on the trade of the country. On the 18th of December, Mr. Jefferson sent to the Senate the very shortest message known. to our history, consisting of two sentences, recommending "the inhibition of the departure of our vessels from the ports of the United States" in order to "keep in safety these essential resources." Obedient to this behest, the Senate passed the necessary act through all its stages in four hours, under a suspension of the rules. In the House it occupied rather more time, but was carried by a strict party vote. The effect of this measure on the prosperity of the northern States, and especially of New England, was most calamitous. It was a blow dealt not merely at the prosperity of the rich, but at the daily bread of the poor. And they were told that all this was for their protection and their own good!

On the eve of the adjournment of Congress, the next April, the ruling party saw that it was necessary to give the President some power over the embargo during the recess; and an act was introduced authorizing him to suspend its operation in the event of peace between the European belligerents, or of such a change of policy on their part as to make our commerce safe. It was on this bill that Mr. Quincy made the following speech. He did not object to investing the President with the proposed power of suspending the embargo. He wished, on the contrary, to make this power absolute, so that he could exercise it in case the pressure of the embargo should endanger the internal peace of the country. The danger of insurrection at home he regarded as a very possible one, while he looked upon the occurrence of the conditions contained in the bill as morally impossible, under the existing relations of England and France. — Ed.]

Mr. Chairman, — The amendment proposed to this bill by the gentleman from Virginia (Mr. Randolph) has for its object to limit the executive discretion in suspending the embargo to certain specified events, — the removal of the French decrees; the revocation of the British orders. It differs from the bill, as it restricts the range of the President's power to relieve the people from this oppressive measure. In this point of view, it appears to me even more objectionable than the bill itself. To neither can I yield my sanction. And, as the view which I shall offer will be different from any which has been taken of this subject, I solicit the indulgence of the committee.

A few days since, when the principle of this bill was under discussion, in the form of a resolution, a wide field was opened. Almost every subject had the honors of debate except that which was the real object of it. Our British and French relations, the merits and demerits of the expired and rejected treaty, as well as those of the late negotiators, and of the present administration, — all were canvassed. I enter not upon these topics. They are of a high and most interesting nature; but their connection with the principle of this bill is, to say the least, remote. There are considerations intimately connected with it, enough to interest our zeal, and to awaken our anxiety.

The question referred to our consideration is, shall the President be authorized to suspend the embargo on the occurrence of certain specified contingencies? The same question is included in the proposed amendment and the bill. Both limit the exercise of the power of suspension of the embargo to the occurrence of certain events. The only difference is, that the discretion given by the former is more limited; that given by the latter is more liberal.

In the course of the former discussion, a constitutional objection was raised, which, if well founded, puts an end to both bill and amendment. It is impossible, therefore, not to give it a short examination. It was contended that the Constitution had not given this House the power to authorize the President at his discretion to suspend a law. The gentleman from Maryland (Mr. Key), and the gentleman from Virginia (Mr. Randolph), both of great authority and influence in this House, maintained this doctrine with no less

3

zeal than eloquence. I place my opinion, with great diffidence, in the scale, opposite to theirs. But as my conviction is different, I must give the reasons for it, — why I adhere to the old canons; those which have been received as the rule, both of faith and practice, by every political sect which has had power, ever since the adoption of the Constitution, rather than to these new dogmas.

The Constitution of the United States, as I understand it, has in every part reference to the nature of things and the necessities of society. No portion of it was intended as a mere ground for the trial of technical skill or verbal ingenuity. The direct, express powers, with which it invests Congress, are always to be so construed as to enable the people to attain the end for which they were given. This is to be gathered from the nature of those powers, compared with the known exigencies of society and the other provisions of the Constitution. If a question arise, as in this case, concerning the extent of the incidental and implied powers vested in us by the Constitution, the instrument itself contains the criterion by which it is to be decided. We have authority to make " laws necessary and proper for carrying into execution " powers unquestionably vested. Reference must be had to the nature of these powers to know what is " necessary and proper " for their wise execution. When this necessity and propriety appear, the Constitution has enabled us to make the correspondent provisions. To the execution of many of the powers vested in us by the Constitution, a discretion is necessarily and properly incident. And when this appears from the nature of any particular power, it is certainly competent for us to provide by law that such a discretion shall be exercised. Thus, for instance, the power to borrow money must in its exercise be regulated, from its very nature, by circumstances, not always to be anticipated by the legislature at the time of passing a law authorizing a loan. Will any man contend that the legislature is necessitated to direct either absolutely that a certain sum shall be borrowed, or to limit the event on which the loan is to take place? Cannot it vest a general discretion to borrow or not to borrow, according to the view which the executive may possess of the state of the Treasury, and of the general exigencies of the country; particularly in cases where the loan is contemplated at some future day, when perhaps Congress is not in session, and when the state of the Treasury, or of the country, cannot be foreseen? In the case of the two millions appropriated for the purchase of the Floridas, such a discretion was invested in the executive. He was authorized, " if necessary, to borrow the sum, or any part thereof." This authority he never exercised, and thus, according to the argument of gentlemen on the other side, he has made null a legislative act. For, so far as it depended upon his discretion, this not being exercised, it is a nullity. The power " to pay the debts of the United States " will present a case in which, from the nature of the power, a discretion to suspend the operation of a law may be necessary and proper to its execution. Congress by one law directs the executive to pay off the eight per cent stock. Will gentlemen seriously contend that by another it may not invest him with a general discretion to stop the payment; that is, to suspend the operation of the former

law, if the state of the Treasury, or even more generally
if the public good should in his opinion require it ?   An
epidemic prevails in one of our commercial cities ; intercourse is prohibited with it ; Congress is about to terminate its session, and the distemper still rages.   Can it
be questioned that it is within our constitutional power
to authorize the President to suspend the operation of
the law, whenever the public safety will permit?
whenever, in his opinion, it is expedient?   The meanest
individual in society, in the most humble transactions of
business, can avail himself of the discretion of his confidential agent, in cases where his own cannot be applied.   Is it possible that the combined wisdom of the
nation is debarred from investing a similar discretion,
whenever, from the nature of the particular power, it is
necessary and proper to its execution?

The power of suspending laws, against which we have
so many warnings in history, was a power exercised contrary to the law, or in denial of its authority, and not
under the law and by virtue of its express enactment.
Without entering more minutely into the argument, I
cannot doubt but that Congress does possess the power
to authorize the President by law to exercise a discretionary suspension of a law.   A contrary doctrine would
lead to multiplied inconveniences, and would be wholly
inconsistent with the proper execution of some of the
powers of the Constitution.   It is true that this, like
every other power, is liable to abuse.   But we are not
to forego a healthy action, because, in its excess, it may
be injurious.

The expediency of investing the executive with such
an authority is always a critical question.   In this case,

from the magnitude of the subject and the manner in which the embargo oppresses all our interests, the inquiry into our duty in relation to it is most solemn and weighty. It is certain some provision must be made touching the embargo previous to our adjournment. A whole people is laboring under a most grievous oppression. All the business of the nation is deranged. All its active hopes are frustrated. All its industry stagnant. Its numerous products hastening to their market, are stopped in their course. A dam is thrown across the current, and every hour the strength and the tendency towards resistance is accumulating. The scene we are now witnessing is altogether unparalleled in history. The tales of fiction have no parallel for it. A new writ is executed upon a whole people. Not, indeed, the old monarchial writ, *ne exeat regno*, but a new republican writ, *ne exeat republicâ*. Freemen, in the pride of their liberty, have restraints imposed on them which despotism never exercised. They are fastened down to the soil by the enchantment of law ; and their property vanishes in the very process of preservation. It is impossible for us to separate and leave such a people at such a moment as this, without administering some opiate to their distress. Some hope, however distant, of alleviation must be proffered ; some prospect of relief opened. Otherwise, justly might we fear for the result of such an unexampled pressure. Who can say what counsels despair might suggest, or what weapons it might furnish? Some provision, then, in relation to the embargo, is unavoidable. The nature of it, is the inquiry. Three courses have been proposed, — to repeal it; to stay here and watch it ; to

leave with the executive the power to suspend it.
Concerning repeal I will say nothing. I respect the
known and immutable determination of the majority of
this House. However convinced I may be that repeal
is the only wise and probably the only safe course, I
cannot persuade myself to urge arguments which have
been often repeated, and to which, so far from granting
them any weight, very few seem willing to listen. The
end to which I aim will not counteract the settled plan
of policy. I consider the embargo as a measure from
which we are not to recede, at least not during the
present session. And my object of research is, in what
hands, and under what auspices it shall be left, so as
best to effect its avowed purpose and least to injure
the community. Repeal, then, is out of the question.
Shall we stay by and watch? This has been recommended. Watch! what? "Why, the crisis!" And
do gentlemen seriously believe that any crisis which
events in Europe are likely to produce will be either
prevented or ameliorated, by such a body as this remaining, during the whole summer, perched upon this
bill? To the tempest which is abroad we can give no
direction : over it we have no control. It may spend
its force on the ocean, now desolate by our laws, or it
may lay waste our shores. We have abandoned the
former, and for the latter, though we have been six
months in session, we have prepared no adequate
shield. Besides, in my apprehension, it is the first duty
of this House to expedite the return of its members to
their constituents. We have been six months in continued session. We begin, I fear, to lose our sympathies for those whom we represent. What can we

know, in this wilderness, of the effects of our measures
upon civilized and commercial life ?   We see nothing,
we feel nothing, but through the intervention of news-
papers, or of letters.   The one obscured by the filth of
party ; the other often distorted by personal feeling or
by private interest.   It is our immediate, our indispensable duty, to mingle with the mass of our brethren
and by direct intercourse to learn their will ; to realize
the temperature of their minds ; to ascertain their sentiments concerning our measures.   The only course
that remains is to leave with the executive the power
to suspend the embargo.   But the degree of power with
which he ought to be vested is made a question.   Shall
he be limited only by his sense of the public good, to
be collected from all the unforeseen circumstances
which may occur during the recess ; or shall it be exercised only on the occurrence of certain specified contingencies ?   The bill proposes the last mode.   It also
contains other provisions highly exceptionable and dangerous ; inasmuch as it permits the President to raise
the embargo, " in part or in whole," and authorizes him
to exercise an unlimited discretion as to the penalties
and restrictions he may lay upon the commerce he shall
allow.   My objections to the bill, therefore, are first,
that it limits the exercise of the executive as to the
whole embargo, to particular events, which if they do
not occur, no discretion can be exercised, and let the
necessity of abandoning the measure be, in other respects, ever so great, the specified events not occurring,
the embargo is absolute at least until the ensuing session ; next, that if the events do happen, the whole of
the commerce he may in his discretion set free is en-

tirely at his mercy : the door is opened to every species
of favoritism, personal or local. This power may not be
abused, but it ought not to be intrusted. The true,
the only safe ground on which this measure, during our
absence, ought to be placed is that which was taken
in the year 1794. The President ought to have authority to take off the prohibition whenever, in his judgment, the public good shall require ; not partially, not
under arbitrary bonds and restrictions, but totally, if at
all. I know that this will be rung in the popular ear
as an unlimited power. Dictatorships, protectorships,
" shadows dire, will throng into the memory." But let
gentlemen weigh the real nature of the power I advocate, and they will find it not so enormous as it first
appears, and in effect much less than the bill itself proposes to invest. In the one case he has the simple and
solitary power of raising or retaining the prohibition,
according to his view of the public good. In the other
he is not only the judge of the events specified in the
bill, but also of the degree of commerce to be permitted, of the place from which and to which it is to
be allowed ; he is the judge of its nature, and has
the power to impose whatever regulation he pleases.
Surely there can be no question but that the latter
power is of much more magnitude and more portentous
than the former. I solicit gentlemen to lay aside their
prepossessions and to investigate what the substantial
interest of this country requires ; to consider by what
dispositions this measure may be made least dangerous
to the tranquillity and interests of this people, and most
productive of that peculiar good which is avowed to be
its object. I address not those who deny our constitu-

tional power to invest a discretion to suspend, but I
address the great majority who are friendly to this bill,
who, by adopting it, sanction the constitutionality of
the grant of fresh authority, to whom, therefore, the
degree of discretion is a fair question of expediency.
In recommending that a discretion, not limited by
events, should be vested in the executive, I can have
no personal wish to augment his power.   He is no
political friend of mine.   I deem it essential, both for
the tranquillity of the people and for the success of the
measure, that such a power should be committed to
him.   Neither personal nor party feelings shall prevent
me from advocating a measure, in my estimation, salutary to the most important interests of this country.
It is true that I am among the earliest and the most
uniform opponents of the embargo.   I have seen nothing to vary my original belief, that its policy was
equally cruel to individuals and mischievous to society.
As a weapon to control foreign powers, it seemed to me
dubious in its theory, uncertain in its operation ; of all
· possible machinery the most difficult to set up and the
most expensive to maintain.   As a means to preserve
our resources, nothing could, to my mind, be more ill
adapted.   The best guarantees of the interest society
has in the wealth of the members which compose it, are
the industry, intelligence, and enterprise of the individual proprietors, strengthened as they always are by
knowledge of business, and quickened by that which
gives the keenest edge to human ingenuity, — self-interest.   When all the property of a multitude is at hazard,
the simplest and surest way of securing the greatest
portion is not to limit individual exertion, but to stim-

ulate it; not to conceal the nature of the exposure, but, by giving a full knowledge of the state of things, to leave the wit of every proprietor free to work out the salvation of his property, according to the opportunities he may discern. Notwithstanding the decrees of the belligerents, there appeared to me a field wide enough to occupy and reward mercantile enterprise. If we left commerce at liberty we might, according to the fable, lose some of her golden eggs; but if we crushed commerce, the parent which produced them, with her our future hopes perished. Without entering into the particular details whence these conclusions resulted, it is enough that they were such as satisfied my mind as to the duty of opposition to the system in its incipient state, and in all the restrictions which have grown out of it. But the system is adopted. May it be successful! It is not to diminish but to increase the chance of that success that I urge that a discretion, unlimited by events, should be vested in the executive. I shall rejoice if this great miracle be worked. I shall congratulate my country if the experiment shall prove that the old world can be controlled by fear of being excluded from the commerce of the new. Happy shall I be if, on the other side of this dark valley of the shadow of death through which our commercial hopes are passing, shall be found regions of future safety and felicity.

Among all the propositions offered to this House, no man has suggested that we ought to rise and leave this embargo, until our return, pressing upon the people, without some power of suspension vested in the executive. Why this uniformity of opinion? The reason is obvious. If the people were left six months without hope, no man could anticipate the consequences. All agree that such an experiment would be unwise and dangerous. Now, precisely the same reasons which induce the majority not to go away without making some provision for its removal, on which to feed popular expectation, is conclusive in my mind that the discretion proposed to be invested should not be limited by contingencies. The embargo power, which now holds in its palsying gripe all the hopes of this nation, is distinguished by two characteristics of material import, in deciding what control shall be left over it during our recess. I allude to its greatness and its novelty.

As to its greatness, nothing is like it. Every class of men feels it. Every interest in the nation is affected by it. The merchant, the farmer, the planter, the mechanic, the laboring poor, — all are sinking under its weight. But there is this that is peculiar to it, that there is no equality in its nature. It is not like taxation, which raises revenue according to the average of wealth ; burdening the rich and letting the poor go free. But it presses upon the particular classes of society, in an inverse ratio to the capacity of each to bear it. From those who have much, it takes indeed something. But from those who have little, it takes all. For what hope is left to the industrious poor when enterprise, activity, and capital are proscribed their legitimate exercise ? This power resembles not the mild influences of an intelligent mind balancing the interests and condition of men, and so conducting a complicated machine as to make inevitable pressure bear upon its strongest parts ; but it is like one of the blind visitations of nature, — a

tornado or a whirlwind. It sweeps away the weak; it
only shakes the strong. The humble plant, uprooted,
is overwhelmed by the tempest. The oak escapes with
the loss of nothing except its annual honors. It is
true the sheriff does not enter any man's house to collect
a tax from his property. But want knocks at his door,
and poverty thrusts its face in at the window. And what
relief can the rich extend? They sit upon their heaps
and feel them mouldering into ruins under them. The
regulations of society forbid what was once property to
be so any longer. For property depends on circulation,
on exchange; on ideal value. The power of property
is all relative. It depends not merely upon opinion
here, but upon opinion in other countries. If it be cut
off from its destined market, much of it is worth nothing, and all of it is worth infinitely less than when circulation is unobstructed.

This embargo power is, therefore, of all powers the
most enormous, in the manner in which it affects the
hopes and interests of a nation. But its magnitude is
not more remarkable than its novelty. An experiment,
such as is now making, was never before — I will not
say tried — it never before entered into the human
imagination. There is nothing like it in the narrations
of history or in the tales of fiction. All the habits of a
mighty nation are at once counteracted. All their
property depreciated. All their external connections
violated. Five millions of people are encaged. They
cannot go beyond the limits of that once free country;
now they are not even permitted to thrust their own
property through the grates. I am not now questioning
its policy, its wisdom, or its practicability: I am merely

stating the fact. And I ask if such a power as this, thus great, thus novel, thus interfering with all the great passions and interests of a whole people, ought to be left for six months in operation, without any power of control, except upon the occurrence of certain specified and arbitrary contingencies? Who can foretell when the spirit of endurance will cease? Who, when the strength of nature shall outgrow the strength of your bonds? Or if they do, who can give a pledge that the patience of the people will not first be exhausted. I make a supposition, Mr. Chairman. You are a great physician; you take a hearty, hale man, in the very pride of health, his young blood all active in his veins, and you outstretch him on a bed; you stop up all his natural orifices, you hermetically seal down his pores, so that nothing shall escape outwards, and that all his functions and all his humors shall be turned inward upon his system. While your patient is laboring in the very crisis of this course of treatment, you, his physician, take a journey into a far country, and you say to his attendant, — "I have a great experiment here in process, and a new one. It is all for the good of the young man, so do not fail to adhere to it. These are my directions, and the power with which I invest you. No attention is to be paid to any internal symptom which may occur. Let the patient be convulsed as much as he will, you are to remove none of my bandages. But, in case something external should happen, — if the sky should fall, and larks should begin to abound, if three birds of Paradise should fly into the window, — the great purpose of all these sufferings is answered. Then, and then only, have you my authority to administer relief."

The conduct of such a physician, in such a case, would not be more extraordinary than that of this House in the present, should it adjourn and limit the discretion of the executive to certain specified events arbitrarily anticipated; leaving him destitute of the power to grant relief should internal symptoms indicate that nothing else would prevent convulsions. If the events you specify do not happen, then the embargo is absolutely fixed until our return. Is there one among us that has such an enlarged view of the nature and necessities of this people as to warrant that such a system can continue six months longer? It is a proposition which no known facts substantiate, and which the strength and the universality of the passions such a pressure will set at work in the community render, to say the least, of very dubious issue. My argument in this part has this prudential truth for its basis : if a great power is put in motion, affecting great interests, the power which is left to manage it should be adequate to its control. If the power be not only great in its nature, but novel in its mode of operation, the superintending power should be permitted to exercise a wise discretion ; for if you limit him by contingencies, the experiment may fail, or its results be unexpected. In either case, nothing but shame or ruin would be our portion.

But I ask the House to view this subject in relation to the success of this measure, which the majority have justly so much at heart. Which position of invested power is the most auspicious to a happy issue ?

As soon as this House has risen, what think you will be the first question every man in this nation will put to his neighbor? Will it not be, — " What has Congress

done with the embargo?" Suppose the reply should
be, — "They have made no provision. This corroding
cancer is to be left to prey on our vitals six months
longer." Is there a man who doubts but that such a
reply would sink the heart of every owner of property,
and of every laborer in the community? No man can
hesitate. The magnitude of the evil, the certain prospect of so terrible a calamity thus long protracted,
would itself tend to counteract the continuance of the
measure by the discontent and despair it could not fail
to produce in the great body of the people. But suppose in reply to such a question, it should be said —
" the removal of the embargo depends upon events.
France must retrace her steps. England must apologize
and atone for her insolence. Two of the proudest and
most powerful nations on the globe must truckle for our
favor, or we shall persist in maintaining our dignified
retirement." What, then, would be the consequence?
would not every reflecting man in the nation set himself at work to calculate the probability of the occurrence of these events? If they were likely to happen,
the distress and discontent would be scarcely less than
in the case of absolute certainty for six months' perpetuation of it. For if the events do not happen, the
embargo is absolute. Such a state of popular mind all
agree is little favorable either to perseverance in the
measure, or to its ultimate success. But suppose that
the people should find a discretionary power was invested
in the executive, to act as in his judgment, according to
circumstances, the public good should require. Would
not such a state of things have a direct tendency to
allay fear, to tranquillize discontent, and encourage

endurance of suffering? Should experience prove that it is absolutely insupportable, there is a constitutional way of relief. The way of escape is not wholly closed. The knowledge of this fact would be alone a support to the people. They would endure it longer. They would endure it better. They would be secure of a more cordial co-operation in the measure as the people would ' see they were not wholly hopeless, in case the experiment was too oppressive. Surely, nothing can be more favorable to its success than producing such a state of public sentiment.

We are but a young nation. The United States are scarcely yet hardened into the bone of manhood. The whole period of our national existence has been nothing else than a continued series of prosperity. The miseries of the Revolutionary war were but as the pangs of parturition. The experience of that period was of a nature not to be very useful after our nation had acquired an individual form and a manly constitutional stamina. It is to be feared we have grown giddy with good fortune; attributing the greatness of our prosperity to our own wisdom, rather than to a course of events and a guidance over which we had no influence. It is to be feared that we are now entering that school of adversity, the first blessing of which is to chastise an overweening conceit of ourselves. A nation mistakes its relative consequence, when it thinks its countenance, or its intercourse, or its existence, all important to the rest of the world. There is scarcely any people, and none of any weight in the society of nations, which does not possess within its own sphere all that is essential to its exist-

ence. An individual who should retire from conversation with the world for the purpose of taking vengeance
on it for some real or imaginary wrong would soon find
himself grievously mistaken : notwithstanding the delu-
sions of self-flattery, he would certainly be taught that
the world was moving along just as well, after his dignified retirement, as it did while he intermeddled with its
concerns. The case of a nation which should make a
similar trial of its importance to other nations would
not be very different from that of such an individual.
The intercourse of human life has its basis in a natural
reciprocity, which always exists, although the vanity of
nations, as well as of individuals, will often suggest to
inflated fancies that they give more than they gain in
the interchange of friendship, of civilities, or of business. I conjure gentlemen not to commit the nation as
to the purpose of this embargo measure, but, by leaving
a wise discretion during our absence with the executive,
neither to admit nor deny by the terms of our law that
its object is to coerce foreign nations. Such a state of
things is safest for our own honor and the wisest to
secure success for this system of policy.

4

SPEECH

ON THE FIRST RESOLUTION REPORTED BY THE COMMITTEE ON FOREIGN RELATIONS.

Nov. 28, 1808.

SPEECH

Nov. 28, 1808.

[THE necessity of some more important protection of the sea-board cities than that provided by Mr. Jefferson's government grew more and more apparent, as the relations of the United States with France and England became more and more complicated. To resent the injury done to American commerce by the new rulings of Lord Stowell in the Court of Admiralty, and the insult to the American flag in the right claimed and exercised by England of searching our merchant-ships for English sailors and impressing them wherever found, the law known as the Non-importation Act had been passed shortly before the speech of April 14th, 1806, was delivered. By this act the importation from Great Britain, or any of her dependencies, of all the articles of her commerce with the United States was forbidden. As this measure did not have the desired effect of bringing England to her senses, Mr. Jefferson prepared to push still further his attempt to conquer her by a war of commercial restrictions. The governing party had most exaggerated notions of the dependence of England upon the commerce of America, and believed that she would submit to any terms rather than lose it. In retaliation for the Berlin decree of Bonaparte, declaring the British Islands in a state of blockade and forbidding all neutral intercourse with them, the British government in November, 1807, issued the famous Orders in Council, forbidding any commercial intercourse with France or her allies,

excepting through some port of Great Britain or Ireland. All
ships engaged in this trade were to touch at one of the ports of
the United Kingdom and pay certain fees and take out a license
for permission to proceed on their voyage. To these orders
Bonaparte soon replied by the Milan decree, by which he
declared every vessel which complied with their conditions to be
" denationalized," and lawful prize. As the Americans were
the only neutrals, inasmuch as all the continent was either in
alliance with or in subjection to Bonaparte, their commerce was
very effectually destroyed. But as if the agreement in policy of
the two great belligerents of Europe were not sufficient for its
utter extinction, Mr. Jefferson devised his celebrated embargo to
hinder adventurous merchants from taking the chance of capture
at their own risk. On the 18th of December, 1807, he sent the
shortest presidential message on record, of two sentences only,
to both Houses, recommending an embargo, or prohibition of all
vessels from leaving the ports of the United States. This message was received and discussed in secret session, and was
despatched in *four hours* by the Senate, and had its preliminary
reading despatched in the House with even greater speed,
though the discussion in the committee of the whole continued
for three days and nearly three nights, — the more recent
application of the previous question as a daily instrument for
the suppression of debate not having then been imagined. The
act finally passed by a vote of eighty-two yeas to forty-four
nays. The promulgation of this law carried dismay and ruin
to the whole seaboard. Massachusetts, which then included
Maine, felt the blow most severely, which struck not merely at
her wealth, but at her daily bread. And the victims of this cruel
measure were told that its object was only their own protection
and advantage! And although both belligerents were ostensibly
included in the recital of grievances which led to the measure,
yet it was scarcely denied that it was aimed chiefly at England, the trade with France being comparatively of no importance. And Bonaparte himself took this view of the matter,
regarding the American embargo as a necessary complement of
his continental system, for the destruction of England through

that of her commerce. Before the adjournment of Congress, in April, 1808, an act was passed authorizing the President, in case of peace between the belligerents, or such other change in their measures as to neutral commerce as should in his judgment justify such action, to suspend the operation of the embargo. Mr. Quincy moved to invest the President with full powers, unrestricted by any conditions, and made the following speech in support of his motion. It came to nothing, of course. Congress soon after adjourned.

When it reassembled, by adjournment, at the beginning of November, 1808, the embargo and the state of our relations with foreign powers formed the staple of debate, as it had of men's thoughts and talk in the interval. The committee to which so much of the President's message as treated of foreign relations having reported the following resolution : " Resolved : that the United States cannot without a sacrifice of their rights, honor, and independence, submit to the late edicts of Great Britain and France," upon this hint Mr. Quincy spoke as follows, on the 28th of November. — Ed.]

Mr. Chairman, — I am not, in general, a friend to abstract legislation. Ostentatious declaration of general principles is so often the resort of weakness and of ignorance ; it is so frequently the subterfuge of men who are willing to amuse or who mean to delude the people, that it is with great reluctance I yield to such a course my sanction.

If, however, a formal annunciation of a determination to perform one of the most common and undeniable of national duties be deemed by a majority of this House essential to their character, or to the attainment of public confidence, I am willing to admit that the one now offered, is as unexceptionable as any it would be likely to propose.

In this view, however, I lay wholly out of sight the

report of the committee, by which it is accompanied
and introduced.   The course advocated in that report
is. in my opinion, loathsome ; the spirit it breathes disgraceful ; the temper it is likely to inspire, neither
calculated to regain the rights we have lost, nor to
preserve those which remain to us. It is an established
maxim that, in adopting a resolution offered by a committee in this House, no member is pledged to support
the reasoning, or made sponsor for the facts which they
have seen fit to insert in it. I exercise, therefore, a
common right, when I subscribe to the resolution, not
on the principles of the committee, but on those which
obviously result from its terms, and are the plain meaning of its expressions.

I agree to this resolution, because, in my apprehension, it offers a solemn pledge to this nation — a pledge
not to be mistaken, and not to be evaded — that the
present system of public measures shall be totally abandoned. Adopt it, and there is an end of the policy of
deserting our rights, under a pretence of maintaining
them. Adopt it, and we no longer yield to the beck of
haughty belligerents the rights of navigating the ocean,
that choice inheritance bequeathed to us by our fathers.
Adopt it. and there is a termination of that base and
abject submission by which this country has for these
eleven months been disgraced and brought to the brink
of ruin.

That the natural import and necessary implication of
the terms of this resolution are such as I have suggested will be apparent from a very transient consideration. What do its terms necessarily include ? They
contain an assertion and a pledge. The assertion is,

that the edicts of Great Britain and France are contrary
to our rights, honor, and independence.   The pledge is,
that we will not submit to them.

Concerning the assertion contained in this resolution, I would say nothing, were it not that I fear that
those who have so long been in the habit of looking at
the orders and decrees of foreign powers as the measure of the rights of our own citizens, and have been
accustomed, in direct subserviency to them, of prohibiting commerce altogether, might apprehend that there
was some lurking danger in such an assertion.   They
may be assured there can be nothing more harmless.
Neither Great Britain or France ever pretended that
those edicts were consistent with American rights.   On
the contrary, both these nations ground those edicts on
the principle of imperious necessity, which admits the
injustice done, at the very instant of executing the act
of oppression.   No gentleman need have any difficulty
in screwing his courage up to this assertion.   Neither
of the belligerents will contradict it.   Mr. Turreau and
Mr. Erskine will both of them countersign the declaration to-morrow.

With respect to the pledge contained in this resolution, understood according to its true import, it is a
glorious one.   It opens new prospects.   It promises a
change in the disposition of this House.   It is a solemn
assurance to the nation, that it will no longer submit to
these edicts.

It remains for us, therefore, to consider what submission is, and what the pledge not to submit implies.

One man submits to the order, decree, or edict of
another, when he does that thing which such order,

decree, or edict commands; or when he omits to do that
thing which such order, decree, or edict prohibits.
This, then, is submission. It is to do as we are bidden.
It is to take the will of another as the measure of our
rights. It is to yield to his power; to go where he
directs, or to refrain from going where he forbids us.

If this be submission, then the pledge not to submit
implies the reverse of all this. It is a solemn declaration, that we will not do that thing which such order,
decree, or edict commands, or that we will do what
it prohibits. This, then, is freedom. This is honor.
This is independence. It consists in taking the nature
of things, and not the will of another, as the measure
of our rights. What God and nature offer us, we will
enjoy in despite of the commands, regardless of the
menaces of iniquitous power.

Let us apply these correct and undeniable principles
to the edicts of Great Britain and France, and the consequent abandonment of the ocean by the American
government. The decrees of France prohibit us from
trading with Great Britain. The orders of Great
Britain prohibit us from trading with France. And
what do we? Why — in direct subserviency to the
edicts of each — we prohibit our citizens from trading
with either. We do more, as if unqualified submission
was not humiliating enough, we descend to an act of
supererogation in servility: we abandon trade altogether; we not only refrain from that particular trade,
which their respective edicts proscribe, but lest the
ingenuity of our merchants should enable them to evade
their operation, to make submission doubly sure, the
American government virtually re-enact the edicts of

the belligerents, and abandon all the trade which, not-withstanding the practical effects of their edicts, remains to us. The same conclusion will result if we consider our embargo in relation to the objects of this belligerent policy. France by her edicts would compress Great Britain, by destroying her commerce and cutting off her supplies. All the continent of Europe, in the hand of Bonaparte, is made subservient to this policy. The embargo law of the United States, in its operation, is an union with this continental coalition against British commerce, at the very moment most auspicious to its success. Can any thing be more in direct subserviency to the views of the French emperor? If we consider the orders of Great Britain, the result will be the same. I proceed at present on the supposition of a perfect impartiality in our administration towards both belliger-ents, so far as relates to the embargo law. Great Britain had two objects in issuing her orders. First, to excite discontent in the people of the continent, by depriving them of their accustomed colonial supplies. Second, to secure to herself that commerce of which she deprived neutrals. Our embargo co-operates with the British views in both respects. By our dereliction of the ocean, the continent is much more deprived of the advantages of commerce than it would be possible for the British navy to effect, and, by removing our compe-tition, all the commerce of the continent which can be forced, is wholly left to be reaped by Great Britain. The language of each sovereign is in direct conformity with these ideas. Napoleon tells the American minister, virtually, that we are very good Americans; that although he will not allow the property he has in his hands to escape him, nor desist from burning and capturing our vessels on every occasion, yet that he is, thus far, satisfied with our co-operation. And what is the language of George the Third, when our minister presents to his consideration the embargo laws. Is it *Le Roi s'avisera?* The king will reflect upon them. No, it is the pure language of royal approbation. *Le Roi le veut.* The king wills it. Were you colonies, he could expect no more. His subjects as inevitably get that commerce which you abandon, as the water will certainly run into the only channel which remains after all the others are obstructed. In whatever point of view you consider these embargo laws in relation to those edicts and decrees, we shall find them co-operating with each belligerent in its policy. In this way, I grant, our conduct may be impartial; but what has become of our American rights to navigate the ocean? They are abandoned in strict conformity to the decrees of both belligerents. This resolution declares that we will no longer submit to such degrading humiliation. Little as I relish, I will take it as the harbinger of a new day, the pledge of a new system of measures.

Perhaps here, in strictness, I ought to close my observations. But the report of the committee, contrary to what I deem the principle of the resolution, unquestionably recommends the continuance of the embargo laws. And such is the state of the nation, and in particular that portion of it which in part I represent, under their oppression, that I cannot refrain from submitting some considerations on that subject.

When I enter on the subject of the embargo, I am struck with wonder at the very threshold. I know not

with what words to express my astonishment. At the
time I departed from Massachusetts, if there was an
impression which I thought universal, it was that, at
the commencement of this session, an end would be put
to this measure. The opinion was not so much that it
would be terminated as that it was then at an end.
Sir, the prevailing sentiment, according to my apprehension, was stronger than this, — even that the pressure
was so great that it could not possibly be endured ; that
it would soon be absolutely insupportable. And this
opinion, as I then had reason to believe, was not confined to any one class or description or party, — that
even those who were friends of the existing administration, and unwilling to abandon it, were yet satisfied
that a sufficient trial had been given to this measure.
With these impressions, I arrive in this city. I hear the
incantations of the great enchanter. I feel his spell. I
see the legislative machinery begin to move. The scene
opens. And I am commanded to forget all my recollections, to disbelieve the evidence of my senses, to contradict what I have seen and heard and felt. I hear that
all this discontent was mere party clamor, electioneering
artifice ; that the people of New England are able and
willing to endure this embargo for an indefinite, unlimited period ; some say for six months ; some a year,
some two years. The gentleman from North Carolina
(Mr. Macon) told us that he preferred three years of
embargo to a war. And the gentleman from Virginia
(Mr. Clopton) said expressly, that he hoped we should
never allow our vessels to go upon the ocean again,
until the orders and decrees of the belligerents were
rescinded. In plain English, until France and Great

Britain should, in their great condescension permit. Good Heavens! Mr. Chairman, are men mad? Is this House touched with that insanity which is the never-failing precursor of the intention of Heaven to destroy! The people of New England, after eleven months deprivation of the ocean, to be commanded still longer to abandon it, for an undefined period; to hold their unalienable rights, at the tenure of the will of Britain or of Bonaparte! A people, commercial in all aspects, in all their relations, in all their hopes, in all their recollections of the past, in all their prospects of the future: a people whose first love was the ocean, the choice of their childhood, the approbation of their manly years, the most precious inheritance of their fathers, in the midst of their success, in the moment of the most exquisite perception of commercial prosperity, to be commanded to abandon it, not for a time limited, but for a time unlimited; not until they can be prepared to defend themselves there (for that is not pretended), but until their rivals recede from it; not until their necessities require, but until foreign nations permit! I am lost in astonishment, Mr. Chairman. I have not words to express the matchless absurdity of this attempt. I have no tongue to express the swift and headlong destruction which a blind perseverance in such a system must bring upon this nation.

But men from New England, representatives on this floor, equally with myself the constitutional guardians of her interests, differ from me in these opinions. My honorable colleague (Mr. Bacon) took occasion in secret session, to deny that there did exist all that discontent and distress, which I had attempted in an

humble way to describe. He told us he had travelled
in Massachusetts, that the people were not thus dissat-
isfied, that the embargo had not produced any such
tragical effects. Really, sir, my honorable colleague
has travelled all the way from Stockbridge to Hudson;
from Berkshire to Boston; from inn to inn; from county
court to county court; and doubtless he collected all
that important information which an acute intelligence
never fails to retain on such occasions. He found tea,
sugar, salt, West India rum, and molasses dearer; beef,
pork, butter, and cheese cheaper. Reflection enabled
him to arrive at this difficult result, that in this way
the evil and the good of the embargo equalize one
another. But has my honorable colleague travelled on
the seaboard? Has he witnessed the state of our
cities? Has he seen our ships rotting at our wharves,
our wharves deserted, our stores tenantless, our streets
bereft of active business; industry forsaking her beloved
haunts, and hope fled away from places where she had
from earliest time been accustomed to make and to fulfil her most precious promises? Has he conversed with
the merchant, and heard the tale of his embarrassments,
— his capital arrested in his hands, forbidden by your
laws to resort to a market, with property four times
sufficient to discharge all his engagements, obliged to
hang on the precarious mercy of moneyed institutions
for that indulgence which preserves him from stopping
payment, the first step towards bankruptcy? Has he
conversed with our mechanics? Has he seen them
either destitute of employment or obliged to seek it in
labors odious to them, because they were not educated
to them? That mechanic, who the day before this em-

bargo passed, the very day that you took this bit, and
rolled it like a sweet morsel under your tongue, had
more business than he had hands or time or thought
to employ in it, now soliciting at reduced prices
that employment which the rich, owing to the uncertainty in which your laws have involved their capital,
cannot afford. I could heighten this picture. I could
show you laboring poor in the almshouse, and willing industry, dependent upon charity. But I confine myself to particulars which have fallen under my
own observation, and of which ten thousand suffering
individuals on the seaboard of New England are living
witnesses.

Mr. Chairman, — Other gentlemen must take their
responsibilities : I shall take mine. This embargo must
be repealed. You cannot enforce it for any important
period of time longer. When I speak of your inability
to enforce this law, let no gentleman misunderstand me.
I mean not to intimate insurrections or open defiances
of them. Although it is impossible to foresee in what
acts that "oppression" will finally terminate which, we
are told, "makes wise men mad." I speak of an inability resulting from very different causes.

The gentleman from North Carolina (Mr. Macon),
exclaimed the other day in a strain of patriotic ardor,
"What! shall not our laws be executed? Shall their
authority be defied? I am for enforcing them at every
hazard." I honor that gentleman's zeal ; and I mean
no deviation from that true respect I entertain for him,
when I tell him that, in this instance, "his zeal is not
according to knowledge."

I ask this House, is there no control to its authority,

is there no limit to the power of this national legislature? I hope I shall offend no man, when I intimate that two limits exist, — *nature* and the *Constitution*. Should this House undertake to declare that this atmosphere should no longer surround us, that water should cease to flow, that gravity should not hereafter operate, that the needle should not vibrate to the pole, I do suppose, Mr. Chairman, — sir, I mean no disrespect to the authority of this House; I know the high notions some gentlemen entertain on this subject, — I do suppose, — sir, I hope I shall not offend, — I think I may venture to affirm, that such a law to the contrary notwithstanding the air would continue to circulate, the Mississippi, the Hudson, and the Potomac would hurl their floods to the ocean, heavy bodies continue to descend, and the mysterious magnet hold on its course to its celestial cynosure.

Just as utterly absurd and contrary to nature is it, to attempt to prohibit the people of New England, for any considerable length of time, from the ocean. Commerce is not only associated with all the feelings, the habits, the interests, and relations, of that people, but the nature of our soil and of our coasts, the state of our population and its mode of distribution over our territory, renders it indispensable. We have five hundred miles of sea-coast; all furnished with harbors, bays, creeks, rivers, inlets, basins, with every variety of invitation to the sea, with every species of facility to violate such laws as these: our people are not scattered over an immense surface, at a solemn distance from each other, in lordly retirement, in the midst of extended plantations and intervening wastes. They are collected

5

on the margin of the ocean, by the sides of rivers, at the heads of bays, looking into the water or on the surface of it for the incitement and the reward of their industry.   Among a people thus situated, thus educated, thus numerous, laws prohibiting them from the exercise of their natural rights will have a binding effect not one moment longer than the public sentiment supports them.   Gentlemen talk of twelve revenue cutters additional to enforce the embargo laws. Multiply the number by twelve, multiply it by an hundred, join all your ships of war, all your gunboats, and all your militia, in despite of them all, such laws as these are of no avail when they become odious to public sentiment.   Continue these laws any considerable time longer, and it is very doubtful if you will have officers to execute, juries to convict, or purchasers to bid for your confiscations.   Cases have begun to occur.   Ask your revenue officers, and they will tell you that already at public sales in your cities, under these laws, the owner has bought his property at less than four per cent upon the real value.   Public opinion begins to look with such a jealous and hateful eye upon these laws, that even self-interest will not co-operate to enforce their penalties.

But where is our love of order ?   Where our respect for the laws ?   Let legislators beware lest, by the very nature of their laws, they weaken that sentiment of respect for them, so important to be inspired, and so difficult to be reinstated when it has once been driven from the mind.   Regulate not the multitude to their ruin.   Disgust not men of virtue by the tendency of your laws, lest when they cannot yield them the sanc-

tion of their approbation, the enterprising and the
necessitous find a principal check upon their fears of
violating them removed. It is not enough for men in
place to exclaim, " the worthless part of society."
Words cannot alter the nature of things. You cannot
identify the violator of such laws as these, in our part
of the country, for any great length of time, with the
common smuggler, nor bring the former down to the
level of the latter. The reason is obvious. You bring
the duties the citizen owes to society into competition,
not only with the strongest interests, but, which is more,
with the most sacred private obligations. When you
present to the choice of a citizen, bankruptcy, a total
loss of the accumulated wealth of his whole life, or a
violation of a positive law, restrictive of the exercise of
the most common rights, it presents to him a most critical alternative. I will not say how sublime casuists
may decide. But it is easy to foretell that nature will
plead too strong in the bosom to make obedience long
possible. I state no imaginary case. Thousands in
New England see in the continuance of this embargo and
in obedience to it irremediable ruin to themselves and
families. But where is our patriotism? Sir, you call
upon patriotism for sacrifices to which it is unequal;
and require its operation in a way in which that passion
cannot long subsist. Patriotism is a great comfort to
men in the interior, to the farmer and the planter, who
are denied a market by your laws, whose local situation
is such that they can neither sell their produce, nor
scarcely give it away, and who are made to believe that
their privations will ultimately redound to the benefit of
the country. But on the seaboard, where men feel not

only their annual profit, but their whole capital perishing, where they know the utter inefficacy of your laws
to coerce foreign nations, and their utter futility as a
means of saving our own property; to such laws in such
a situation, patriotism is, to say the least, a very inactive
assistant.   You cannot lay a man upon the rack and
crack his muscles, by a slow torment, and call patriotism
to soothe the sufferer.

But there is another obstacle to a long and effectual
continuance of this law, — the doubt which hangs over
its constitutionality.   I know I shall be told that the
sanction of the judiciary has been added to this act of
the legislature. Sir, I honor that tribunal. I revere the
individual whose opinion declared in this instance the
constitutionality of the law.   But it is one thing to venerate our courts of justice ; it is one thing to deem this
law obligatory upon the citizen, while it has all these
sanctions ; it is another, on this floor, in the high court
of the people's privileges, to advocate its repeal on the
ground that it is an invasion of their rights.   The embargo laws have unquestionable sanction.   They are
laws of this land.   Yet, who shall deny to a representative of this people the right, in their own favorite tribunal, of bringing your laws to the test of the principles
of the Constitution ?

Is there any principle more wise, or more generally
received among statesmen, than that a law, in proportion to its pressure upon the people, should have its
basis in unquestionable authority, as well as necessity ?
A legislature may sport with the rights of an individual.
It may violate the constitution to the ruin of whole
classes of men.   But once let it begin, by its laws, to

crush the hopes of the great mass of the citizens; let it bring every eye in the land to the scrutiny of its laws and its authority, to be permanent those laws must possess no flaw in their foundation.

I ask in what page of the Constitution you find the power of laying an embargo? Directly given it is nowhere. You have it, then, by construction or by precedent. By construction of the power to regulate. I lay out of the question the common-place argument, that regulation cannot mean annihilation; and that what is annihilated cannot be regulated. I ask this question, Can a power be ever obtained by construction which had never been exercised at the time of the authority given; the like of which had not only never been seen, but the idea of which had never entered into human imagination, I will not say in this country, but in the world? Yet such is this power which by construction you assume to exercise. Never before did society witness a total prohibition of all intercourse like this in a commercial nation. Did the people of the United States invest this House with a power of which, at the time of investment, that people had not and could not have had any idea? for even in works of fiction it had never existed. But we have precedent. Precedent is directly against you. For the only precedent, that in 1794, was in conformity to the embargo power, as it had been exercised in other countries. It was limited. Its duration was known. The power passed from the representatives of this House only for sixty days. In that day the legislature would not trust even Washington, amid all his well-earned influence, with any other than a limited power. But away, sir, with such deduc-

4

tions as these: I appeal to the history of the times when this national compact was formed. This Constitution grew out of our necessities, and it was in every stage of its formation obstructed by the jealousies and diverse interests of the different States. The gentlemen of the South had certain species of property with the control of which they would not trust us in the North. And wisely; for we neither appreciate it as they do, nor could regulate it safely for them. In the east our sentiment concerning their interest in commerce, and their power to understand its true interests, was in a great degree similar. The writings of that period exhibit this jealousy, and the fears excited by it formed in that portion of the United States a formidable objection to its adoption. In this state of things, would the people of New England consent to convey to a legislature, constituted as this in time must be, a power, not only to regulate commerce, but to annihilate it, for a time unlimited, or altogether? Suppose, in 1788, in the Convention of Massachusetts, while debating upon the adoption of this Constitution, some hoary sage had arisen, and with an eye looking deep into futurity, with a prophet's ken, had thus addressed the assembly. " Fellow-citizens of Massachusetts, to what ruin are you hastening? Twenty years shall not elapse before, under a secret and dubious construction of the instrument now proposed for your adoption, your commerce shall be annihilated; the whole of your vast trade prohibited; not a boat shall cross your harbor, not a coaster shall be permitted to go out of your ports, unless under permission of the distant head of your nation, and after a grievous visitation of a custom-house officer?" Sir, does any man believe that, with such a prospect into futurity, the people of that State would have for one moment listened to its adoption? Rather would they not have rejected it with indignation? Yet this, now, is not prophecy. It is history. But this law is not perpetual, it is said. Show the limit to it. Show by what terms it can be made more perpetual.

The universal opinion entertained in New England among commercial men of the total imbecility of this law, as a measure of coercion of either belligerent, is another cause pregnant with discontent in that country. It may do well enough to amuse ourselves with calculations of this kind on this floor; but intelligent merchants, masters of vessels, seamen, who are acquainted with the West Indies, and with the European dominions of both powers, speak with sovereign contempt of the idea of starving either of these powers into submission to our plans of policy. The entire failure of this scheme, after a trial of eleven months, would, I should suppose, have satisfied the most obstinate of its hopelessness. Yet it is revived again at this session. We are told from high authority of the failure of the wheat harvest in Great Britain, and this has been urged as a farther reason for a continuance of this measure. Have gentlemen who press this argument informed themselves how exceedingly small a proportion our export of wheat bears to the whole consumption of the British dominions? Our whole export to all the world of wheat in its natural and manufactured state does not amount to seven millions of bushels. The whole consumption of the British dominions exceeds one hundred and fifty millions. Let gentlemen consider what a small object this amount is, in a national point of view, even could the attainment of the whole supply be assumed, as the condition of her yielding to the terms we should prescribe. Are not the borders of the Black Sea, the coast of Africa, and South America, all wheat countries, open to her commerce?

But the embargo saves our resources. It may justly be questioned, whether, in this point of view, the embargo is so effectual as, at first, men are led to imagine. It may be doubted if the seed wheat for this harvest is not worth more than the whole crop. I say nothing of the embarrassments of our commerce, of the loss of our seamen, of the sunken value of real estate. But our dead, irredeemable loss, by this embargo, during the present year, cannot be stated at less than ten per cent on account of interest and profit on the whole export of our country, — that is, on the one hundred and eight millions, — ten million eight hundred thousand dollars.

Nor can our loss upon a million tons of unemployed shipping be stated at less than at twenty dollars the ton, twenty millions of dollars. Thirty millions of dollars is a serious outfit for any voyage of salvation, and the profit ought to be very unquestionable, before a wise man would be persuaded to renew or prolong it. Besides, is it true that the articles the embargo retains are in the common acceptation of the term resources? I suppose that by this word, so ostentatiously used, on all occasions, it is meant to convey the idea that the produce thus retained in the country will be a resource for use or defence in case of war, or any other misfortune happening to it. But is this true? Our exports are surplus products, — what we raise beyond what we consume. Because we cannot use them, they are surplus. Of course in this country they have little or no value in use, but only in exchange. Take away the power of exchange, and how can they be called resources? Every year produces sufficient for its own consumption, and a surplus. Suppose an embargo of ten years, — will gentlemen seriously contend that the accumulating surplus of fish, cotton, tobacco, and flour would be a resource for any national exigencies? We cannot consume it, because the annual product is equal to our annual consumption. Our embargo forbids us to sell it. How, then, is it a resource; are we stronger or richer for it? The reverse, we are weaker and poorer. Weaker by all the loss of motive to activity, by all the diminution of the industry of the country, which such a deprivation of the power to exchange produces. And what can be poorer than he who is obliged to keep what he cannot use, and to labor for that which profiteth not?

But the inequality of the pressure of this measure of embargo upon the people of the Eastern States is another source of great discontent with it. Every gentleman who has spoken upon the subject has seemed to take it for granted that this was a burden which pressed equally. But is this the case? I shall confine myself to a single fact, although the point admits of other elucidations. Compare the State of Virginia with that of Massachusetts, in the single particular of the amount of capital embarrassed by this law. Virginia with a population, according to the last census, of nine hundred thousand souls, has four million seven hundred thousand dollars in exports, forty thousand eight hundred tons of registered shipping at thirty dollars the ton, amounting to one million seven hundred dollars in value ; constituting an aggregate capital of six millions of dollars, obstructed by this embargo. Massachusetts, on the other hand, has in exports twenty millions one hundred thousand dollars, and three hundred and six thousand tons of registered shipping, equal nearly to ten millions of dollars, in value ; constituting an aggregate of capital, in Massachusetts, equal to thirty millions of dollars, obstructed by this law. By the last census, the population of Massachusetts is about six hundred thousand souls. So that in Virginia, nine hundred thousand souls have to bear a pressure of embarrassed capital equal to six millions of dollars, and in Massachusetts six hundred thousand souls a pressure of thirty millions. To equalize the pressure of Virginia with Massachusetts, the capital of the former ought to be forty-five millions instead of six millions. I wish not to bring into view any unpleasant comparisons, but when gentlemen wonder at our complaints they ought rightly to appreciate their causes. The pressure resulting from the embarrassments of this immense capital is the more sensibly felt, inasmuch as it is not divided in great masses among rich individuals, but in moderate portions among the middling classes of our citizens, who have many of them the earnings of a whole life invested in single articles destined for a foreign market, from which your embargo alone prohibits them.

It is in vain to say that if the embargo was raised there would be no market. The merchants understand that subject better than you ; and the eagerness with

which preparations to load were carried on previous to
the commencement of this session speaks, in a language
not to be mistaken, their opinion of the foreign markets.
But it has been asked in debate, " Will not Massachusetts, the cradle of liberty, submit to such privations ? "
An embargo liberty was never cradled in Massachusetts.
Our liberty was not so much a mountain as a sea
nymph. She was free as air. She could swim, or she
could run. The ocean was her cradle. Our fathers
met her as she came, like the goddess of beauty, from
the waves. They caught her as she was sporting on
the beach. They courted her whilst she was spreading
her nets upon the rocks. But an embargo liberty, — a
hand-cuffed liberty ; a liberty in fetters ; a liberty trav-
ersing between the four sides of a prison and beating
her head against the walls, is none of our offspring.
We abjure the monster. Its parentage is all inland.

The gentleman from North Carolina (Mr Macon)
exclaimed the other day, " Where is the spirit of '76 ? "
Aye, sir ; where is it ? Would to heaven, that at our
invocation it would condescend to alight on this floor.
But let gentlemen remember that the spirit of '76 was
not a spirit of empty declaration, or of abstract propositions. It did not content itself with non-importation
acts or non-intercourse laws. It was a spirit of active
preparation, of dignified energy. It studied both to
know our rights and to devise the effectual means of
maintaining them. In all the annals of '76, you will
find no such degrading doctrine as that maintained in
this report. It never presented to the people of the
United States the alternative of war or a suspension of
our rights, and recommended the latter rather than to

incur the risk of the former. What was the language of that period in one of the addresses of Congress to Great Britain? " You attempt to reduce us, by the sword, to base and abject submission. On the sword, therefore, we rely for protection." In that day there were no alternatives presented to dishearten, — no abandonment of our rights under the pretence of maintaining them, — no gaining the battle by running away. In the whole history of that period there are no such terms as " embargo, — dignified retirement, — trying who can do each other the most harm." At that time we had a navy, that name so odious to the influences of the present day. Yes, sir, in 1776, though but in our infancy, we had a navy scouring our coasts, and defending our commerce, which was never for one moment wholly suspended. In 1776 we had an army also ; and a glorious army it was ! not composed of men halting from the stews, or swept from the jails, but of the best blood, the real yeomanry of the country, noble cavaliers, men without fear and without reproach. We had such an army in 1776, and Washington at its head. We have an army in 1808, and a head to it.

I will not humiliate those who lead the fortunes of the nation at the present day by any comparison with the great men of that period. But I recommend the advocates of the present system of public measures to study well the true spirit of 1776, before they venture to call it in aid of their purposes. It may bring in its train some recollections not suited to give ease or hope to their bosoms. I beg gentlemen who are so frequent in their recurrence to that period to remember that, among the causes which led to a separation from Great

Britain, the following are enumerated, — unnecessary restrictions upon trade; cutting off commercial intercourse between the colonies; embarrassing our fisheries; wantonly depriving our citizens of necessaries; invasion of private property by governmental edicts; the authority of the commander-in-chief, and under him of the brigadier-general, being rendered supreme in the civil government; the commander-in-chief of the army made governor of a colony; citizens transferred from their native country for trial. Let gentlemen beware how they appeal to the spirit of '76, lest it come with the aspect, not of a friend, but of a tormentor; lest they find a warning, when they look for support, and instead of encouragement they are presented with an awful lesson.

But repealing the embargo will be submission to tribute. The popular ear is fretted with this word "tribute." And an odium is attempted to be thrown upon those who are indignant at this abandonment of their rights, by representing them as the advocates of tribute. Sir, who advocates it? No man, in this country, I believe. This outcry about tribute is the veriest bugbear that was ever raised, in order to persuade men to quit rights which God and nature had given them. In the first place, it is scarce possible that, if left to himself, the interest of the merchant could ever permit him to pay the British re-exportation duty, denominated tribute. France, under penalty of confiscation, prohibits our vessels from receiving a visit from an English ship, or touching at an English port. In this state of things, England pretends to permit us to export to France certain articles, paying her a duty. The statement of the case shows the futility of the attempt. Who will pay a duty to England for permission to go to France to be confiscated? But, suppose there is a mistake in this, and that it may be the interest of the merchant to pay such duty, for the purpose of going to certain destruction, have not you full powers over this matter? Cannot you, by pains and penalties, prohibit the merchant from the payment of such a duty? No man will obstruct you. There is, as I believe, but one opinion upon this subject: I hope, therefore, that gentlemen will cease this outcry about tribute.

However, suppose that the payment of this duty is inevitable, which it certainly is not. Let me ask, is embargo independence? Deceive not yourselves. It is palpable submission. Gentlemen exclaim, Great Britain "smites us on one cheek;" and what does administration? "It turns the other also." Gentlemen say, Great Britain is a robber; she "takes our cloak;" and what say administration? "Let her take our coat also." France and Great Britain requires you to relinquish a part of your commerce, and you yield it entirely. Sir, this conduct may be the way to dignity and honor in another world, but it will never secure safety and independence in this.

At every corner of this great city we meet some gentlemen of the majority, wringing their hands and exclaiming, "What shall we do? Nothing but embargo will save us. Remove it, and what shall we do?" Sir, it is not for me, an humble and uninfluential individual, at an awful distance from the predominant influences, to suggest plans of government. But, to my eye, the path of our duty is as distinct as the milky way; all studded with living sapphires; glowing with cumulating light. It is the path of active preparation, of dignified energy. It is the path of 1776. It consists, not in abandoning our rights, but in supporting them, as they exist, and where they exist, — on the ocean, as well as on the land. It consists, in taking the nature of things as the measure of the rights of your citizens, not the orders and decrees of imperious foreigners. Give what protection you can. Take no counsel of fear. Your strength will increase with the trial, and prove greater than you are now aware.

But I shall be told, " This may lead to war." I ask, " Are we now at peace ? " Certainly not, unless retiring from insult be peace, unless shrinking under the lash be peace. The surest way to prevent war is not to fear it. The idea that nothing on earth is so dreadful as war is inculcated too studiously among us. Disgrace is worse. Abandonment of essential rights is worse.

Sir, I could not refrain from seizing the first opportunity of spreading before this House the sufferings and exigencies of New England under this embargo. Some gentlemen may deem it not strictly before us. In my opinion, it is necessarily. For, if the idea of the committee be correct, and embargo is resistance, then this resolution sanctions its continuance. If, on the contrary, as I contend, embargo is submission, then this resolution is a pledge of its repeal.

SECOND SPEECH

ON THE REPORT OF THE COMMITTEE OF FOREIGN
RELATIONS; IN REPLY TO THE OBSERVATIONS
OF MR. BACON.

Dec. 7, 1808.

6

SECOND SPEECH

ON THE REPORT OF THE COMMITTEE ON FOREIGN RELATIONS; IN REPLY TO THE OBSERVATIONS OF MR. BACON.

DEC. 7, 1808.

[THE speech of the 28th of November made Mr. Quincy for the time being what Daniel O'Connell said of himself, " the best abused man living," both in Congress and by the Democratic press throughout the country. He was consoled, however, by Federal praise, quite as warm as the Democratic censure. On the 7th of the next month he took or made occasion for the following speech, in reply to his chief assailants. — ED.]

MR. SPEAKER, — I offer myself to the view of this House with very sensible embarrassment, in attempting to follow the honorable member from Tennessee (Mr. Campbell), — a gentleman who holds so distinguished a station on this floor, through thy blessing, Mr. Speaker, on his talents and industry. I place myself, with much reluctance, in competition with this our great political Æneas, — an illustrious leader of antiquity, whom in his present relations, and with his present projects, the gentleman from Tennessee not a little resembles. Since, in order to evade the ruin impending over our cities, taking my honorable colleague (Mr. Bacon) by one hand, and the honorable gentleman from Maryland (Mr. Montgomery) by the other, little Iulus, and wife Creusa, he is posting away into the woods, with Father Anchises and all the household gods.

When I had the honor of addressing this House, a few days ago, I touched this famous report of our committee on foreign relations, perhaps, a little too carelessly; perhaps, I handled it a little too roughly, considering its tender age and the manifest delicacy of its constitution. But, sir, I had no idea of affecting very exquisitely the sensibilities of any gentleman. I thought that this was a common report of one of our ordinary committees, which I had a right to canvass, or to slight, to applaud, or to censure, without raising any extraordinary concern, either here or elsewhere. But, from the general excitement which my inconsiderate treatment of this subject occasions, I fear that I have been mistaken. This can be no mortal fabric, Mr. Speaker. This must be that image which fell down from Jupiter, — present or future. Surely nothing but a being of celestial origin would raise such tumult in minds attempered like those which lead the destinies of this House.

Sir, I thought that this report had been a common piece of wood, — " *Inutile lignum*." Sir, just such a piece of wood as any day laborer might have hewed out, in an hour, had he health and a hatchet. But it seems that our honorable chairman of the committee of foreign relations " *maluit esse Deum*." Well, sir, I have no objections. If the workmen will, a god it shall be. I only wish, when gentlemen bring their sacred things upon this floor, that they would " blow a trumpet before them, as the heathens do," on such occasions, to the end that all true believers may prepare themselves to adore and tremble, and that all unbelievers may turn aside, and not disturb their devotions.

I assure gentlemen that I meant to commit no sacrilege. I had no intention, sir, of canvassing very strictly this report. I supposed that, when it had been published and circulated, it had answered all the purposes of its authors, and I felt no disposition to interfere with them. But the House is my witness that I am compelled, by the clamor raised, on all sides, by the friends of administration, to descend to particulars, and to examine it somewhat minutely.

My honorable colleague (Mr. Bacon) was pleased the other day to assert : . . . Sir, in referring to his observations on a former occasion, I beg the House not to imagine that I am about to follow him. No, sir, I will neither follow nor imitate him. I hang upon no man's skirts. I run barking at no man's heel. I canvass principles and measures, solely with a view to the great interests of my country. The idea of personal victory is lost in the total absorption of sense and mind in the importance of impending consequences. I say he was pleased to assert that I had dealt in general allegations against this report, without pointing out any particular objection. And the honorable chairman (Mr. Campbell) has reiterated the charge. Both have treated this alleged omission with no little asperity. Yet, sir, it is very remarkable that, so far from dealing in general allegations, I explicitly stated my objections. The alternatives presented by the report — war or suspension of our rights, and the recommendation of the latter, rather than take the risk of the former — I expressly censured. I went farther, — I compared these

alternatives with an extract from an address made by
the first Continental Congress to the inhabitants of Great
Britain, and attempted to show, by way of contrast,
what I thought the disgraceful spirit of the report.
Yet these gentlemen complain that I dealt in general
allegations. Before I close, sir, they will have, I hope,
no reason to repeat such objections. I trust I shall be
particular to their content.

Before entering upon an examination of this report, it
may be useful to recollect how it originated.

By the 3d section of the 2d article of the Constitution,
it is declared that the President of the United States
" shall, from time to time, give to Congress information
of the state of the Union, and recommend to their consideration such measures as he shall judge necessary and
expedient." It is, then, the duty of the President to
recommend such measures as in his judgment Congress
ought to adopt. A great crisis is impending over our
country. It is a time of alarm and peril and distress.
How has the President performed this constitutional
duty ? Why, after recapitulating, in a formal message,
our dangers and his trials, he expresses his confidence
that we shall, " with an unerring regard to the essential
rights and interests of the nation, weigh and compare
the painful alternatives out of which a choice is to be
made," and that " the alternative chosen will be maintained with fortitude and patriotism." In this way our
chief magistrate performs his duty. A storm is approaching, — the captain calls his choice hands upon
deck, leaves the rudder swinging, and sets the crew to
scuffle about alternatives. This message, pregnant with
nondescript alternatives, is received by this House.

And what do we ? Why, constitute a great committee
of foreign relations, and, lest they should not have their
attention completely occupied by the pressing exigencies
of those with France and Great Britain, they are en-
dowed with the whole mass, British, Spanish, and
French ; Barbary powers and Indian neighbors. And
what does this committee ? Why, after seven days'
solemn conclave, they present to this House an illustrious report, loaded with alternatives, — nothing but
alternatives. The cold meat of the palace is hashed and
served up to us, piping hot, from our committee room.

In considering this report, I shall pay no attention to
either its beginning or its conclusion. The former consists of shavings from old documents, and the latter of
birdlime for new converts. The twelfth page is the
heart of this report. That I mean to canvass. And I do
assert that there is not one of all the principal positions
contained in it which is true, in the sense and to the
extent assumed by the committee. Let us examine
each separately.

" Your committee can perceive no other alternative
but abject and degrading submission, — war with both
nations, or a continuance and enforcement of the present suspension of our commerce." Here is a trifurcate
alternative. Let us consider each branch, and see if
either be true in the sense assumed by the committee.
The first, " abject and degrading submission," takes two
things for granted, — that trading, pending the edicts of
France and Great Britain, is submission ; and next, that
it is submission in its nature, abject and degrading.
Neither is true. It is not submission to trade, pending
those edicts, because they do not command you to trade.

They command you not to trade. When you refuse to trade you submit, not when you carry on that trade, as far as you can, which they prohibit. Again, it is not true that such trading is abject and disgraceful, and that, too, upon the principles avowed by the advocates of this report. Trading, while these edicts are suspended over our commerce, is submission, say they, because we have not physical force to resist the power of these belligerents; of course, if we trade, we must submit to these restrictions; not having power to evade, or break through them. Now, admit for the sake of argument what, however, in fact I deny, that the belligerents have the power to carry into effect their decrees so perfectly that, by reason of the orders of Great Britain, we are physically disabled from going to France, and that by the edicts of France, we are, in like manner, disabled from going to Great Britain. If such be our case, in relation to these powers, the question is, whether submitting to exercise all the trade which remains to us, notwithstanding the edicts, is " abject and degrading."

In the first place, I observe that submission is not to beings constituted as we are always " abject and degrading." We submit to the decrees of providence, — to the laws of our nature, — absolute weakness submits to absolute power, — and there is nothing, in such submission, shameful or degrading. It is no dishonor, for finite, not to contend with infinite. There is no loss of reputation if creatures such as men perform not impossibilities. If, then, it be true, in the sense asserted by some of the advocates of this report, that it is physically impossible for us to trade with France and Great Britain and their dependencies by reason of these edicts, still there is nothing "abject or degrading" in carrying on such trade as these edicts leave open to us, let it be never so small or so trifling ; which, however, it might be easily shown, as it has been, that it is neither the one nor the other.   Sir, in this point of view, it is no more disgraceful for us to trade to Sweden, to China, to the North-West coast, or to Spain and her dependencies, not one of which countries is now included in those edicts, than it is disgraceful for us to walk, because we are unable to fly ; no more than it is shameful for man to use and enjoy the surface of this globe, because he has not at his command the whole circle of nature, and cannot range at will over all the glorious spheres which constitute the universe.

The gentleman from Tennessee (Mr. Campbell) called upon us just now to tell him what was disgraceful submission, if carrying on commerce under these restrictions was not such submission.   I will tell that gentleman. That submission is "abject and disgraceful," which yields to the decrees of frail and feeble power, as though they were irresistible, — which takes counsel of fear, and weighs not our comparative force, — which abandons the whole at a summons to deliver up a part, — which makes the will of others the measure of rights which God and nature, not only have constituted eternal and unalienable, but have also indued us with ample means to maintain.

My argument, on this clause of the report of the committee, may be presented in this form.   Either the United States have, or they have not, physical ability to carry on commerce, in defiance of the edicts of both, or of either, of these nations.   If we have not physical ability to carry on the trade which they prohibit, then it is no disgrace to exercise that commerce which these irresistible decrees permit. If we have such physical ability, then to the degree in which we abandon that commerce which we have the power to carry on, is our submission " abject and disgraceful." It is yielding without struggle. It is sacrificing our rights, not because we have not force, but because we have not spirit, to maintain them. It is in this point of view that I am disgusted with this report. It abjures what it recommends. It declaims in heroics against submission, and proposes in creeping prose a tame and servile subserviency.

It cannot be concealed, let gentlemen try as much as they will, that we can trade, not only with one, but with both these belligerents, notwithstanding these restrictive decrees. The risk to Great Britain against French capture scarcely amounts to two per cent. That to France against Great Britain is, unquestionably, much greater. But what is that to us? It is not our fault, if the power of Britain on the ocean is superior to that of Bonaparte. It is equal and exact justice, between both nations, for us to trade with both as far as it is in our power. Great as the power of Britain is on the ocean, the enterprise and intrepidity of our merchants are more than a match for it. They will get your products to the Continent, in spite of her navy. But suppose they do not? Suppose they fail, and are captured in the attempt? What is that to us after we have given them full notice of all their dangers, and perfect warning, either of our inability or of our determination not to protect them? If they take the risk it is at their peril. And upon whom does the loss fall? As it does now, through the operation of your embargo, on the planter, on the farmer, on the mechanic, on the day laborer? No, sir. On the insurer, on the capitalist, on those who, in the full exercise of their intelligence, apprised of all circumstances, are willing to take the hazard for the sake of the profit.

I will illustrate my general idea by a supposition. There are two avenues to the ocean from the harbor of New York, — by the Narrows and through Long Island Sound. Suppose the fleets both of France and Great Britain should block up the Narrows, so that to pass them would be physically impossible in the relative state of our naval force. Will gentlemen seriously contend that there would be any thing " abject or disgraceful " if the people of New York should submit to carry on their trade through the Sound ? Would the remedy for this interference with our rights be abandoning the ocean altogether? Again, suppose that, instead of both nations blockading the same, each should station its force at a different one, — France at the mouth of the Sound, Britain at the Narrows. In such case would staying at home and refusing any more to go upon the sea be exercise of independence in the citizens of New York ? Great philosophers may call it " dignified retirement " if they will. I call it, and I am mistaken if the people would not also call it, " base and abject submission." Sir, what in such a case would be true honor ? Why, to consider well which adversary is weakest, and cut our way to our rights through the path which he obstructs. Having removed the smaller impediment, we should return with courage strengthened by trial and animated by success, to the relief of our rights from the pressure of the strongest assailant. But all this is war. And war is never to be incurred. If this be the national principle, avow it. Tell your merchants you will not protect them. But for heaven's sake do not deny them the power of relieving their own and the nation's burdens by the exercise of their own ingenuity. Sir, impassable as the barriers offered by these edicts are in the estimation of members on this floor, the merchants abroad do not estimate them as insurmountable. Their anxiety to risk their property in defiance of them is full evidence of this. The great danger to mercantile ingenuity is internal envy ; the corrosion of weakness or prejudice. Its external hazard is ever infinitely smaller. That practical intelligence which this class of men possesses beyond any other in the community, excited by self-interest, the strongest of human passions, is too elastic to be confined by the limits of exterior human powers, however great or uncommon. Build a Chinese wall, the wit of your merchants, if permitted freely to operate, will break through it, or overleap it, or under-creep it.

> . . . "mille adde catenas,
> Effugiet tamen hæc sceleratus vincula Proteus."

The second branch of the alternatives under consideration is equally deceptive : " War with both nations." Can this ever be an alternative ? Did you ever read in history, can you conceive in fancy, a war with two nations, each of whom is at war with the other, without an union with one against the other immediately resulting ? It cannot exist in nature. The very idea is absurd. It never can be an alternative whether we

shall fight two nations, each hostile to the other. But
it may be, and, if we are to fight at all, it is a very
serious question, which of the two we are to select as
an adversary. As to the third branch of these celebrated alternatives, " a continuance and enforcement of
the present system of commerce," I need not spend
time to show that this does not include all the alternatives which exist under this head, since the committee
immediately admit that there does exist another alternative, " partial repeal," about which they proceed to
reason.

The report proceeds : " The first " (abject and degrading submission) " cannot require any discussion."
Certainly not. Submission of that quality which the
committee assume, and with the epithets of which they
choose to invest it, can never require discussion at any
time. But whether trading under these orders and decrees be such submission, whether we are not competent
to resist them, in part, if not in whole, without a total
abandonment of the exercise of all our maritime rights,
the comparative effects of the edicts of each upon our
commerce, and the means we possess to influence or
control either, are all fair and proper subjects of discussion, some of which the committee have wholly neglected, and none of which have they examined as the
House had a right to expect.

The committee proceed " to dissipate the illusion "
that there is any " middle course," and to reassert the
position before examined, that " there is no other alternative than war with both nations, or a continuance
of the present system." This position they undertake
to support by two assertions: First, that " war with

one of the belligerents only would be submission to the edicts and will of the other ; " second, that " repeal, in whole or in part, of the embargo must necessarily be war or submission."

As to the first assertion, it is a miserable fallacy, confounding coincidence of interest with a subjection of will ; things in their nature palpably distinct. A man may do what another wills, nay, what he commands, and not act in submission to his will or in obedience to his command. Our interest or duty may coincide with the line of conduct another presumes to prescribe. Shall we vindicate our independence at the expense of our social or moral obligations ? I exemplify my idea in this way : Two bullies beset your door, from which there are but two avenues. One of them forbids you to go by the left, the other forbids you to go by the right avenue. Each is willing that you should pass by the way which he permits. In such case, what will you do ? Will you keep house for ever rather than make choice of the path through which you will resume your external rights ? You cannot go both ways at once ; you must make your election. Yet in making such election you must necessarily coincide with the wishes and act according to the commands of one of the bullies. Yet who, before this committee, ever thought an election of one of two inevitable courses made under such circumstances " abject and degrading submission " to the will of either of the assailants. The second assertion, that " repeal, in whole or in part, of the embargo must necessarily be war or submission " the committee proceed to maintain by several subsidiary assertions : First, " A general repeal, without arming, would be submission to both nations." So far from this being true, the reverse is the fact: it would be submission to neither. Great Britain does not say, "You shall trade with me." France does not say, "You shall trade with me." If this was the language of their edicts, there might be some cause for the assertion of the committee, If we trade with either we submit. The edicts of each declare you shall not trade with my adversary. Our servile, knee-crooking embargo says, "You shall, therefore, not trade." Can any submission be more palpable, more "abject, more disgraceful!" A general repeal without arming would be only an exercise of our natural rights under the protection of our mercantile ingenuity, and not under that of physical power. Whether our merchants shall arm or not is a question of political expediency and of relative force. It may be very true that we can fight our way to neither country, and yet it may be also very true that we may carry on a very important commerce with both. The strength of the national arm may not be equal to contend with either, and yet the wit of our merchants may be an overmatch for the edicts of all. The question of arming or not arming has reference only to the mode in which we shall best enjoy our rights, and not at all to the quality of the act of trading during these edicts. To exercise commerce is our absolute right. If we arm, we may possibly extend the field beyond that which mere ingenuity would open to us. Whether the extension thus required be worthy of the risk and expense is a fair question. But, decide it either way, how is trading as far as we have ability made more abject than not trading at all.

I come to the second subsidiary assertion : " A general repeal and arming of merchant vessels would be war with both, and war of the worst kind, suffering the enemies to plunder us without retaliation upon them."

I have before exposed the absurdity of a war with two belligerents, each hostile to the other. It cannot be true, therefore, that " a general repeal and arming . our merchant vessels " would be such a war. Neither if war resulted would it be " war of the worst kind." In my humble apprehension a war in which our enemies are permitted to plunder us and our merchants not permitted to defend their property, is somewhat worse than a war like this, in which, with arms in their hands, our brave seamen might sometimes prove too strong for their piratical assailants. By the whole amount of property which we might be able to preserve by these means, would such a war be better than that in which we are now engaged. For the committee assure us (page 14) that the aggressions to which we are subject " are to all intents and purposes a maritime war, waged by both nations against the United States."

The last assertion of the committee in this most masterly page is, that " a partial repeal must, from the situation of Europe, necessarily be actual submission to one of the aggressors, and war with the other." In the name of common sense, how can this be true ? The trade to Sweden, to Spain, to China, are not now affected by the orders or decrees of either belligerent. How is it submission, then, to these orders for us to trade to Gottenburg, when neither France nor Britain command nor prohibit it ? Of what consequence is it to us in what way the Gottenburg merchant disposes of

our products after he has paid us our price? I am not
about to deny that a trade to Gottenburg would defeat
the purpose of coercing Great Britain through the want
of our supplies. But I reason on the report upon its
avowed principles. If gentlemen adhere to their system
as a means of coercion, let the administration avow it as
such, and support the system by arguments such as their
friends use every day on this floor. . Let them avow, as
those friends do, that this is our mode of hostility against
Great Britain; that it is better than "ball and gun-
powder." Let them show that the means are adequate
to the end; let them exhibit to us, beyond the term of
all this suffering, a happy salvation and a glorious victory, and the people may then submit to it, even without murmur. But while the administration support their
system only as a municipal regulation, as a means of
safety and preservation, those who canvass their principle are not called upon to contest with them on ground
which not only they do not take, but which officially
they disavow. As partial repeal would not be submission to either, so also it would not be war with either.
A trade to Sweden would not be war with Great Britain;
that nation is her ally, and she permits it: nor with
France; though Sweden is her enemy, she does not
prohibit it. "Ah! but," say the committee (page 13),
"a measure which would supply exclusively one of the
belligerents would be war with the other." This is the
state secret; this is the master-key to the whole policy.
You must not only not do what the letter of these orders
prohibits, but you must not sin against the spirit of them.
The great purpose is to prevent your products from
getting to our enemy; and to effect this you must not

7

only so act as to obey the terms of the decrees; but, keeping the great purpose of them always in sight, you must extend their construction to cases which they cannot by any rule of reason be made to include.

Sir, I have done with this report. I would not have submitted to the task of canvassing it if gentlemen had not thrown the gauntlet with the air of sturdy defiance. I willingly leave to this House and the nation to decide whether the position I took in the commencement of my argument is not maintained, — that there is not one of the principal positions contained in this twelfth page, the heart of this report, which is true in the sense and to the extent assumed by the committee.

It was under these general impressions that I used the word "loathsome," which has so often been repeated. Sir, it may not have been a well-chosen word. It was that which happened to come to hand first. I meant to express my disgust at what appeared to me a mass of bold assumptions and of ill-cemented sophisms.

I said, also, that "the spirit which it breathed was disgraceful." Sir, I meant no reflection upon the committee. Honest men and wise men may mistake the character of the spirit which they recommend, or by which they are actuated. When called upon to reason concerning that which by adoption is to become identified with the national character, I am bound to speak of it as it appears to my vision. I may be mistaken, yet I ask the question, Is not the spirit which it breathes disgraceful? Is it not disgraceful to abandon the exercise of all our commercial rights because our rivals interfere with a part? not only to refrain from exercising that trade which they prohibit, but for fear of giving

offence to decline that which they permit ? Is it not
disgraceful, after inflammatory recapitulation of insults
and plunderings and burnings and confiscatious and
murders and actual war made upon us, to talk of
nothing but alternatives, of general declarations, of
still longer suspension of our rights, and retreating
further out of " harm's way " ? If this course be
adopted by my country, I hope I am in error concerning its real character. But to my sense this whole
report is nothing else than a recommendation to us of
the abandonment of our essential rights, and apologies
for doing it.

Before I sit down, I feel myself compelled to notice
some observations which have been made in different
quarters of this House on the remarks which, at an early
stage of this debate, I had the honor of submitting to
its consideration. My honorable colleague (Mr. Bacon)
was pleased to represent me as appealing to the people,
over the heads of the whole government, against the
authority of a law which had not only the sanction of
all the legislative branches of the government, but also
of the judiciary. Sir, I made no such appeal. I did
not so much as threaten it. I admitted expressly the
binding authority of the law. But I claim a right,
which I ever will claim and ever will exercise, to urge
on this floor my opinion of the unconstitutionality of a
law and my reasons for that opinion as a valid ground
for its repeal. Sir, I will not only do this, I will do
more. If a law be, in my apprehension, dangerous in
its principles, ruinous in its consequences, above all if
it be unconstitutional, I will not fail, in every fair and
honorable way, to awaken the people to a sense of their

peril, and to quicken them, by the exercise of their constitutional privileges, to vindicate themselves and posterity from ruin.

My honorable colleague (Mr. Bacon) was also pleased
to refer to me as a man of divisions and distinctions,
waging war with adverbs and dealing in figures. Sir, I
am sorry that my honorable colleague should stoop " from
his pride of place " at such humble game as my poor style
presents to him. Certainly, Mr. Speaker, I cannot but
confess that " deeming high" of this station which I
hold ; standing, as it were, in the awful presence of an
assembled people, — I am more than ordinarily anxious,
on all occasions, to select the best thoughts in my narrow storehouse, and to adapt to them the most appropriate dress in my intellectual wardrobe. I know not
whether on this account I am justly obnoxious to the
asperity of my honorable colleague. But on the subject
of figures, Mr. Speaker, this I know, and cannot refrain
from assuring this House, that as, on the one hand, I
shall, to the extent of my humble talents, always be
ambitious, and never cease striving, to make a decent
figure on this floor, so, on the other, I never can be ambitious, but, on the contrary, shall ever strive chiefly
to avoid cutting a figure like my honorable colleague.

The gentleman from Georgia (Mr. Troup), the other
day, told this House that, if commerce were permitted,
such was the state of our foreign relations, none but
bankrupts would carry on trade. Sir, the honorable
gentleman has not attained correct information in this
particular. I do not believe that I state any thing
above the real fact when I say that, on the day this legislature assembled, one hundred vessels, at least, were

lying in the different ports and harbors of New England, loaded, riding at single anchor, ready and anxious for nothing so much as for your leave to depart. Certainly, this does not look much like any doubt that a field of advantageous commerce would open if you would unbar the door to our citizens. That this was the case in Massachusetts, I know. Before I left that part of the country, I had several applications from men who stated that they had property in such situations, and soliciting me to give them the earliest information of your probable policy. The men so applying, sir, I can assure the House, were not bankrupts, but intelligent merchants, shrewd to perceive their true interests, keen to pursue them. An honorable gentleman (Mr. Troup, of Georgia) was also pleased to speak of "a paltry trade in potash and codfish," and to refer to me as the representative of men who raised "beef and pork, and butter and cheese, and potatoes and cabbages." Well, sir, I confess the fact. I am the representative, in part, of men the products of whose industry are beef and pork, and butter and cheese, and potatoes and cabbages. And let me tell that honorable gentleman that I would not yield the honor of representing such men to be the representative of all the growers of cotton and rice and tobacco and indigo in the whole world. Sir, the men whom I represent not only raise these humble articles, but they do it with the labor of their own hands, with the sweat of their own brows. And by this, their habitual mode of hardy industry, they acquire a vigor of nerve, a strength of muscle, and a spirit and intelligence somewhat characteristic. And let me assure that honorable gentleman that the men of whom I speak will not, at his call nor at the invitation of any set of men from his quarter of the Union, undertake to " drive one another into the ocean." But, on the contrary, whenever they once realize that their rights are invaded, they will unite, like a band of brothers, and drive their enemies there.

The honorable gentleman from Kentucky (Mr. Johnson), speaking of the embargo, said that this was the kind of conflict which our fathers waged ; and my honorable colleague (Mr. Bacon) made a poor attempt to confound this policy with the non-intercourse and non-importation agreement of 1774 and 1775. Sir, nothing can be more dissimilar. The non-intercourse and non-importation agreement of that period, so far from destroying commerce, fostered and encouraged it. The trade with Great Britain was, indeed, voluntarily obstructed, but the enterprise of our merchants found a new incentive in the commerce with all the other nations of the globe, which succeeded immediately on our escape from the monopoly of the mother country. Our navigation was never suspended. The field of commerce, at that period, so far from being blasted by pestiferous regulations, was extended by the effect of the restrictions adopted.

But, let us grant all they assert. Admit, for the sake of argument, that the embargo which restrains us now from communication with all the world is precisely synonymous with that non-intercourse and non-importation which restrained us then from Great Britain. Suppose the war which we now wage with that nation is in every respect the same as that which our fathers waged with her in 1774 and 1775. Have we, from the

effects of their trial, any lively hope of success in our
present attempt? Did our fathers either effect a change
in her injurious policy, or prevent a war, by non-importation and non-intercourse? Sir, they did neither the
one nor the other.   Her policy was never changed
until she had been beaten on our soil in an eight years'
war.   Our fathers never relied upon non-intercourse
and non-importation as measures of hostile coercion.
They placed their dependence upon them solely as
means of pacific influence among the people of that
nation.   The relation in which this country stood at
that time, with regard to Great Britain, gave a weight
and a potency to these measures then which, in our
present relation to her, we can neither hope nor imagine
possible.   At that period we were her colonies, a part
of her family.   Our prosperity was essentially hers.   So
it was avowed in this country, so it was admitted in
Great Britain.   Every refusal of intercourse which had
a tendency to show the importance of these, then colonies, to the parent country, of the part to the whole,
was a natural and a wise means of giving weight to our
remonstrances.   We pretended not to control, but to
influence, by making her feel our importance.   In this
attempt, we excited no national pride on the other side
of the Atlantic.   Our success was no national degra-
dation ; for the more we developed our resources and
relative weight, the more we discovered the strength
and resources of the British power.   We were then
component parts of it.   All the measures of the colonies,
antecedent to the Declaration of Independence, had this
principle for its basis.   As such, non-importation and
non-intercourse were adopted in this country.   As such,

they met the co-operation of the patriots of Great
Britain, who deemed themselves deviating from none of
their national duties when they avowed themselves the
allies of American patriots, to drive, through the influence of the loss of our trade, the ministry from their
places or their measures. Those patriots did co-operate
with our fathers, and that openly, in exciting discontent
under the effect of our non-intercourse agreements. In
so doing, they failed in none of their obligations to their
sovereign. In no nation, can it ever be a failure of duty
to maintain that the safety of the whole depends on
preserving its due weight to every part. Yet, notwithstanding the natural and little suspicious use of these
instruments of influence ; notwithstanding the zeal of
the American people coincided with the views of the
Congress, and a mighty party existed in Great Britain
openly leagued with our fathers to give weight and
effect to their measures, — they did not effect the purposes for which they were put into operation. The
British policy was not abandoned. War was not prevented. How, then, can any encouragement be drawn
from that precedent, to support us under the privations of the present system of commercial suspension ? Can any nation admit that the trade of another
is so important to her welfare as that, on its being
withdrawn, any obnoxious policy must be abandoned,
without at the same time admitting that she is no
longer independent ? Sir, I could indeed wish that
it were in our power to regulate not only Great Britain
but the whole world by opening or closing our ports. It
would be a glorious thing for our country to possess
such a mighty weapon of offence. But, acting in a

public capacity, with the high responsibilities resulting from the great interests dependent upon my decision, I cannot yield to the wishes of love-sick patriots, or the visions of teeming enthusiasts. I must see the adequacy of means .to their ends. I must see not merely that it is very desirable that Great Britain should be brought to our feet by this embargo, but that there is some likelihood of such a consequence to the measure, before I can concur in that universal distress and ruin which, if much longer continued, will inevitably result from it. Since, then, every dictate of sense and reflection convinces me of the utter futility of this system, as a means of coercion on Great Britain, I shall not hesitate to urge its abandonment. No, sir, not even, although, like others, I should be assailed by all the terrors of the outcry of British influence.

Really, Mr. Speaker, I know not how to express the shame and disgust with which I am filled when I hear language of this kind cast out upon this floor, and thrown in the faces of men standing justly at no mean height in the confidence of their countrymen. Sir, I did indeed know that such vulgar aspersions were circulating among the lower passions of our nature. I knew that such vile substances were ever tempering between the paws of some printer's devil. I knew that foul exhalations, like these, daily rose in our cities, and crept along the ground, just as high as the spirits of lamp-black and saline oil could elevate ; falling soon, by native baseness, into oblivion. I knew, too, that this species of party insinuation was a mighty engine in this quarter of the country on an election day, played off from the top of a stump, or the top of a hogshead, while the gin circulated, while barbecue was roasting; in those happy, fraternal associations and consociations, when those who speak utter without responsibility and those who listen hear without scrutiny. But little did I think that such odious shapes would dare to obtrude themselves on this national floor, among honorable men, and select representatives, the confidential agents of a wise, a thoughtful, and a virtuous people. I want language to express my contempt and indignation at the sight.

So far as respects the attempt which has been made to cast such aspersion on that part of the country which I have the honor to represent, I beg this honorable House to understand that, so long as they who circulated such insinuations deal only in generals and touch not particulars, they may gain among the ignorant and the stupid a vacant and a staring audience. But when once these suggestions are brought to bear upon those individuals who, in New England, have naturally the confidence of their countrymen, there is no power in these calumnies. The men who now lead the influences of that country, and in whose councils the people on the day when the tempest shall come will seek refuge, are men whose stake is in the soil, whose interests are identified with those of the mass of their brethren, whose private lives and public sacrifices present a never-failing antidote to the poison of malicious invectives. On such men, sir, party spirit may indeed cast its odious filth, but there is a polish in their virtues to which no such slime can adhere. They are owners of the soil, real yeomanry; many of them men who led in the councils of our country in the dark day which preceded national independence ; many of them men who, like my honorable friend from Connecticut, on my left (Colonel Talmage), stood foremost on the perilous edge of battle, making their breasts in the day of danger a bulwark for their country.

True it is, Mr. Speaker, there is another and a much more numerous class, composed of such as, through defect of age, can claim no share in the glories of our Revolution : such as have not yet been blest with the happy opportunity of " playing the man " for their country ; generous sons of illustrious sires ; men not to be deterred from fulfilling the high obligations they owe to this people by the sight of these foul and offensive weapons.   Men who, with little experience of their own to boast, will fly to the tombs of their fathers, and questioning concerning their duties the spirit which hovers there, will no more shrink from maintaining their native rights, through fear of the sharpness of malevolent tongues, than they will, if put to the trial, shrink from defending them, through fear of the sharpness of their enemies' swords.

SPEECH

ON THE BILL FOR RAISING FIFTY THOUSAND VOLUNTEERS.

DEC. 30, 1808.

SPEECH

ON THE BILL FOR RAISING FIFTY THOUSAND VOLUNTEERS.

Dec. 30, 1808.

———

[In the course of December, 1808, a bill was introduced for raising fifty thousand volunteers. It caused excited discussions between the two parties. The administration affirmed that this force should be provided in case the embargo should fail of its purpose and war should ensue. The Federalists were willing to vote for the bill provided its object was defined. If the administration contemplated war, they would vote for any necessary force to carry it on. But, if the purpose of the proposed army was to enforce the embargo, they should resist it to the utmost of their ability. It was on this occasion that Mr. Quincy made the following speech, on the 30th of December, 1808, which caused a great excitement, as will be seen by the interruptions of the friends of the bill. — Ed.]

I AGREE with the gentleman from Virginia (Mr. Eppes) that the present is a period in which it becomes members of this legislature to maintain their independence and not to shrink from responsibility. I agree that it is a time in which all men in places of trust should weigh well the principles by which they are actuated and the ends at which they aim; and that they should mark both so distinctly as that they may be fully understood by the people. But I hope it is not, and that there never will be, a time in which it becomes the duty of any man or set of men on this floor, under pretence of national exigencies. to concur in an infringement of the limits of the Constitution. I trust it is not a time, for a member of such a legislature as this, thoughtlessly to strengthen hands which already hold powers inconsistent with civil liberty, by our surrender of authority, especially intrusted to us by the people, into the exclusive possession of another department of the government.

The gentleman from Virginia (Mr. Eppes) alleges that the men whom he calls Federalists have, for party purposes, represented the embargo as a permanent measure. He disclaims such an idea, both on his own account and on that of a majority of this House. On this head, I am ready to maintain that the embargo law, as it was originally passed, was an abuse of the powers vested in this branch of the legislature, and, as it has been subsequently enforced by supplementary laws, is a manifest violation of the Constitution, and an assumption of powers vested in the States ; and that, until I have some satisfaction on these points, I am not disposed to pass a law for raising such an additional military force as this bill contemplates.

Concerning the permanency of the embargo, about which so much wire-drawing ingenuity has been exercised, this I assert. that, so far as relates to the powers of this House, the embargo is permanent. That control over commerce which the Constitution has vested in us, we have transferred to the executive. Whether the people shall ever enjoy any commerce again, or whether we shall ever have any power in its regulation, depends

not upon the will of this House, but upon the will of
the President and of twelve members of the Senate.
The manner in which the powers vested in this branch
of the legislature have been exercised, I hesitate not to
declare a flagrant abuse of those powers and a violation
of the most acknowledged safeguards of civil liberty.

Sir, what is the relation in which this House, in the
eye of the Constitution, stands to the people ? Is it not
composed of men emanating from the mass of the community ? Are not our interests peculiarly identified with
theirs ? Is not this the place in which the people have
a right naturally to look for the strongest struggle for
our constitutional privileges, and the last surrender of
them unconditionally to the executive ? Is not the
power to regulate commerce one of the most important
of all the trusts reposed in us by the people ? Yet how
have we exercised this most interesting power ? Why,
sir, we have so exercised it as not only to annihilate
commerce for the present, but so as that we can never,
hereafter, have any commerce to regulate, until the
President and twelve Senators permit. Gentlemen,
when pressed upon the constitutional point resulting
from the permanent nature of this embargo, repel it, as
the gentleman from Virginia (Mr. Eppes) did just now,
by a broad denial. " It is not permanent," say they.
" It was never intended to be permanent." Yet it has
every feature of permanency. It is impossible for terms
to give it a more unlimited duration. With respect to intentions, the President and Senate have a right to speak
on that subject. They have a power to permit
commerce again to be prosecuted, or to continue its
prohibition. But what right have we to talk in this

8

manner? I know that we every day amuse ourselves in making some law about commerce. Sir, this is permitted. It is a part of the delusion which we practise upon the people, and perhaps upon ourselves. While engaged in debate, we feel as if the power to regulate commerce was yet in this House. But put this matter to the test. Pass a law unanimously to-morrow repealing the embargo. Let two-thirds of the Senate concur. Let the President and twelve men determine not to repeal. I ask, is there any power in this House to prevent them from continuing this embargo for ever? The fact is undeniable. Let the President and twelve men obstinately persist in adherence to this measure, and, in spite of the intentions of this House, the people can alone again obtain their commerce by a revolution. It follows, from what I have stated, that those may well enough talk about what they intend who have the power of fulfilling their intentions. But on that subject it becomes the members of this House to be silent, since that power which we once possessed has by our own act departed. So far as this House can ever hereafter enjoy the opportunity of again regulating commerce. it depends not upon the gift it received from the people, but upon the restoration to us of that power which, the people having intrusted to our care, we have without limitation transferred to the executive.

Yes, sir. The people *once* had a commerce. *Once* this House possessed the power to regulate it. Of all the grants in the Constitution, perhaps this was most highly prized by the people. It was truly the apple of their eye. To their concern for it the Constitution almost owes its existence. They brought this, the object of their choice affections, and delivered it to the custody of this House, as a tender parent would deliver the hope of his declining years, with a trembling solicitude, to its selected guardians. And how have we conducted in this sacred trust? Why, delivered it over to the care of twelve dry-nurses, concerning whose tempers we know nothing; for whose intentions we cannot vouch; and who, for any thing we know, may some of them have an interest in destroying it.

Yes, sir, the people did intrust us with that great power, — the regulation of commerce. It was their most precious jewel. Richer than all the mines of Peru and Golconda. But we have sported with it as though it were common dust. With a thoughtless indifference, — in the dead of the night, not under the cover of the cheering pinions of our eagle, but under the mortal shade of the bat's wing, — we surrendered this rich deposit. It is gone. And we have nothing else to do than to beg back, at the footstool of the executive, the people's patrimony. Sir, I know the answer which will, and it is the only one which can, be given. "There is no fear of an improper use of this power by the President and Senate. There is no danger in trusting this most excellent man." Why, sir, this is the very slave's gibberish. What other reason could the cross-legged Turk or the cringing Parisian give for that implicit confidence they yield to their sovereigns, except that it is impossible they should abuse their power.

The state of things I mention does not terminate in mere verbal precision or constructive distinctions. The very continuance of the measure has, in my opinion, its root in the situation which results from this, as I deem it, abuse of our constitutional powers. Does any man believe, if the embargo had been originally limited, that a bill continuing it could now be passed through all the branches? I know that gentlemen who originally voted for this embargo, and will probably for the enforcement of it, have urged the situation of this House, in relation to it, as a reason for farther adherence. "It is a measure of the executive," say they. "Suppose this House should pass a law repealing it. Should he negative, what effect would result but to show distracted councils. In the present situation of our country, nothing is so desirable as unanimity." I know that, substantially, such arguments have been urged.

[Mr. J. G. Jackson wished the gentleman to name the persons to whom he alluded.

Mr. Quincy said that he did not deem himself bound to state names connected with facts by which he had acquired the knowledge of particular dispositions in the House. It was enough for him to state them, and leave the nation to judge if there were, under the circumstances, any thing improbable or unnatural in them.

Mr. Nicholas called the gentleman from Massachusetts to order. He regretted to say that throughout the whole session there had been a total departure from the idea which he had of order. When it was attempted to palm upon those with whom he acted opinions which all must disclaim, he was compelled to object to the disorderly course pursued.

Mr. Quincy said that he had no intention to palm upon any gentlemen sentiments which they disavowed. We did not suppose that the gentlemen who entertained such sentiments would disavow them. He said he should certainly not mention names. He did not think that the argument derived any strength from the fact that such expressions had been used by any gentleman. They are natural and inevitable from the situation in which gentlemen are placed in relation to the executive. Men willing to take off the embargo, yet not willing to counteract the system of the President, were necessitated to adopt such reasoning as this. It was unavoidable when they came to reflect upon the powers which remained to this House in relation to the repeal of this law.

Mr. Nicholas required that the gentleman should observe order.

Mr. G. W. Campbell said that, as the gentleman had made a reflection on members in the majority, he must be permitted to observe that he utterly disclaimed any such opinion as the gentleman had charged indiscriminately upon the majority.

Mr. Quincy said that he had made no such indiscriminate charge on the majority. An attempt had been made to give the discussion a turn which he neither anticipated nor intended. I understand, said Mr. Quincy, the cause of this interruption. It is not the fact intimated, but the force of the argument stated, which startles gentlemen from their seats. They like not to hear the truth elucidated concerning their abuse of power intrusted to them by the people. In reply to the gentleman from Virginia (Mr. Eppes), who alleged that for party purposes the embargo had been represented permanent, I undertook to show that, as far as respects this House, it was to all intents permanent. This is the insupportable position. The embargo —

Mr. J. G. Jackson called Mr. Quincy to order. This disorder, he said, had progressed too long. There had not only been disorder on the floor of the House, but in the galleries, and from British subjects too, which had interrupted the gentleman from Virginia (Mr. Eppes), whilst he had been speaking a few moments ago. It was not in order to discuss the subject of embargo on this question. Every thing which presented itself to the House was made a question of embargo. It was the watchword of the day.

The Speaker requested Mr. Quincy to take his seat, and asked Mr. Jackson to put down in writing the words to which he objected.

Mr. Jackson said he could not specify particular words to which he had objected, unless, indeed, he were to include the gentleman's whole speech. He wished, however, to know of the Speaker, is it in order, on a question for raising volunteer troops, to discuss the constitutionality of the embargo?

The Speaker observed that a very wide range had been taken in debate, and that, excluding personal matter, the gentleman was in order to reply to observations of other gentlemen.

Mr. Quincy said that he had been drawn unexpectedly into this course of debate by following the gentleman from Virginia (Mr. Eppes). He said that he wished to lay before the House and the nation —

Mr. Eppes said that he had said nothing concerning the supplementary embargo law, now before the House, which he conceived the gentleman was about to introduce into the discussion. He hoped the gentleman would suspend his observations upon the subject until

it came before the House, when, notwithstanding all
the clamor on the subject, it would be found that there
was not a provision contained in it which was not to
be found in the present revenue laws.

MR. QUINCY said he was not about to bring the supplementary embargo bill into debate. The gentleman
had asserted that the embargo law was not permanent;
that the Constitution had not been violated. He had
taken the gentleman upon that ground. And the course
of his observations had been to prove that the embargo
was permanent, so far as respected the powers of this
House to repeal, and that the Constitution had been
violated.

MR. EPPES said that he had not said that the Constitution had not been violated.

MR. QUINCY said that he had no particular inclination to speak at that moment, and if gentlemen did not
wish to hear —

MR. EPPES said he had no objection to hear the gentleman state any violations of the Constitution, and he
should take the privilege of a member to answer them,
if they were plausible.

MR. MASTERS made some observations upon the point
of order; and, as the House was rather in a state of
agitation, moved to adjourn. Mr. Quincy having given
way for the purpose, — negatived; ayes, 22.]

Notwithstanding all the interruptions I have experienced, my observations have been perfectly in order.
The reason I am opposed to the resolution is, that the
force proposed to be raised is, in my opinion, intended
not to meet a foreign enemy, but to enforce the embargo
laws. Now is it not the most pertinent and strongest

of all arguments against the adoption of such a·resolution, to prove that the powers of the executive, in these respects, already transcend the limits of the Constitution, and that these laws proposed thus to be enforced are open violations of it? Considering, however, the temper of the House, I shall limit myself to the statement and elucidation of a single position. And the argument I shall offer will be only in outline. I will not enter into the wide field which the greatness of the question naturally opens. I know that, as soon as my position is stated, gentlemen advocating the present measures will be ready to exclaim, It is a small objection! But I warn gentlemen that, small as it may appear to them, if the principle receive the sanction of the people and the support of the State legislatures, there is an end of this destructive system of embargo.

The position I take, and which I mean to maintain is, that those provisions of the embargo laws which assume to regulate the coasting trade, between ports and ports of the same State, are gross invasions of the rights of the States, and palpable grasps of power beyond the limits of the Constitution. I ask the attention of the House to a very short argument upon this subject. I present it, not by way of crimination, but as worthy of its consideration and candid examination. I feel no passions on the question. If any have been exhibited by me, they were caught at the flame enkindled by the gentleman from Virginia (Mr. Eppes).

The powers granted to Congress, in relation to commerce, are contained in the eighth section of the first article of the Constitution, in these words: " The Congress shall have power to regulate commerce with foreign

nations, and among the several States, and with the
Indian tribes." The particular power to which I object,
as being assumed, if granted at all, is contained within
the terms, "commerce among the several States." In
reference to which I ask this question : Can the grant of
a power to regulate commerce among the States, by any
fair construction, be made to include a power to regulate commerce within a State? It is a simple question.
The strength and certainty of the conclusion results
from its simplicity. There is no need of any refined
argument to arrive at conviction. It is a plain appeal
to the common-sense of the people, — to that common-
sense which, on most practical subjects, is a much surer
guide than all the reasoning of the learned. It is scarce
possible, there can be but one answer to this question.
To bring the subject more directly into the course of
the reasonings of common life, suppose that ten house-
holders who live in a neighborhood should agree upon
a tribunal which should possess powers to regulate
commerce or intercourse among their houses, could
such an authority be fairly extended to the regulation
of the intercourse of the members of their families
within their respective houses? Under a grant of
power like this, would such a tribunal have a right to
regulate the intercourse between room and room within
each dwelling-house? It is impossible. Nothing can
be plainer. The general government has no color for
interfering with the interior commerce of each State,
let it be carried on by water or by land. The regulation of the commerce between ports and ports of the
same State belongs exclusively to the States respectively.

In farther support of this position, a strong argument results from the ninth section of the first article: " No tax or duty shall be laid on articles exported from any State. No preference shall be given by any regulation of commerce or revenue to the ports of one State over those of another, nor shall vessels bound to or from one State be obliged to enter, clear, or pay duties in another." In this clause of the Constitution, the people restrict the general power over commerce granted to Congress. And to what objects do these restrictions apply? To exports from a State; to preferences of the ports of one State over those of another; to vessels bound to or from another State. Not one word of restriction of the powers of Congress touching that great portion of commerce between ports and ports of the same State. Now can any thing be more conclusive that the general power of regulating commerce did not, in the opinion of the people, include the right to regulate commerce between ports and ports of the same State than this fact, that they have not thought it necessary even to enumerate it among these restrictions? If it were included in the grant of the general power, can a reason be shown why it was not, as well as the others, included within these restrictions? That it is not provided for among these restrictions is perfect conviction, to my mind, that it was never included in the general power. A contrary doctrine leads to this monstrous absurdity, that Congress, which, in consequence of these constitutional restrictions, can neither grant any preference to the ports of one State over those of another State, nor oblige vessels to enter, clear, or pay duties when bound to or from the ports of one State in another, yet that it may grant preferences to the ports of one State over ports in the same State, and may oblige vessels to enter, clear, and pay duties when bound from port to port within the same State. This enormous consequence is inevitable. The conclusion, therefore, to my mind, is perfectly clear, that the reason why the people did not restrict the abuse of this species of power was, that the power itself was not granted to Congress.

I shall state only one other corroborative argument, drawn from another part of the Constitution. By the second clause of the tenth section and first article, it is provided that " no State shall, without the consent of Congress, lay any imposts or duties on imports or exports, except what may be absolutely necessary for executing its inspection laws, &c. Now can it for one moment be admitted that, in consequence of this restriction, the individual States are prohibited from laying transit duties on articles passing from port to port within their State limits? Can the States lay no toll upon ferries across their rivers? no tax upon vessels plying up and down their rivers, or across their bays? May not the State of New York impose a duty upon vessels going from Hudson or Albany to New York? Yet, if it be true that the general power of regulating commerce among the States includes the power of regulating commerce between ports and ports of the same State, all this great branch of State prerogative is absolutely gone from the individual States, — a construction of the Constitution in which, if realized by the people and the legislature of the States in all its consequences, they never can acquiesce. The language of this clause

is in strict consonance with that construction of the
Constitution for which I contend. It strongly, and con-
clusively to my mind, implies that the general power
does not include the power to regulate commerce between ports and ports of the same State. The language
of this clause is, " no State shall lay any imposts or
duties on imports or exports." These terms " imports
and exports " are exclusively appropriate to duties upon
goods passing into a State or passing out of a State, and
can never be made, by any fair construction, to extend
to duties upon goods passing wholly within the limits of
a State. On goods in this situation, — that is, on goods
passing between ports and ports of the same State, — the
individual States have, notwithstanding this restriction
in the Constitution, the power to lay transit duties. Of
consequence, the regulation of this branch of trade is not
included in the grant to Congress of the general power
over commerce among the States.

This is the point of view which I take in this matter,
of the limits of the Constitution. On this ground it is,
that I asserted that the rights of the States have been
invaded in your embargo laws, and that this legislature
has grasped a power not given to it by the Constitution.
And, so far as the liberties of this people are dependent
upon the preservation of the State and national authori-
ties in their respective orbits, I hesitate not to declare
the embargo laws a manifest infringement of those liberties.

On a question of this magnitude, I cannot condescend
to inquire whether, in the early revenue laws, any regulations were made affecting this particular branch of

trade.   A practice in direct violation of the Constitution can have no binding force.   Violations of the
Constitution touching only a few solitary individuals,
small in amount or in inconvenience, may for a long
period be submitted to without a struggle or a murmur.
When the extension of the principle begins to affect
whole classes of the community, the interest of the
nation claims a solemn and satisfactory decision.   The
truth is, I can find but a single attempt in all your revenue laws contrary to the construction for which I
contend.   In the case of carrying distilled spirits, or
imported goods of a specified amount, from port to port
within a State, the master is obliged to make a manifest
and take an oath that the duties have been paid.   The
infringement of the Constitution was in this instance,
and in its immediate consequences, so trifling that it has
passed without notice, and been submitted to without a
question.   But, surely, on the silent acquiescence of
the people in such a practice as this can never be built
the fabric of so enormous a power as your embargo laws
attempt to exercise.

Gentlemen say the embargo is brought into view on
all occasions.   Certainly, sir, it is connected with almost
all national questions.   I have no objection to voting
for fifty thousand men, if I can be informed to what use
they are to be applied.   Let me only understand the
system proposed.   Is it intended to repeal the embargo
and go to war?   Or are these men only intended to
enforce it?   If the former, I have no objection to any
requisite army.   If the latter, I am in direct hostility to
this proposition.   Deeming the embargo laws unconsti-

tutional, and powers vested in the executive which ought never to have passed out of the possession of this House, I will never acquiesce in augmentation of the military until I am satisfied that the system is not to support by it still farther the violations of this Constitution.

SPEECH

ON THE BILL FOR HOLDING AN EXTRA SESSION OF CONGRESS IN MAY NEXT.

Jan. 19, 1809.

SPEECH

ON THE BILL FOR HOLDING AN EXTRA SESSION OF CONGRESS IN MAY NEXT.

JAN. 19, 1809.

––––––––––

[THE discontents caused by the embargo had grown so fierce that the Democrats themselves had become alarmed by them. The Northern public men, who had stood by Mr. Jefferson in his favorite policy of conquering England through the ruin of American commerce, began, towards the close of his administration, to tremble for themselves, if not for their country. He still remained firm in his faith, and saw with grief the approaching defection of his followers. Even sight could not shake his faith. After the first disturbance of trade arising from an embargo was past, the English merchants, far from asking for the restoration of American commerce through the repeal of the Orders in Council, wished them to be made more rigid yet, so that they themselves might have the monopoly of the continental trade; thus literally fulfilling Mr. Quincy's prophecy at the time the embargo was first proposed. The importation of cotton into England was first absolutely prohibited, in order to cripple the manufacturing of the continent, which Bonaparte wished to establish as a part of his system. Then, as the Democratic orators and presses denounced the duty which England demanded for the privilege of re-exportation to the continent, as a tribute to that haughty power, the British government removed this particular ground of complaint by forbidding any importation whatever from America for the purpose of reshipment. And

9

Mr. Canning called the particular attention of the American government, through Mr. Pinkney, its representative, "to this concession to the sensibilities of the American people"!

Mr. Jefferson's reign was drawing to a close, and the allegiance of his partisans naturally grew weaker and weaker; and during the short session of 1808-9, previous to the accession of Mr. Madison, the unquestioning obedience of the Democratic majority in Congress to the behests of Mr. Jefferson was greatly though secretly shaken. The New England and New York members showed strong symptoms of rebellion, which Mr. Jefferson attributed to "an unaccountable revolution of opinion and kind of panic" among them. The revolution in opinion and the panic grew out of their observation of the effects of the embargo on the interests of their constituents and their apprehensions of its influence at the polls. In this state of things, an extra session of Congress was proposed, in May, 1809, by way of pacifying the growing discontent under the embargo with the prospect of its removal, but with the additional pretence that the time would then have arrived for substituting an open war for that by commercial restrictions. It was on this bill that Mr. Quincy made the following speech, which caused a great excitement in the House, and made a strong impression on the country. — Ed.]

Mr. Speaker, — If the bill under consideration had no other aspect on the fates of this country than its terms indicate, I should have continued silent. If the question upon it involved no other consequences than those of personal inconvenience to us and of expense to the public, I would not now ask the indulgence of the House. But I deem this bill to be a materially component part of that system of commercial restriction under which the best hopes of this nation are oppressed. I consider this measure as intended to induce this people still longer to endure patiently the embargo, and all the evils which it brings in its train, by exciting and

fostering in them delusive expectations. A great crisis
is, to all human appearance, advancing upon our country. Gentlemen may attempt to conceal it from the
nation, perhaps from themselves, but every step they
take has an influence upon that crisis ; and, small as they
may deem the decision on this bill, in its effects it will
be among the most important of any of the acts of this
session.

It is very painful to me, Mr. Speaker, to be compelled
to place my opposition to this bill on ground resulting
from the conduct of the administration of this nation.
I say, sir, this is very painful to me, because I have no
personal animosity to any individual of that administration. Nor, if I know myself, am I induced to this opposition from any party motive. But, sir, acting in a
public capacity, and reasoning concerning events as
they occur, with reference to the high duties of my
station, I shall not, when I arrive in my conception at
a just conclusion, shrink from any proper responsibility
in spreading that conclusion before this House and
nation. One thing I shall hope and certainly shall
deserve from the friends of administration, — the ac-
knowledgment that I shall aim no insidious blow. It
shall be made openly, distinctly, in the daylight. Be
it strong or be it weak, I invite those friends to parry
it. If they are successful, I shall rejoice in it not less
than they.

This is the position in relation to the conduct of administration which I take, and on which I rest my
opposition to this bill : that this House, when it passed
the embargo law, was under a deception touching the
motives of administration in recommending that meas-

ure ; that it has been, in adopting that measure, instrumental in deceiving this people as to the motives which induced that law ; that if it passes this bill it will again act under a deception touching those motives, and again be instrumental, unwarily and unwillingly, as I believe, in deceiving this people in relation to them. I think I have stated my ground of opposition so clearly as to admit of no misconception, and invite gentlemen to meet me candidly upon it. When I speak of deception, I beg gentlemen not to misunderstand me. I will be as just to the administration as I mean to be true and fearless in the performance of my duty to the people. By this term, I do not mean any moral obliquity, any direct falsehood or palpable misrepresentation. But I intend by it political deception, — that species of cunning, not uncommon among politicians, which Lord Bacon calls "left-handed wisdom." This is exhibited when ostensible and popular motives are presented as inducements to a particular line of conduct, and the real and critical ones are kept behind the curtain. This is practised when those who have obtained an influence over others troll them by the means of fair promises upon trundles in a downhill path, and so are enabled gradually to shove them, by gentle motions, farther than at first they had any intention to go. We witness this species of political deception when we see men meshed in the toils of a complicated policy, and then dragged whithersoever their leaders will, through sheer shame at breaking the cords of that net in which they have suffered themselves incautiously to be entangled.

In support of my first position, — that this House, when it passed the embargo law, was under a deception

touching the motives of administration, — I shall ask
the House to recollect, as far as possible, all the motives
which induced it to pass the embargo law, and then I
will attempt to show that the motives of administration
were different, in kind or in degree, from those which
operated on this floor.   I will recapitulate them as distinctly as possible, excluding no one which I have any
reason to think had an influence in the House, imput-
ing none which did not exist.   One motive was the preservation of our resources ; that is, the saving of our
seamen and navigation.   This was the ostensible and
popular motive, — that avowed by administration.   Another motive was, that many thought war was inevitable,
and that embargo would give an opportunity to prepare
for it.   Again : some thought that it would have a
good effect on the negotiation then daily expected, and
frighten Mr. Rose.   Again : others supposed that it
would straiten Great Britain at a moment the most
favorable to make her feel the importance of the United
States.   The system of commercial pressure was in full
operation in Europe ; and, should this country complete
the circle of compression, they thought that it would
be impossible for her not to yield to our pretensions.
Again : some thought that the French emperor was contending for maritime rights, and that it was time for us
to co-operate.   [Here Messrs. Smilie and Eppes required
of Mr. Quincy to know to whom he had allusion.]   I
am surprised, said Mr. Quincy, to hear that question
asked by the gentleman from Pennsylvania.   If, however, it be denied as a motive, I have no objection to
withdraw it.   What I am now doing ought to excite no
passion.   I am not about to question the motives of this

House. I am only recapitulating all those which there is any reason to believe existed. If any gentlemen say a particular one did not exist, for the present argument I reject it. My present object only is to be complete in my enumeration, in order to make more forcible the bearing of my principal argument, that it does not include those which principally had an influence with administration in recommending the measure. I do not recollect but two other motives besides those already mentioned. Some voted for this embargo, because they thought this House ought to do something, and they did not know what else to do. Others intimated that it might have an effect to injure France in the few West India possessions which remained to her. But this was urged so faintly, and with such little show of reason, that I doubt if it were an influential motive with any man. The preceding enumeration includes all the motives, as I believe, either urged on this floor, or in any way silently operative in producing that measure. Now I do not think I state my position too strongly when I say that not a man in this House deemed the embargo intended chiefly as a measure of coercion on Great Britain; that it was to be made permanent at all hazards, until it had effected that object; and that nothing else effectual was to be done for the support of our maritime rights. If any individual was influenced by such motives, certainly they were not those of a majority of this House. Now, sir, on my conscience, I do believe that these were the motives and intentions of administration when they recommended the embargo to the adoption of this House. Sir, I believe these continue to be still their motives and intentions. And if this were fairly understood by the people to be the fact, I do not believe that they would countenance the continuance of such an oppressive measure for such a purpose without better assurance than has ever yet been given to them, that, by adherence to this policy, the great and real object of it will be effected.

The proposition which I undertake to maintain consists of three particulars: first, that it was and is the intention of administration to coerce Great Britain by the embargo, and that this, and not precaution, is and was the principal object of the policy; second, that it was and is intended to persevere in this measure until it effect, if possible, the proposed object; third, that it was and is the intention of administration to do nothing else effectual in support of our maritime rights.

Having in my own mind a perfect conviction of the truth of every one of these propositions, I should be false to myself and to my country at such a crisis as this if I did not state that conviction to this House, and through it to my fellow-citizens. I shall not, however, take refuge in mere declaration of individual opinion, or content myself simply with assertions. I shall state the grounds and the reasonings by which I arrive at this result. I invite gentlemen to reply to them in the spirit in which they are offered, not with the design of awakening any personal or party passion, but to fulfil the high duties which, according to my apprehension of them, I owe to this people.

When we attempt to penetrate into the intentions of men, we are all sensible how thick and mysterious is that veil which, by the law of our nature, is spread over

them. At times it is scarcely permitted to an individual
to be absolutely certain of his own motives. But when
the question is concerning the purposes of others, experience daily tells how hard a task it is to descend into
the hidden recesses of the mind, and pluck intentions
from that granite cell in which they delight to incrust
themselves. The only mode of discovery is to consider
language and conduct in their relation to the real and
avowed object, and thence to conclude, as fairly as we
can, which is the one and which the other. This course
I shall adopt. If there be any thing fallacious, let the
friends of administration oppose it.

When I state that precaution was not, but that coercion on Great Britain was, the principal motive with
administration in advising the embargo, I do not mean
to aver that precaution did not enter into the view, but
only that it was a minor consideration, and did by no
means bear so great a proportion in producing that
policy in the cabinet as it did before the world. This
will appear presently. That the principal object of
the embargo policy was coercion on Great Britain, I
conclude from the language of the friends of administration in this country and the language which the minister of administration was directed to hold across the
Atlantic, as also from their subsequent conduct. Here
all the leading calculations had relation to coercion.
The dependence of Great Britain upon her manufactures, and their dependence upon us for supply and
consumption ; the greatness of her debt ; her solitary
state, engaged with a world in arms ; the fortunes and
the power of the French emperor ; the certain effect of
the commercial prohibitions of combined Europe upon

her maritime power, — such were the uniform considerations in support of this policy adduced by the friends of
administration on this floor or in this nation.

There, on the contrary, the considerations urged as
the motive for it were altogether different.   Let us
recur to the language which our minister was directed
to hold to the court of Great Britain on this subject.
The Secretary of State, in his letter of the 23d of
December, 1807, to Mr. Pinkney, thus dictates to him
the course he is to pursue in impressing on the British
cabinet the objects of the embargo : " I avail myself of
the opportunity to enclose you a copy of a message from
the President to Congress, and their act, in pursuance
of it, laying an embargo on our vessels and exports.
The policy and causes of the measure are explained in
the message itself.   But it may be proper to authorize
you to assure the British government, as has been just
expressed to its minister here, that the act is a measure
of precaution only, called for by the occasion ; that it is
to be considered as neither hostile in its character, nor
as justifying or inviting or leading to hostility with
any nation whatever, and particularly as opposing no
obstacle whatever to amicable negotiations and satisfactory adjustments with Great Britain on the subjects
of difference between the two countries."   Here our
administration expressly declare that " the policy and
causes of the measure are explained in the message
itself."   And in that message the " dangers with which
our vessels, our seamen, and merchandise are threat-
ened ; " and " the great importance of keeping in safety
these essential resources,"— are the sole causes enumerated as explanatory of that policy.   At the court of

Great Britain, then, our minister was directed to represent this measure as merely intended to save our essential resources.   But administration were not content
with the direct assertion of this motive : they abjure any
other.   They expressly direct our minister " to assure
the British government that the act is a measure of
precaution only," and " that it opposes no obstacle
whatever to amicable negotiations between the two
countries."   Here, then, the friends of administration,
speaking, as is well known, its language allege in this
country that the embargo is a measure of coercion, and
that, if persisted in vigorously, it will reduce Great
Britain to our terms ; whereas the minister of the United
States, speaking also the language of administration,
is directed, unequivocally, to deny all this in Great
Britain, and to exclude the idea of coercion by declaring it to be a measure of precaution only.   Certainly,
never was there a policy more perfectly characteristic.
It is precisely that policy which one deeply skilled in
the knowledge of the human character described as " a
language official and a language confidential," — a language for the ear of the American people, an opposite
for the ear of the British cabinet.   If this had been, as
the minister of the United States was directed to assure
the British cabinet, " a measure of precaution only,"
why were the friends of administration permitted to
advocate it as a measure of coercion ?   Why is it
continued after all pretence of precaution has ceased ?
Did not administration know that, if it were supported
here on the ground of coercion, this fact would necessarily be understood in Great Britain, and that it must
form " an obstacle to negotiation," notwithstanding

all their declarations? If, therefore, it had been truly " a measure of precaution only," would not administration have been the first to have counteracted such an opinion, and not permitted it to have gained any ground here or elsewhere? Yet they countenance this opinion in America at the moment they are denying it in Great Britain. And why? The reason is obvious, and is conclusive in support of the position that it was at first, as it is now, simply a measure of coercion. The mode adopted by administration is the only one they could adopt with any hope of success in case the object was coercion, and the very mode they would avoid had it been really precaution. There is not an individual in the United States so much of a child as not to know that the argument of precaution was good only for ninety, or, at farthest, an hundred and twenty days. After our ships and seamen were in port, which within that time would have been principally the case, the reason of precaution was at an end. Upon the principle that the self-interest and intelligence of the merchant and navigator are the best guides and patrons of their own concerns, and that the stake which society has in the property of the citizen is better secured by his own knowledge and activity than by any general regulations whatsoever, it was necessary, therefore, in the United States, to resort early to the idea of coercion, and to press it vigorously: otherwise the people of America could not be induced to endurance beyond the time when the reason of precaution had ceased. In America, therefore, it was coercion. But in Great Britain the state of things was altogether the reverse. Administration knew perfectly well, not only from the

character of the British nation, but also from the most
common principles of human nature, that once present
this embargo to it as a measure of coercion, to compel
it to adopt or retract any principle of adopted policy,
and there was an end of negotiation. It would have
been like laying a drawn sword upon the table, and
declaring, " Yield us what we demand, or we will push
it to the hilt into your vitals." In such case, it was
perfectly apparent that there could be received from an
independent nation but one answer. " Take away your
sword ; withdraw your menace : while these continue
we listen to nothing. Aware of this inevitable consequence, administration not only aver that it is precaution, but even condescend to deny it is any thing else,
by declaring that it is this, and this only. Thus in
Great Britain precaution was the veil under which a
sword was passed into her side. But in the United
States coercion was the palatable liquor with which
administration softened and gargled the passage, while
it thrust, at the point of the bayonet, the bitter pill of
embargo down the throats of the American people. It
is this variation of the avowed motive to suit the unquestionable diversity of the state of things in this
country and Great Britain, combined with the fact that
the embargo is continued long after the plea of precaution has ceased to be effectual, that produces a perfect
conviction in my mind that precaution was little more
than the pretext, and that coercion was in fact the principal purpose, of the policy. Indeed, how is it possible
to conclude otherwise when the very mode of argument adopted in each country was the only one which
could have made coercion successful, and the very one

which would have been avoided if precaution had been the real and only motive? I cheerfully submit the correctness of this conclusion to the consideration of the people.

I come now to my second proposition, — that it was the intention of administration to persevere in this measure of embargo until it should effect, if possible, the proposed object, and, as I believe, at all hazard. The evidence of this intention I gather not only from the subsequent perseverance in this system, in spite of the cries of distress heard in one quarter of the Union, and the dangers not to be concealed resulting from an adherence to it, but from the very tenor of the law, from its original form and feature. If this had been, as it was asserted by administration, originally a measure of precaution only, there was every reason why it should be limited, and none why its duration should be unlimited. A limited embargo was conformable to precedent in this country. It was conformable to practice in others. There was less question of its constitutionality; and, certainly, much less reason to be jealous of it as a transfer of power to the executive. The question of precaution having reference to the interests of the merchant, and of the other classes of the community, was naturally one which the members of this House, emanating directly from the people, were best qualified to decide, and was the last which they ought or would, in such case, have submitted to the entire control of another branch of the legislature. But as, notwithstanding assertions, it was in fact a measure of coercion, a very different principle operated in its formation. It was to be used as a weapon against Great Britain. If drawn against her, it was necessary to be put into such a situation as most certainly to effect its purpose. If drawn, it was not to be sheathed, until this had been done, or until it had reached the marrow and the vitals of the enemy. But, with such a purpose, a limited embargo would have been a nerveless weapon. At every term of its limitation, it would have been under the control of this House ; a body deeply responsible to the people, liable intimately to be affected by their feelings and passions. These would have instantly operated upon this House, which never could have been brought to continue the measure one moment longer than it was for the interest and consentaneous to the wishes of the mass of their fellow-citizens. But if the intention was to keep if possible these restrictions upon the people, until they effected their object at all hazards, then no other course could be adopted but that of unlimited embargo. The whole commercial power given to us by the Constitution was thus transferred absolutely to the President and twelve men in the other branch of the legislature,[1] — men, from their situation and their tenure of office, not so likely to be affected by the interests of the people, or so able to sympathize with them, as the members of this House. If it were intended, then, to keep this instrument of coercion aloof from the influence of the people, so that it might be maintained long after they had ceased to approve of it, this was the only course which could be adopted. This House could not be trusted with the power of re-enacting it. The weapon would be shortened and weakened, if it re-

[1] Twelve senators held the balance of power in the Senate, who could be depended upon to support the administration.

mained in our control. But, in the exclusive possession of the President and twelve men, its whole force might be wielded with the greatest possible efficacy. It is from this feature of the embargo law, reconcilable to no other intention than a predetermination to persevere in it regardless of the people's sufferings until it had effected, if possible, its object, as well as from the actual obstinacy of adherence after the most manifest symptoms of discontent in the commercial States, that I draw the conclusion that such was the original determination of administration. And not only so, but I am perfectly of opinion that such is still their intention, and that, if the people will bear it, this embargo will be continued not only until next May, but until next September; yes, sir, to next May twelvemonth. Having this conviction, a sense of duty obliges me to declare it, and thus to state the reasons of it.

I come now to my third position, — not only that embargo was resorted to as a means of coercion; but that, from the first, it was never intended by administration to do any thing else effectual for the support of our maritime rights. Sir, I am sick, sick to loathing, of this eternal clamor of "war, war, war," which has been kept up almost incessantly on this floor, now for more than two years, sir. If I can help it, the old women of this country shall not be frightened in this way any longer. I have been a long time a close observer of what has been done and said by the majority of this House; and, for one, I am satisfied that no insult, however gross, offered to us by either France or Great Britain, could force this majority into the declaration of war. To use a strong but common expression, it could not be kicked into such a declaration by either nation. Letters are read from the British minister. Passions are excited by his sarcasms. Men get up and recapitulate insults. They rise and exclaim " perfidy," " robbery," " falsehood," " murder " !

> . . . " Unpacking hearts with words,
> And fall a cursing, like a very drab,
> A scullion."

Sir, is this the way to maintain national honor or dignity ? Is it the way to respect abroad or at home ? Is the perpetual recapitulation of wrongs the ready path to redress, or even the means to keep alive a just sense of them in our minds ? Are those sensibilities likely to remain for a long time very keen which are kept constantly under the lash of the tongue ?

The grounds on which I conclude that it was the intention of administration to do nothing else effectual, in support of our maritime rights, are these, that, if it had ever been contemplated to fight for them, less would have been said about war, and more preparation made for it. The observation is common and just as true of collective bodies of men as- of individuals, that those fight the best who make the least noise upon the subject. The man of determined character shows his strength in his muscles, in the attitude he assumes, in the dignified position in which he places himself. Just so is it with men determined to maintain the rights and honor of the nation. They consider the nature of the exigency, the power of the nation with which they are likely to involve their country, what preparations are necessary to its ultimate success. They do not content themselves with evaporating words of passion. They look to the end, and devise and put in train such means as are suited to a safe and honorable issue. This conduct speaks more terribly than any words to the fears of foreign nations. And as to our citizens, they find in it an assurance, which can be given them by no enumeration of wrongs, however accurate or eloquent. But it is not merely by what has been said, but by what has been done, that my mind is satisfied that administration never seriously contemplated a war with any nation under heaven. That all this clamor so ostentatiously raised, and all this detail of the horrors of war, are nothing else than the machinery by which it is intended to keep this people quiet, through apprehension of a worse state, under their most oppressive evil, the embargo. We have been told from divine authority, " By their deeds ye shall know them." The rule is just as true in relation to professors in politics as to professors in religion. I ask, sir, what has this majority done, during the two years past, in every moment of which the people have been kept under almost a daily anticipation of war, towards an effectual maintenance of their rights, should war in fact result? Why, we have built seventy gunboats; we have in requisition one hundred thousand militia. Are either of these intended to fight Great Britain? or competent to maintain our maritime rights? But we have an army of five thousand men. And how have you appointed officers to that army? Have you done it in a manner to create that sentiment of unanimity so necessary to be inspired, if your intention be to fight seriously a foreign enemy? In the last session, when the proposal to raise that army was before

the House, no cry was so universal as that of " Union."
Well, sir, and how did those gentlemen whose sentiments usually coincide with mine act upon that occasion? Did we make a party question of it? No: it
was supported very generally by us. Now, upon what
principle have you conducted in your appointment of
officers to that army? as though you wished to unite
every heart and hand in the nation in opposition to a
foreign enemy? No: but as though you had no other
project than to reward political adherents or to enforce
the embargo laws. I mean not unjustly to charge any
member of the administration. But I am obliged to
state that I have satisfactory evidence to my mind that
it has been established as a principle by the Secretary
at War not to appoint any man to a command in that
army who was not an open partisan of the existing
administration. If I am in an error, appoint a committee
of inquiry; and I will be the happiest, if it be proved, to
acknowledge it. [Mr. LOVE asked if Mr. Quincy was
in order. Mr. SPEAKER conceived he was not.] Mr.
QUINCY continued: I am performing what I deem a great
duty; and, if the connection between this topic and the
subject before the House be denied, I am prepared to
establish it. I am contending that if the purpose for
which this army was raised were to meet a foreign
enemy, this principle would never have been adopted in
the appointment of officers. I do not believe the fact I
state will be denied. But if it should be, it is easily to be
ascertained by comparing the applications for appointments to those offices with the list of those appointments.
Now, sir, if the intention were to unite the nation as
one man against a foreign enemy, is not this the last

policy which any administration ought ever to have adopted? Of all engines, is not a party army the most dreadful and detestable? Is it not the most likely to awaken suspicion, and to sow discontent rather than concord? This is one reason on which I rest my opinion, that it was not the intention to go to war, or they would have adopted a principle more harmonizing in relation to the organization of that army.

Again, sir, you talk of going to war against Great Britain with, I believe, only one frigate and five sloops-of-war in commission! And yet you have not the resolution to meet the expense of the paltry little navy which is rotting in the Potomac! Already we have heard it rung on this floor that if we fit out that little navy our treasury will be emptied. If you had ever a serious intention of going to war, would you have frittered down the resources of this nation in the manner we witness? you go to war, with all the revenue to be derived from commerce annihilated, and possessing no other resource than loans, or direct or other internal taxes! you, a party that rose into power by declaiming against direct taxes and loans! Do you hope to make the people of this country, much more foreign nations, believe that such is your intention, when you have reduced your revenue to such a condition? [Mr. G. W. CAMPBELL asked the gentleman if he could tell how much money there was now in the treasury.] MR. QUINCY continued: My memory has not at present at command the precise sum, but perhaps twelve or thirteen millions of dollars, charged with the expenses and appropriations for the year. But what is this? Make any material preparation for such a war as you must wage, if you engage with either of the European powers, and your whole treasury is exhausted. I am not now examining the present state of our finances. But I would address myself to men of sense, and ask them to examine the adequacy of our revenues in their future product to the inevitable exigencies of war. Sir, you have no other resources, commerce being gone, than loans or internal taxes. Great Britain and France know this fact as well as you. Nothing can be conducted in such a country as ours without public notoriety. The general resources of our country are as well known in Europe as they are here. But we are about to raise an army of fifty thousand volunteers. For what purpose? I have heard gentlemen say, "We can invade Canada." But, sir, does not all the world, as well as you, know that Great Britain holds, as it were, a pledge for Canada? and one sufficient to induce you to refrain from such a project, when you begin seriously to weigh all the consequences of such invasion. I mean that pledge which results from the defenceless state of your seaport towns. For what purpose would you attack Canada? For territory? No: you have enough of that. Do you want citizen refugees? No: you would be willing to dispense with them. Do you want plunder? This is the only hope an invasion of Canada can offer you. And is it not very doubtful whether she could not in one month destroy more property on your seaboard than you can acquire by the most successful invasion of that province? Sir, in this state of things, I cannot hear such perpetual outcries about war without declaring my opinion concerning them.

When I say, sir, that this administration could not be

induced into a war, I mean by its own self-motion. War may — I will not assert that it will not — come. But such a state administration do not contemplate, nor are they prepared for it.   On the contrary, I do believe that the very tendency of all imbecile measures is to bring on the very event their advisers deprecate.   Well did the gentleman from Georgia (Mr. Troup) warn you the other day not to get into war.   He told you it was the design of the Federalists to lead you into that state, in order that they might get your places.   Now, I agree with the gentleman that, if by your measures you get this country into a war, that you will lose your places. But I do not agree that in such case the Federalists would get them.   No, sir.   The course of affairs in popular revolutions proceeds, not from bad to better, but from bad to worse.   After Condorcet and Brissot came Danton and Robespierre.   Well may gentlemen dread, on account of their places, being involved in war !   For let the people once begin to look on the state of the country with that anxiety which the actual per- ception of present danger never fails to awaken : let them realize the exigencies which that state involves, and compare with them your preparations for it : let them see an army in which, perhaps, a full half of your citizens cannot confide ; a small navy, rendered less by natural decay, and even the few ships we have not in a state to give battle ; our treasury exhausted, as it will soon be, and all the ordinary sources of commercial sup- ply dried away, — and they will hurl you from your seats with as little remorse, with as much indifference, as a mischievous boy would shy so many blind and trembling kittens, six to a litter, into a horse-pond.

Yes, sir, be assured that war is the termination of your political power, unless you have the prescience to prepare an effectual force, worthy of this nation, worthy of either adversary you may elect to engage. But remember you must rely upon something else than the paltry surpluses of your treasury, — which, in fact, in one year will not exist, — upon something else than loans or direct taxes.

This bill I consider as a continuation of the same deception as to the motive as that which operated in the passage of the original embargo law. If we pass it, I fear we shall again be instrumental in deceiving this people. The effect of this bill, whatever may be its avowed design, is calculated to soothe the people, impatient under the embargo, until the spring elections are passed, and until the first session of the State legislatures are finished. By a new session of the next Congress, in May, the people are to be led to hope that next May will bring them relief. But let the embargo be kept on until May, and, as the honorable gentleman from North Carolina (Mr. Macon) told you very ingenuously, it will then be found necessary to keep it on until September, and perhaps for another year. This is the keystone of the whole policy of this bill, as I apprehend. If it be your real intention to remove this embargo after May, why do you not adopt a provision similar to that proposed the other day by the gentleman from Connecticut (Mr. Sturges), and annex it to this bill? Why not limit the continuance of the embargo law until next June, and thereby leave the new Congress free, relative to this measure, from the power of the executive? Give the people a pledge that the embargo shall be removed at a limited time. At least put it into the power of your successors, by refusing to re-enact the law, to control the executive's will. This pledge the people have a right to claim, if it be your real purpose to abandon the measure after May. If, however, this be not your policy, avow your intentions. Tell the people at once that it is a power of coercion, in which you mean to persevere until it has effected its object. Show them the reasons on which you rely that it will be successful. Perhaps they will consent to endure it. But with the present state of things they cannot, they ought not to, be satisfied. At least get back, by limiting the present law, your commercial power, which you have absolutely surrendered to the President and twelve men. Permit your successors to be as independent of the executive in continuing this system as you were when you consented to adopt it.

The only consistent advocates of the embargo system are such gentlemen as those from North and South Carolina (Messrs. Macon and D. R. Williams), and they are opposed to this bill. They tell you that this is an effectual weapon against Great Britain, and believing this, as they do, they say truly that a session in May will evidence timidity and defeat the effect of the wea-pon. You ought to take one or the other ground de-cidedly. Either you still confide in its efficacy, or you begin to doubt of it. If the former, show your con-fidence to be rational, and leave the weapon to have its full operation, not unnerved by the hope of a May session. If the latter, either repeal it instantly, or give the people an assurance that it will be done in May.

The course you are pursuing has no other tendency than to excite suspicions, to agitate and embarrass.

I ask gentlemen to consider what will be their situation in May. Will you be in a better condition to go to war then than you are now? No: you will be in a worse. You will be more embarrassed; you will have less revenue; you will have more discontent. Your efficient force will not be materially greater. Will you have more encouragement then to strike at the Canadas than exists at present? and what other point of attack have you on Great Britain? Will you be a whit more inclined in May or June to remove the embargo than you are at this moment? No: it will be stepping back then just as it is now. That dreadful thought will be, I fear, sufficient to induce then, as now, adherence to the measure six months longer. And, after abundance of war speeches, Congress will rise, and leave that measure bending down the people until next December.

Sir, these are the general reasons which I have to urge against the adoption of this bill. In what I have said, my only view has been to exhibit to this House and nation the real motives which, as I apprehend, caused the original imposition of the embargo, and which still operate in support of this bill. I do not believe that it is the intention of a majority of this House at present to continue this system after May. But I do believe that it is the intention of administration. My design has been to recall the recollection of gentlemen to the difference between the arguments now urged for its continuance and the official reasons at first given for its adoption. And I would warn them that, if they mean to gain credit with the people for the intention of repealing the embargo in May, they will not obtain it, if they leave the next Congress at the mercy of the executive, by rising without affixing some limitation to it.

SPEECH

ON THE RESOLUTION OF CENSURE ON FRANCIS J.
JACKSON, THE BRITISH MINISTER.

Dec. 28, 1809.

SPEECH

ON THE RESOLUTION OF CENSURE ON FRANCIS J. JACKSON, THE BRITISH MINISTER.

DEC. 28, 1809.

[IN the winter of 1809, just before Mr. Jefferson gave way to Mr. Madison, his favorite measure of the embargo was repealed. It had answered none of the expectations of its inventors. It had paralyzed American commerce, ruined multitudes of merchants, and reduced the laboring classes, who depended on trade for their support, to hopeless poverty, while in England its effects had been the very opposite of what had been hoped from it. After the first disturbance caused by the withdrawal of the American trade was over, the British merchants found that the monopoly of the trade of the world which it secured to them much more than overbalanced any loss it occasioned. Mr. Jefferson had lost none of his faith in his policy of conquering England by ruining the commerce of America, and he lamented the conversion of his own partisans to "the fatal measure of repeal." But the tide was too strong to be stemmed, and Mr. Jefferson had to see the policy which he had identified with his political life end with it. The mortification attending this compulsion, however, was mitigated by the substitution of an Act of Non-intercourse with both belligerents. Though this measure was far enough from restoring the prosperity the embargo had destroyed, it was an improvement upon what it replaced, as it opened the rest of the world to American commerce, and removed the worst of the restrictions on the coastwise trade.

Mr. Madison, on his accession to the Presidency in March, 1809, naturally and justly wished to signalize the beginning of his administration by the restoration of friendly commercial relations with Great Britain. Accordingly, he entered into negotiations with this view with Mr. David Erskine, the eldest son of the great Lord Erskine, who had been made minister to Washington by the administration of "All the Talents" in 1806. He was a man of about thirty, of small diplomatic experience, and by no means a match for such experienced hands as Mr. Madison and Mr. Gallatin, who wished to cover their own retreat from the position taken up under Mr. Jefferson as gracefully as they could.   In this they were seconded by Mr. Erskine, who was connected by marriage with this country and naturally wished to be the means of reconciling the two nations, to both of which he, in a manner, belonged.   But, unfortunately, his discretion was not equal to his zeal.   The administration of the Duke of Portland, in which Mr. Canning was Secretary for Foreign Affairs, gave Mr. Erskine very exact instructions as to the conditions on which it would revoke the Orders in Council, which were carefully guarded so as to save the pride of the English nation.   The particulars will be found in the histories of the times, and need not be recapitulated here.   Mr. Erskine was authorized to show the despatch to the American government, which, however, he omitted to do, fearing, probably, that this would stop the negotiation on this side the Atlantic, and hoping that the advantages of the Arrangement, as it was called, would cause his departure from his instructions to be overlooked on the other.   The announcement of the Erskine Arrangement, made by proclamation on the 17th of April, diffused a general joy throughout the country, as it provided for the repeal of the Orders in Council.   But the joy was soon damped by another proclamation of the 9th of August, announcing that the English administration had repudiated the Arrangement, as made in direct violation of their express instructions.   They were technically justified in thus acting, but it may be doubted whether it was a wise and statesmanlike step.   By the Arrangement England would have gained every thing she demanded, without re-

nouncing the right of search and impressment. The war of
1812 would not have occurred, and the irritation of spirit and
bitterness of feeling which it left behind it — hardly yet ap-
peased — would have been avoided.

Mr. Erskine was recalled in disgrace, and he was replaced by
Mr. Francis J. Jackson, an experienced diplomatist, known at
the time as " Copenhagen Jackson," from the part he played as
minister to Denmark at the time of the seizure of the Danish
fleet by Nelson in 1807. Mr. Madison was deeply mortified by
the result of his negotiations with Mr. Erskine, and was ill disposed to give a gracious reception to his successor. A quarrel
was soon established between them, and on the ground that Mr.
Jackson had intimated — which he denied — that the President
knew at the time of the negotiation of the Arrangement that Mr.
Erskine had no authority to make it, all diplomatic communication with him was broken off, and his recall demanded of his government. Of course the Democratic party in Congress sustained
Mr. Madison, and it was on a joint resolution, approving his
course and severely censuring that of Mr. Jackson, that Mr.
Quincy delivered the following speech, December the 28th, 1809.

It may be proper to say here that Mr. Jackson, previous to
his return to England, had an edition of this speech printed to
take home with him, as the best defence of himself. A copy of
this edition is in the possession of the family. — Ed.]

It is not my intention, Mr. Speaker, to offer any
common-place apology for the few observations I shall
submit to the House on the subject now under consideration. Such is the character, and such the consequences of these resolutions, that no man, who has at
heart the honor and happiness of this country, ought
to continue silent, so long as any topic of illustration
is unexhausted, or any important point of view unoc-
cupied.

It is proposed, sir, that this solemn assembly, the rep-

resentative of the American people, the depositary of
their power, and, in a constitutional light, the image
of their wisdom, should descend from the dignity of
its legislative duties to the task of uttering against
an individual the mingled language of indignation and
reproach. Not satisfied with seeing that individual
prohibited the exercise of his official character, we are
invited to pursue him with the joint terrors of legislative wrath, couched in terms selected to convey oppro-
brium and infix a stigma. " Indecorum," " insolence,"
" affront," " more insolence," " more affront," " direct
premeditated insult and affront," " disguises, fallacious
and false," — these are the stains we are called upon to
cast, these the wounds we are about to inflict. It is
scarcely possible to comprise, within the same compass,
more of the spirit of whatever is bitter in invective and
humiliating in aspersion. This heaped-up measure of
legislative contumely is prepared for whom? For a
private, unassisted, insulated, unallied individual? No,
sir. For the accredited minister of a great and powerful sovereign, whose character he in this country rep-
resents, whose confidence he shares; of a sovereign
who is not bound, and perhaps will not be disposed, to
uphold him in misconduct, but who is bound by the
highest moral obligations and by the most impressive
political considerations to vindicate his wrongs, whether
they affect his person or reputation; and to take care
that whatever treatment he shall receive shall not exceed the measure of justice, and, above all, that it does
not amount to national indignity.

Important as is this view of these resolutions, it is
not their most serious aspect. This bull of anathemas,

scarcely less than papal, is to be fulminated in the name
of the American people from the high tower of their
authority, under the pretence of asserting their rights
and vindicating their wrongs.   What will that people
say, if, after the passions and excitements of this day
shall have subsided, they shall find, and find I fear they
will, that this resolution is false ; in fact, that a falsehood is the basis of these aspersions upon the character
of a public minister ?   What will be their just indignation when they find national embarrassment multiplied,
perhaps their peace gone, their character disgraced, for
no better reason than that you, their representatives,
following headlong a temporary current, insist on making assertions, as they may then, and, I believe, will,
realize to be not authorized by truth, under circumstances and in terms not warranted by wisdom ?

Let us not be deceived.   It is no slight responsibility
which this House is about to assume.   This is not one
of those holiday resolutions which frets and fumes its
hour upon the stage and is forgotten for ever.   Very different is its character and consequences.   It attempts
to stamp dishonor and falsehood on the forehead of a
foreign minister.   If the allegation itself be false, it will
turn to plague the accuser.   In its train will follow
severe retribution, perhaps in war ; certainly in additional embarrassments ; and most certainly in, worst of
all, the loss of that sentiment of self-esteem which to
nations as well as individuals is the " pearl of great
price," which power cannot purchase nor gold measure.

In this point of view, all the other questions, which
have been agitated in the course of this debate, dwin-
dle into utter insignificance.   The attack or defence

11

of administration, the detection of fault, or even the
exposure of crime, are of no importance when brought
into competition with the duty of rescuing this House
and nation from the guilt of asserting what is false, and
making that falsehood the basis of outrage and virulence. I avoid, therefore, all questions of censure or
reproach, on either the British minister or the American
Secretary of State. I confine myself to an examination
of this resolution, particularly of the first branch of it.
This is the foundation of all that follows. I shall submit it to a rigid analysis, not for the purpose of discov-
ering how others have performed their duties, but of
learning how we shall perform ours. The obligation to
truth is the highest of moral and social duties.

It is remarkable, Mr. Speaker, that of all the gentlemen who have spoken, no one has taken the precise
terms of the resolution as the basis of his argument, and
followed that course of investigation which those terms
naturally prescribe. Yet the obvious and only safe
course in a case of such high responsibility is first to
form a distinct idea of the assertion we are about to
make, and then carefully to examine how that assertion
is supported, if supported at all, by the evidence. With
this view I recur to the resolution in the form in which
it is proposed for our adoption, and make it the basis of
my inquiries.

"*Resolved*, By the Senate and House of Representatives of the United States of America, in Congress
assembled, That the expressions contained in the official
letter of Francis J. Jackson, minister plenipotentiary of
his Britannic Majesty near the United States, dated the
twenty-third day of October, 1809, and addressed to

Mr. Smith, Secretary of State, conveying the idea that the executive government of the United States had a knowledge that the arrangement lately made by Mr. Erskine, his predecessor, in behalf of his government, with the government of the United States was entered into without competent powers on the part of Mr. Erskine for that purpose, were highly indecorous and insolent."

This part of the resolution, it will not be denied, is the foundation of the whole : for if no such "idea was conveyed" in the letter of the 23d of October, then there could be no "repetition" of that idea in the letter of the 4th of November; and if, in the former part of his correspondence, Mr. Jackson had made no such "insinuation," then the assertion in this letter that he had made none was perfectly harmless and justifiable. This part, therefore, includes the pith of the resolution. If we analyze it, we shall find that it contains two distinct assertions. First, that the expressions alluded to convey a certain idea; second, that this idea, so conveyed, is indecorous and insolent. Here, again, we are enabled to limit the field of our investigation ; for if no such idea as is asserted was conveyed, then the inquiry, whether such idea is indecorous and insolent, is wholly superseded. The true and only question, therefore, is, whether the expressions alluded to do convey the asserted idea. I place the subject in this abstract form before the House, to the end that, if possible, we may exclude all those prejudices and partialities which so naturally and imperceptibly bias the judgment. In the light in which it now stands, it must be apparent to every one who will reflect that the question has, so far as it respects the principles on which our decision ought to proceed, no more to do with the relations between Great Britain and the United States than it has with those between the United States and China, and no more connection with Mr. Francis J. Jackson and Mr. Robert Smith than with the late Charles of Sweden and the old Duke of Sudermania. It is a simple philological disquisition, which is to be decided by known rules of construction. The only investigation is touching the power or capacity of certain terms to convey an alleged idea. However ill suited a question like this may be for the discussion of an assembly like the present, yet, if we would be just to ourselves and the people, we must submit to an examination of it in that form in which alone certainty can be attained. It is only by stripping the subject of all adventitious circumstances that we can arrive at that perfect view of its nature which can satisfy minds scrupulous of truth and anxious concerning duty. It is only by such a rigorous scrutiny that we shall be able to form that judgment which will stand the test of time, and do honor to us and our country when the passions of the day are passed away and forgotten.

The natural course of inquiry now is into the idea which is asserted to be conveyed, and the expressions which are said to convey it. Concerning the first there is no difficulty. The idea asserted to be conveyed is, " that the arrangement made between Mr. Erskine and Mr. Smith was entered into by the American government, with a knowledge that the powers of Mr. Erskine were incompetent for that purpose." It would save a world of trouble if the expressions in which this idea is said to be conveyed were equally easy of ascertainment. But on this point those gentlemen who maintain this insult are far from being agreed: some being of opinion that it is to be found in one place ; some in another ; and others, again, assert that it is to be found in the whole correspondence taken together. Never was an argument of this nature before so strangely conducted. Gentlemen seem wholly to lay out of sight that this resolution pledges this House to the assertion of a particular fact, and expresses no general sentiment concerning the conduct of Mr. Jackson or the conduct of his government. Yet, as if the whole subject of the British relations was under discussion, they have deemed themselves at liberty to course through these documents, collect every thing which seems to them indecorous, insolent, or unsuitable in Mr. Jackson's language, and add to the heap thus made the whole list of injuries received from Great Britain, impressments, affair of the Chesapeake, murder of Pierce ; and all this for what purpose? Why, truly, to justify this House in making a solemn asseveration of a particular fact! as if any injury in the world could be even an apology for the deliberate utterance of a falsehood. Let the conduct of Mr. Jackson or of Great Britain be as atrocious as it will, if the fact which we assert do not exist, we and this nation are disgraced. It is evident, then, that irksome as such a task is, it is necessary that we should submit to a precise inquiry into the truth of that to which we are about to pledge our reputation and that of this people.

In our investigation let us follow the natural course pointed out in the resolution. This alleges that the

obnoxious expressions are contained in the letter of
the 23d of October, and to this limits our assertion.
In this letter, therefore, either directly or by way of
reference to some other, this obnoxious idea or insinuation must be found. For if it be not in this, even if it
should be contained in other parts of the correspondence, which is not, however, pretended, still our assertion would be false. Concerning this letter of the
23d of October, I confidently assert, without fear of
contradiction, that the obnoxious idea, if contained
in that letter, is conveyed in the paragraph I am now
about to quote. No man has pretended to cite any
part of this letter as evidence of the asserted insult
except the ensuing ; and although there is not a perfect
coincidence in opinion as to the particular part in which
it resides, yet all agree that it lurks somewhere in this
paragraph, if it have any dwelling-place in this letter.

" I have therefore no hesitation in informing you that
his Majesty was pleased to disavow the agreement concluded between you and Mr. Erskine, because it was
concluded in violation of that gentleman's instructions,
and altogether without authority to subscribe to the
terms of it. These instructions I now understand by
your letter, as well as from the obvious deduction which
I took the liberty of making in mine of the 11th instant, were at the time, in substance, made known to
you ; no stronger illustration, therefore, can be given of
the deviation from them which occurred, than by a
reference to the terms of your agreement. Nothing can
be more notorious than the frequency with which, in
the course of complicated negotiations, ministers are
furnished with a gradation of conditions on which they

may be successively authorized to conclude. So common is the case which you put hypothetically, that in acceding to the justice of your statement I feel myself compelled to make only one observation upon it, which is, that it does not strike me as bearing upon the consideration of the unauthorized agreement concluded here, inasmuch as, in point of fact, Mr. Erskine had no such graduated instructions. You are already acquainted with that which was given, and I have had the honor of informing you that it was the only one by which the conditions on which he was to conclude were prescribed. So far from the terms which he was actually induced to accept having been contemplated in that instruction, he himself states that they were substituted by you in lieu of those originally proposed."

I have quoted the whole paragraph, because in that obscure and general mode of argument in which gentlemen have indulged, it has been read as that entire portion in which the insult is conveyed. It is difficult to conceive how some parts of this paragraph can be thought to convey any insult. However, in prosecution of my plan, I shall first exclude all those parts in which the obnoxious idea cannot be pretended to exist, and then limit my investigation to that part in which it must exist, if in the letter of the 23d of October it be conveyed at all.

With respect to the first sentence in this paragraph, I say confidently that the insult is not contained there. It is simply a declaration of the causes of the disavowal. So far is it from including the obnoxious idea of a knowledge in our government of the incompetency of Erskine's powers, that in a manner it excludes that idea, by enu-

merating violation of instructions and want of authority
as the only causes of the disavowal. In the first sentence, then, the insult is not. I pass by the second, as
it will be the subject of a distinct examination hereafter.
The third and fourth sentences it will not even be pretended convey this obnoxious idea. They simply acknowledge the frequency of graduated instructions, and
assert the fact that Mr. Erskine's were not of that
character. In this there is no insult. As little can it
be pretended to exist in the fifth sentence. It merely
asserts that Mr. Smith "already" — that is, at or before
the time Mr. Jackson was then writing — is acquainted
with the instructions (a fact not denied, and not suggested to be an insult), and that the fact of these
instructions being the only ones, Mr. Smith knows from
the information of Mr. Jackson; an assertion which, so
far from intimating the obnoxious idea of a knowledge
in Mr. Smith at the time of the arrangement with Mr.
Erskine, that it conveys a contrary idea, by declaring
that he was indebted for it to his, Mr. Jackson's, information. Here, then, the insult is not. With respect to
the last sentence in this paragraph, the only assertions
it contains are the fact that the terms accepted were not
contained in the instructions, and the evidence of this
fact, derived from the statement of Mr. Erskine, that
those acceded to were substituted by Mr. Smith in lieu
of those originally proposed. In all this, the knowledge
of Mr. Smith of the incompetency of Mr. Erskine's
powers is not so much as intimated. Indeed, no one has
pretended directly to assert that they have found it in
the parts of this paragraph, from which I have thus
excluded the obnoxious idea. Yet as the whole has

been cited and made the basis of desultory declamation, I thought it not time lost to clear out of the way all irrelevant matter, and to leave for distinct examination the only sentence of this paragraph in which the insult lurks, if it have any existence in this letter. This point we have now attained. And as little inclined as gentlemen may be to precise investigation, they must yield to it. I say, therefore, confidently, and without fear of contradiction, that if the assertion contained in this resolution be capable of justification, by any part of the letter of the 23d of October, it is by the following, the only remaining sentence of the cited paragraph which I have not yet examined : " These instructions I now understand by your letter, as well as from the obvious deduction which I took the liberty of making in mine of the 11th instant, were, at the time, in substance made known to you ; no stronger illustration, therefore, can be given of the deviation from them which occurred, than by a reference to the terms of your agreement." The latter part of this sentence being merely a conclusion from the preceding part, and having no relation to the knowledge of our government at the time of the arrangement, will be laid out of consideration, as being, obviously, wholly without the possibility of any agency in conveying the obnoxious idea. There remains only the preceding part of this sentence for the residence of the insult. Here, if anywhere, it must exist. Accordingly, this is usually shown as the spot where the ghost of insinuation first appeared before the eyes of our astonished administration. Here we shall again find it; unless, indeed, it were in fact a mere delusion of the fancy, formed of

"such stuff as dreams are made of." Let us examine
by way of analysis.

The sentence to which the advocates of this insulting insinuation are now reduced contains, first, a fact
asserted ; second, the sources from which a knowledge
of that fact is derived. The fact asserted is, that " the
instructions were, at the time, in substance made known
to you." The sources stated are, Mr. Smith's letter
of the 19th of October, and the obvious deductions in
his (Mr. Jackson's) letter of the 11th." The question is, whether, in either of these branches, or in both
taken together, directly or in the way of reference,
the following idea is by any fair construction conveyed,
viz., " That at the time of the arrangement with Mr.
Erskine the government of the United States had a
knowledge of the incompetency of Erskine's powers."

Previous to proceeding further, I wish to make a
single observation, by way of illustrating the nature
and strength of the argument I shall offer. To induce
this House to adopt a resolution so pregnant with consequences to the hopes and character of this people, it
cannot be sufficient merely to show that the insinuation
on which their assertion is predicated may be conveyed,
it will require certainty that not only this idea is, but
also that no other possibly can be. Surely if it be
possible to show, or even make it probable, that
another and an innocent idea may be conveyed, this
House will never consent to make an assertion of such
high responsibility, on such dubious ground. For the
purpose of defeating this resolution, it would therefore
be amply sufficient for me to show that an idea other
than the obnoxious one may be conveyed. But I do

not limit myself to this task: I undertake to show not
only that another idea than the obnoxious one may be
conveyed, but that another is, and that the idea asserted
in this resolution is not, and by any fair construction of
language cannot possibly be, conveyed by these expressions.

The question recurs in the fact asserted in this sentence, is the knowledge of our government of the incom-
petence of Mr. Erskine's powers intimated? So far from
conveying such an idea that it intimates nothing concerning the knowledge of our government in relation
to the general state of Mr. Erskine's powers, the
simple assertion is, " You knew the substance of those
instructions," because you admit you knew the conditions, and I tell you these were the substance. So far
from this assertion conveying the idea of a knowledge
in our government of the general state of Mr. Erskine's
powers, that if Mr. Jackson had here expressly asserted
that these instructions were shown *in extenso* to our
government, although this, after the denial of Mr. Smith,
might have been an insult, yet it would not have conveyed the obnoxious idea, nor authorized this resolution,
unless he had also asserted, or it was a fact, that those
instructions included an exclusion of all other powers;
because the assertion of the knowledge of a particular
power, which does not include such an exclusion, can
never convey the idea of the general incompetency of
the agent. In order to make my argument distinct, I
will state it more generally: If a particular power contain an exclusion of all other powers, except those
expressed in it, then an assertion that this particular
power was known may convey the idea of a knowledge

of the general incompetency of the agent. But if such particular power do not, in fact, contain an exclusion of all other powers, then to assert that this particular power was known can never convey the idea of a knowledge of such general incompetency. In this case, it is not even suggested that the instructions in question did include any such exclusion of other powers. An assertion, therefore, that they were known can never convey the idea of a general knowledge of the incompetency of the agent, unless a part can be made to include the whole, and an assertion that one thing is known can be made to convey the idea that every thing is known. If, then, an assertion of a knowledge in our government of the instructions *in extenso* would not have conveyed the idea of a general knowledge of Mr. Erskine's powers, by much stronger reason a simple assertion that only the substance of those instructions was known cannot convey that idea. I say, therefore, that, so far as respects the fact here asserted, not only another idea than the obnoxious one may be conveyed, but that another idea is, and that the idea this resolution asserts cannot by any possibility be conveyed. So that if this idea is to be found anywhere in this letter of the 23d of October, it must be in consequence of the reference to the two letters of the 19th and the 11th, which Mr. Jackson says were the sources by means of which he understood the fact he asserts. Into these letters, therefore, we must look after the insulting idea; for we have now shown that it is not in the letter of the 23d of October, unless it be by virtue of this reference.

With respect to Mr. Smith's letter of the 19th, the assertion, " I understand by your letter (that of the

19th) that the substance of these instructions was known to you," has been represented as insolent. So far from being insolent, it is not so much as a contradiction. Mr. Smith says, "I knew the three conditions." "That is what I say," replies Mr. Jackson; "you knew the substance, because I tell you that those three conditions were the substance." Here is no contradiction. The only fact open to dispute is, whether the three conditions were the substance. Mr. Jackson, indeed, asserts, but Mr. Smith does not deny, this fact. He only admits that he knew the three conditions; neither admitting nor controverting the fact asserted by Mr. Jackson that they were the substance. But, taking it for granted that this assertion was insolent, general insolence is no justification to this House for asserting a particular fact. It is enough, however, for the present argument to observe that the obnoxious idea, which is the basis of the resolution, cannot be conveyed by means of this reference to the letter of the 19th, not only from the argument just now adduced, showing that even the assertion that these instructions were known *in extenso*, would not have conveyed that idea, but also from this further consideration, that no gentleman has pretended that it was in consequence of this reference to that letter that this obnoxious idea was conveyed.

The advocates of this insult and of this resolution are, therefore, driven back to the letter of the 11th. If it be not found here, it can be found nowhere, at least to justify this resolution. With respect to this letter of the 11th, we are subjected to the same difficulty to which we were reduced in relation to the letter of the

23d. Many passages have been read for the purpose of general comment, to which, in pursuance of my plan, I shall make no allusion. I confine myself only to those passages which have been cited to prove the particular idea asserted in this resolution. None of these I shall omit. With any thing else under this resolution we have nothing to do, unless we are willing, by suffering extraneous influence to operate, to mislead our own judgments, and to deceive our fellow-citizens.

The following paragraph, in the letter of the 11th of October, is the first, and the one principally relied upon, to prove the existence of that obnoxious insinuation which is the basis of the resolution. " I observe that in the records of this mission there is no trace of complaint on the part of the United States of his Majesty's having disavowed the act of his minister. You have not, in the conferences we have hitherto held, distinctly announced any such complaint ; and I have seen with pleasure, in this forbearance on your part, an instance of that candor which I doubt not will prevail in all our communications, inasmuch as you could not but have thought it unreasonable to complain of the disavowal of an act done under such circumstances as could only lead to the consequences that have actually followed." Here is the insult, the advocates of this resolution assert, in a sort of embryo state. Let us look at it through the spectacles of the friends of the administration, without any disposition to distort or to change any of its proportions. The features of this insult, say these gentlemen, consist in this : first, in referring to the thoughts of Mr. Smith ; second, in intimating that his thoughts must have been such as to satisfy him that it was unreasonable to complain of an act done under such circumstances. In this the insult consists. In other words, in this the obnoxious idea is conveyed; because it implies a knowledge in Mr. Smith that it was done under circumstances which could only lead to a disavowal. Now, say they, the circumstance which could only lead to a disavowal is a knowledge in Mr. Smith, at the time of the arrangement, of the incompetency of Mr. Erskine's powers. Thus, say they, the knowledge of that incompetency is implied, and the idea asserted in this resolution conveyed. This is a fair and full statement of their argument. I reply, I do agree that these expressions do imply a knowledge in Mr. Smith that it was done under circumstances which could only lead to a disavowal. But it does not imply that this knowledge existed in Mr. Smith at the time of the arrangement made; but, on the contrary, does imply, and can imply only, a knowledge in Mr. Smith at the time the disavowal was known. The former is the only implication which can possibly be obnoxious; the latter is most innocent, because, at the time of the disavowal known, the circumstances which led to that disavowal were communicated. An intimation of this knowledge in Mr. Smith could not but be, therefore, perfectly inoffensive. That these expressions cannot imply a knowledge in Mr. Smith at the time of the arrangement made, and can only imply a knowledge in him at the time of disavowal known, I argue from this fact, that the only time intimated is the time when Mr. Smith " could not but have thought it unreasonable to complain of the disavowal." Now, Mr. Smith could not have begun to think of complaining of the disavowal until the disavowal was known to him, and with that knowledge came also the knowledge of the circumstances which led to it. Nothing, therefore, can be more plain than that the time here implied is the time after disavowal known, and not the time of the arrangement made. The fair construction of these expressions is, "You must have thought it, Mr. Smith, unreasonable to complain after you knew of the disavowal; for that knowledge apprised you that the act was done under circumstances which could only lead to a disavowal." I say, therefore, that the idea asserted in this resolution (a knowledge in Mr. Smith at the time of the arrangement) is not conveyed in this paragraph: another idea is conveyed; viz., a knowledge at the time of disavowal known. I say, further, that the idea of knowledge of the incompetency of Mr. Erskine's powers in Mr. Smith at the time of the arrangement cannot by any possibility be conveyed, unless the assertion of a knowledge, existing at a time subsequent, can be made to express such knowledge, limited to a time antecedent. The only knowledge implied is subsequent to disavowal, and so by no possibility can be wrested to express the state of knowledge at a time antecedent to disavowal.

The ensuing paragraph I cite at large, because it has been quoted by some of the advocates of this resolution as containing the obnoxious idea, although it requires only a single perusal to satisfy any mind that it is impossible that the far greatest part of it can contain any thing offensive. It is the only paragraph remaining unexamined which has been thus quoted, and will require a very short elucidation. "It was not known when I left England whether Mr. Erskine had, according to the liberty allowed him, communicated to you *in extenso* his original instructions. It now appears that he did not. But, in reverting to this official correspondence, and particularly to a dispatch addressed, on the 20th of April, to his Majesty's Secretary of State for Foreign Affairs, I find that he there states that he had submitted to your consideration the three conditions specified in those instructions, as the groundwork of an arrangement, which, according to information received from this country, it was thought in England might be made with a prospect of great mutual advantage. Mr. Erskine then reports, *verbatim et seriatim,* your observations upon each of the three conditions, and the reasons which induced you to think that others might be substituted in lieu of them. It may have been concluded between you that these latter were an equivalent for the original conditions; but the very act of substitution evidently shows that those original conditions were in fact very explicitly communicated to you, and by you, of course, laid before the President for his consideration. I need hardly add that the difference between these conditions and those contained in the arrangement of the 18th and 19th of April is sufficiently obvious to require no elucidation; nor need I draw the conclusion, which I consider as admitted, by all absence of complaint on the part of the American government, viz., that under such circumstances his Majesty had an undoubted and incontrovertible right to disavow the act of his minister."

On this passage it is only necessary to remark that, so far as it respects the assertion that Mr. Erskine had submitted to Mr. Smith the three conditions specified in those instructions, the fact is admitted by Mr. Smith, that so far as it respects Mr. Jackson's assertion that Mr. Erskine reports, in his official correspondence, the reasons which induced Mr. Smith to think that others might be substituted in lieu of them, that it is not denied by Mr. Smith. For in his letter of the 19th, Mr. Smith, referring to this subject, expresses himself very cautiously, that Mr. Erskine " on finding his first proposals unsuccessful, the more reasonable terms comprised in the arrangement respecting the orders in council were adopted," without denying, as he would if it had been false, and he had thought it material, that he had offered " reasons to Mr. Erskine, which induced him [Mr. Smith] to think that others might be substituted in lieu of them." But whether true or false, the assertion that Mr. Smith had offered such reasons to Mr. Erskine can never, by any fair construction, be made to convey the idea that Mr. Smith knew that Mr. Erskine's powers were limited to the three conditions, or, in other words, that Erskine's powers were incompetent. Upon the next sentence the gentleman from Pennsylvania (Mr. Milnor) lays great stress, asserting that " it conveys the idea that Mr. Smith had overreached Mr. Erskine." Concerning this sentence, my first assertion is, that whatever else it may convey, it can never convey the idea asserted in this resolution. For, certainly, to say of two classes of conditions under consideration, that Mr. Smith and Mr. Erskine concluded together that the one was equivalent to the other, can only imply a comparison and a knowledge of those classes, and by no possibility can imply the state of Mr. Smith's knowledge in relation to Mr. Erskine's

right to conclude concerning either of them. So that
for all the purposes of supporting this resolution, it is
utterly useless, whatever other demerit it may have.
The strenuousness of the gentleman from Pennsylvania
(Mr. Milnor) on this point shows the crude ideas which
even he, usually so acute and correct, entertains concerning his duties on this occasion. His great aim was
to show that Mr. Jackson here intimates the idea that
Mr. Smith had overreached Mr. Erskine. Well, suppose he had said this directly, in so many words,
would this justify the House in voting that Mr. Jackson had conveyed the idea asserted in this resolution?
It is the universal fallacy, prove any thing rude or insolent, and it is a sufficient justification to this House
for asserting a particular, independent fact. Is it possible for any mode of conduct to be more unjustifiable
or thoughtless ; more calculated to bring shame upon
ourselves and disgrace upon the nation?

The next and last sentence in this paragraph is
merely a declaration of the obvious difference between
the conditions in the instructions and those contained
in the arrangement, accompanied by a reference, by way
of recapitulation to the circumstances alluded to in the
paragraph which has been before considered. As it has
been shown that this paragraph did not contain the
obnoxious idea, it needs no argument to show it is not
contained in this sentence. Indeed, I have not heard it
pretended that this is the place of the insult.

I have thus far proceeded by way of a strict analysis
of every part of the correspondence in which the insulting idea asserted in this resolution has been said to
be conveyed. I have omitted no part which has been

cited in support of this first resolution, and think I
have shown that it exists nowhere in the letter of
the 23d of October, either in direct assertion or by
way of reference. And it is concerning what is contained in that letter alone that the resolution under
consideration has to do. The House' will observe
that, according to all rules of fair reasoning, it would
have been sufficient for me to have limited myself to
show the fallacy of the arguments of the advocates
of this insult, it being always incumbent on those who
assert the existence of any thing to prove it. I have
not, however, thought my duty on so important an
occasion fulfilled, unless I undertook to prove what the
lawyers call " a negative," and to show, with as much
strength of reasoning as I had, the non-existence of the
idea asserted in this resolution. With what success, I
cheerfully leave to the decision of such thoughtful men
in the nation who will take the trouble to understand
the argument. There is, however, a corroborative view
of this subject, which ought not to be omitted.

The insulting idea said to be conveyed is, that Mr.
Smith had a knowledge at the time of the arrangement
of the incompetency of Erskine's powers; and this
because such a knowledge was one of the essential
circumstances which could only lead to a disavowal.
Now it does happen that neither Mr. Erskine nor his
government enumerate this knowledge of our government as one of those essential circumstances. On the
contrary, they constantly omit it, when formally enumerating those circumstances. Mr. Canning places the
disavowal solely on the footing of Mr. Erskine's having "acted not only not in conformity, but in direct

contradiction to his instructions." Mr. Jackson, also, in his letter of the 23d, when formally enumerating the causes of the disavowal, says expressly that the disavowal was " because the agreement was concluded in violation of that gentleman's instructions, and altogether without authority to subscribe to the terms of it." Now is it not most extraordinary that after such formal statements, not including the knowledge of our government among the essential circumstances, that it is on this knowledge the British government intend to rely for the justification of their disavowal? I simply ask this question, if the British did intend thus to rely on the previous knowledge of our government, why do they always omit it in their formal enumerations? And if they do not intend thus to rely, in what possible way could it serve that government thus darkly to insinuate it? But as if it were intended to leave this House wholly without excuse, in passing this resolution, Mr. Jackson expressly asserts, in this very letter of the 23d of October, that the information of that fact was derived from him, the knowledge of which, this resolution asserts, he intended to intimate was known at the time of the arrangement with Mr. Erskine. For he specifically says, " I have had the honor of informing you that it" (Mr. Erskine's instruction) " was the only one by which the conditions on which he was to conclude were prescribed." Now if Mr. Jackson had remotely intended to intimate that Mr. Smith had a previous knowledge of that fact, would he have asserted that he was indebted to him (Mr. Jackson) for the information? Conclusive as this argument is, there is yet another in reserve, which is a clincher;

and that is, that this very knowledge, which we propose solemnly to affirm Mr. Jackson intimated our government possessed at the time of the arrangement, it is, from the nature of things, impossible they should have possessed. The idea asserted to be intended to be conveyed is a knowledge in our government that the arrangement was entered into without competent powers on the part of Mr. Erskine. Now the fact that Mr. Erskine's powers were incompetent, it was impossible for our government to know, except from the confession of Mr. Erskine. But Mr. Erskine before, at the time, and ever since, has uniformly asserted the reverse. So that, besides all the other absurdities growing out of this resolution, there is this additional one, that it accuses Mr. Jackson of the senseless stupidity of insinuating as a fact a knowledge in our government, which, from the undeniable nature of things, it is not possible they should have possessed. Mr. Speaker, can any argument be more conclusive?

1. The idea is not conveyed by the form of expression. 2. Mr. Jackson, though expressly enumerating the only causes which led to disavowal, does not suggest this. 3. Mr. Jackson expressly asserts that the knowledge that these were the only instructions was derived from him; of course it could not have been known previous to the arrangement. 4. Had he been absurd enough to attempt to convey such an idea, the very nature of things shows that it could not exist. I confess I am ignorant by what reasoning the non-existence of an insinuation can be demonstrated, if it be not by this concurrence of arguments.

Before I conclude this part of the subject, it will be

necessary to make a single observation or two on the
following passage in Mr. Jackson's letter of the 4th
of November; for although our assertion has relation,
in the part of the resolution under consideration, only
to the letter of the 23d of October, yet this subsequent passage has been adduced as a sort of accessory
after the fact. " You will find that, in my correspondence with you, I have carefully avoided drawing conclusions that did not necessarily follow from the premises advanced by me, and least of all should I think
of uttering an insinuation where I was unable to substantiate a fact. To facts, as I have become acquainted
with them, I have scrupulously adhered." This the
subsequent part of the resolution under debate denom-
inates " the repetition of the same intimation." But if
the argument I have offered be correct, there was no
such " intimation " in the preceding letters, and of
course no repetition of it here. For if he had, as I
think I have proved in his former letters, uttered no
such insinuation as is asserted, then all the allegations
in this paragraph are wholly harmless and decorous;
neither disrespectful nor improper. " But this," says
the gentleman from Pennsylvania (Mr. Milnor), " is
conclusive to my mind that Mr. Jackson did intend to
insult; for if he had not, would he have refrained from
giving an explanation when it was asked ? " That
gentleman will recollect that the assertion of this
House is as to the idea which Mr. Jackson has conveyed in the letter of the 23d, not as to the idea which
he intended to convey. Suppose he intended it, and
has not done it, our assertion is still false. But will
that gentleman seriously conclude, contrary to so obvi-

ous a course of argument, that he has asserted, or even intended to assert, this particular idea, merely because he does not choose to explain it? Are there not a thousand reasons which might have induced Mr. Jackson not to explain, consistent with being perfectly innocent of the intention originally to convey it? Perhaps he thought that he had already been explicit enough. Perhaps he thought the explanation was asked in terms which did not entitle Mr. Smith to receive it. Perhaps he did not choose to give this satisfaction. Well, that now is "very ungentlemanly," says the gentleman from Pennsylvania (Mr. Milnor). I agree, if he pleases, so it was. But does that justify this resolution? Because he is not a gentleman, shall we assert a falsehood?

I briefly recapitulate the leading points of my argument. When Mr. Jackson asserts " that the substance of the instructions was known to our government," the expression cannot convey the obnoxious idea, because it is not pretended that in those instructions the existence of other powers was excluded. When he says, " you must have thought it unreasonable to complain of disavowal," the time of knowledge implied is confined by the structure of the sentence to the time the disavowal was known, and cannot be limited backwards to the time the arrangement was made. It is also absurd to suppose that Mr. Jackson would intimate, by implication, the knowledge of our government of Mr. Erskine's incompetency of powers at the time of arrangement as an essential circumstance, on which the king's right of disavowal was founded, and yet omit that circumstance in a formal enumeration. And, lastly, it is still more absurd to suppose that he would undertake to insinuate a knowledge which, from the nature of things, could not possibly exist.

I have thus, Mr. Speaker, submitted to a strict and minute scrutiny all the parts of this correspondence which have been adduced by any one in support of the fact asserted in this resolution. This course, however irksome, I thought it my duty to adopt, to the end that no exertion of mine might be wanting to prevent this House from passing a resolution which, in my apprehension, is pregnant with national disgrace and other innumerable evils.

But let us suppose for one moment that the fact asserted in this resolution is true ; that the insult has been offered ; and that the proof is not obscure and doubtful, but certain and clear. I ask, is it wise, is it politic, is it manly for a national legislature to utter on any occasion, particularly against an individual, invectives so full of contumely and bitterness ? Shall we gain any thing by it ? Have such expressions a tendency to strengthen our cause, or add weight and respectability to those who advocate it ? In private life do men increase respect or multiply their friends by using the language of intemperate abuse ? Sudden anger may be an excuse for an individual ; inability to avenge an insult may afford an apology to him for resorting to these women's weapons: but what can excuse a nation for humiliating itself by the use of such vindictive aspersions ? Can we plead sudden rage ? we on whose wrath thirty suns have gone down ? Is this nation prepared to resort for apologies to its weakness, and to confess that, being unable to do any thing else, it will strive to envenom its adversary with the tongue? But our honor is assailed. Is this a medicament for its wounds? If not, why engage in such retaliatory insults? Which is best, to leave the British monarch at liberty to decide upon the conduct of his minister, without any deduction or sympathy on account of our virulence, or to necessitate him, in measuring out justice, to put your intemperance in the scale against his imprudence? Railing for railing is a fair offset all over the world. And I ask gentlemen to consider whether it be not an equivalent for a constructive insinuation.

Mr. Speaker, I do not believe that the hand of the chief magistrate of this nation is in this thing. In every aspect this resolution is at war with that wise and temperate ground on which he has placed this insult in the letter to Mr. Pinkney. "You are particularly instructed, in making those communications, to do it in a manner that will leave no doubt of the undiminished desire of the United States to unite in all the means the best calculated to establish the relations of the two countries on the solid foundation of justice, of friendship, and of mutual interests." Is there a man in this House who can lay his hand on his heart and say that, by adopting this resolution, we are about "to unite in all means the best calculated to establish the relations of the two countries on the solid foundations of justice, friendship, and mutual interest"? I hesitate not to say that there is no man who can make such an asseveration.

But if it would be wise and politic to refrain from uttering this opprobrious resolution, in case the insult

was gross, palpable, and undeniable, how much more
wise and politic if this insult be only dubious, and has,
at best, but a glimmering existence? But suppose the
assertion contained in this resolution be, as it appears to
many minds, — and certainly to mine, — false, I ask, what
worse disgrace, what lower depth of infamy, can there
be for a nation than deliberately to assert a falsehood,
and to make that falsehood the groundwork of a graduated scale of atrocious aspersions upon the character of
a public minister?

When I say that the assertion contained in this resolution is false, I beg gentlemen distinctly to understand
me. I speak only as it respects the effects of evidence
upon my mind. I pretend not to make my perceptions
the standard of those of any other. I know the nature
of the human mind, and how imperceptibly even to
ourselves passion and preconception will throw, as it
were, a mist before the intellectual eye, and bend or
scatter the rays of evidence before they strike on its
vision. On a question of this kind, as I would not trust
the casual impressions of others, so I have been equally
unwilling to trust my own. I have therefore submitted
the grounds of my opinion to a rigid analysis. The
process and the result of my reasonings I have laid
before this House. If that which to me appears a palpable falsehood, to others appeared a truth, I condemn
not them, — I can only lament such a diversity on a
point which, in its consequences, may be so important
to the peace and the character of the country.

But this resolution was devised for the purpose of
promoting unanimity. Is there a man in this House who
believes it? Did you ever hear, Mr. Speaker, that lan-

guage of reproach and of insult was the signal for con-
ciliation ?   Did you ever know contending parties made
to harmonize by terms of insult, of reproach, and contumely?   No, sir.   I deprecate this resolution on this
very account, that it is much more like the torch of the
furies than like the token of friendship.   Accordingly,
it has had the effect of enkindling party passions in the
House, which had begun in some degree to be allayed.
It could not possibly be otherwise.   A question is raised
concerning a constructive insult.   Of all topics of dispute,
those relative to the meaning of terms are most likely
to beget diversity and obstinacy in opinion.   But this
is not all.   On a question merely relative to the construction of particular expressions, all the great and
critical relations of the nation have been discussed.   Is
it possible to conceive that such a question as this, on
which the debate has been thus conducted, could be
productive of any thing else than discord and conten-
tion ?

For my own part, I have purposely avoided all reference to any of the great questions which agitate the
nation.   I should deem myself humiliated to discuss
them under a resolution of this kind, which in truth
decides nothing but our opinion of the meaning of Mr.
Jackson's language, and our sense of its nature ; and has,
strictly speaking, nothing to do with any of the national
questions which have been drawn into debate.

I declare, therefore, distinctly that I oppose and vote
against this resolution from no one consideration relative to Great Britain or the United States ; from none
of friendship or animosity to any one man, or set of men :
but simply and solely for this one reason, that in my

conception the assertion contained in this resolution is a falsehood.

But it is said that this resolution must be taken as "a test of patriotism." To this I have but one answer. If patriotism ask me to assert a falsehood, I have no hesitation in telling patriotism, "I am not prepared to make that sacrifice." The duty we owe to our country is indeed among the most solemn and impressive of all obligations; yet, high as it may be, it is nevertheless subordinate to that which we owe to that Being with whose name and character truth is identified. In this respect, I deem myself acting upon this resolution under a higher responsibility than either to this House or to this people.

SPEECH

ON THE PASSAGE OF THE BILL TO ENABLE THE
PEOPLE OF THE TERRITORY OF ORLEANS TO
FORM A CONSTITUTION AND STATE GOVERNMENT,
AND FOR THE ADMISSION OF SUCH STATE INTO
THE UNION.

Jan. 14, 1811.

SPEECH

JAN. 14, 1811.

[THIS is the most famous speech Mr. Quincy ever delivered.
It made the deepest impression of any at the time it was
delivered, and has continued to be quoted, rightly or wrongly,
almost to the present day. It was recalled to recollection at the
time of the excitement attending the admission of Texas, and,
indeed, at all times when questions as to gross violations of the
Constitution were under discussion. It was cited especially at
the time of the Rebellion, and with an approbation I am sure it
did not deserve, on both sides of the Atlantic, as containing the
same doctrine of secession which was held by the promoters
and defenders of that revolt. I do not apprehend that any
candid reader of the speech will deem this opinion well grounded.
Mr. Quincy did not hold that a State had a constitutional or a
natural right to withdraw from the Union when it thought it best
for its own interests. He did maintain that such a violation of
the fundamental compact might be made that the moral obligation
to maintain it ceased and the right of revolution attached. And
he undoubtedly believed and emphatically affirmed in this speech
that this act was such a violation of the Constitution as released
the States from their constitutional obligations, and remitted
them to their original right anterior to the Constitution, if they
chose to appeal to it, to form such a new government as should

13

be most for their own advantage. Right or wrong, he adhered to the opinions expressed in this speech to the day of his death.

It will be observed that neither he nor his party objected to the admission of Louisiana in itself considered. It was necessary for the protection of the South-western States that the free navigation of the Mississippi should be secured by the United States. His position was, that the provision in the Constitution for the erecting of new States applied only to the territory in the possession of the nation at the time of its adoption, and that it never entered into the hearts of its framers to conceive that the whole continent might be annexed by virtue of that provision; and that such annexation could be constitutionally effected only by an amendment of the Constitution authorizing it. This was also the opinion of Mr. Jefferson himself, as appears from his own letters. In one to Mr. Breckenridge, August 12, 1802, he writes of the purchase of this territory: "They (the two Houses of Congress), I presume, will do their duty to their country in ratifying and paying for it; but I suppose they must then appeal to the *nation* for an additional article in the Constitution approving and confirming an act which the nation had not previously authorized. The Constitution has made no provision for our holding foreign territory, still less for incorporating foreign nations into our Union." And, again, in a letter of Levi Lincoln, August 30, 1803, he says: "The less said about any constitutional difficulty the better. I find but one opinion as to the necessity of shutting up the Constitution for some time."

The object of this *coup d'état*, thus profligately perpetrated, was not merely the acquisition of the vast territory opened to slave labor comprised within the Territory of Orleans. Its design was to place the indefinite extension of slave territory in the hands of a majority of Congress, in which the united South were always sure of holding the balance of power. The purchase of Florida, the annexation of Texas, the Mexican war and the enormous addition of territory consequent upon it, were all effected by acts of Congress, and all in the interest of slavery. By this act the control of the nation was delivered over to the slave powers for fifty years, and it is impossible to say how much longer that domination might have lasted had it not been for the pride going before destruction that it fostered, and which tempted it to take the sword by which it perished. I am not afraid to rest Mr. Quincy's fame, as a sagacious statesman and a true prophet, upon this speech. The history of the next half-century, I think, justifies this claim, by the tale it tells of the supremacy of slavery through the operation of the principle of this very bill, and of the convulsion which followed the first successful resistance to its absolute sway and unlimited extension. — ED.]

MR. SPEAKER, — I address you, sir, with an anxiety and distress of mind, with me, wholly unprecedented. The friends of this bill seem to consider it as the exercise of a common power, as an ordinary affair, a mere municipal regulation which they expect to see pass without other questions than those concerning details. But, sir, the principle of this bill materially affects the liberties and rights of the whole people of the United States. To me it appears that it would justify a revolution in this country ; and that, in no great length of time, it may produce it. When I see the zeal and perseverance with which this bill has been urged along its parliamentary path, when I know the local interests and associated projects which combine to promote its success, all opposition to it seems manifestly unavailing. I am almost tempted to leave, without a struggle, my country to its fate. But, sir, while there is life, there is hope. So long as the fatal shaft has not yet sped, if heaven so will, the bow may be broken and the vigor of the mischief-meditating arm withered. If there be a man in this House or nation who cherishes the Constitution under which we are assembled, as the chief stay of his hope, as the light which is destined to gladden his own day, and to soften even the gloom of the grave by the prospect it sheds over his children, I fall not behind him in such sentiments. I will yield to no man in attachment to this Constitution, in veneration for the sages who laid its foundations, in devotion to those principles which form its cement and constitute its proportions. What, then, must be my feelings, — what ought to be the feelings of a man cherishing such sentiments, when he sees an act contemplated which lays ruin at the root of all these hopes? when he sees a principle of action about to be usurped, before the operation of which the bands of this Constitution are no more than flax before the fire, or stubble before the whirlwind. When this bill passes, such an act is done, and such a principle usurped.

Mr. Speaker, there is a great rule of human conduct which he who honestly observes cannot err widely from the path of his sought duty. It is to be very scrupulous concerning the principles you select as the test of your rights and obligations; to be very faithful in noticing the result of their application; and to be very fearless in tracing and exposing their immediate effects and distant consequences. Under the sanction of this rule of conduct, I am compelled to declare *it as my deliberate opinion that, if this bill passes, the bonds of this Union are virtually dissolved; that the States which compose it are free from their moral obligations; and that as it will be the right of all, so it will be the duty of some to prepare definitely for a separation — amicably, if they can; violently, if they must.*

[Mr. Quincy was here called to order by Mr. Poindexter, delegate from the Mississippi Territory, for the words quoted. After it was decided, upon an appeal to the House, that Mr. Quincy was in order, he proceeded.]

I rejoice, Mr. Speaker, at the result of this appeal; not from any personal consideration, but from the respect paid to the essential rights of the people in one of their representatives. When I spoke of the separation of the States, as resulting from the violation of the Constitution contemplated in this bill, I spoke of it as a necessity deeply to be deprecated, but as resulting from causes so certain and obvious as to be absolutely inevitable, when the effect of the principle is practically experienced. It is to preserve, to guard the Constitution of my country, that I denounce this attempt. I would rouse the attention of gentlemen from the apathy with which they seem beset. These observations are not made in a corner; there is no low intrigue, — no secret machination. I am on the people's own ground; to them I appeal concerning their own rights, their own liberties, their own intent in adopting this Constitution. The voice I have uttered, at which gentlemen startle with such agitation, is no unfriendly voice. I intended it as a voice of warning. By this people and by the event, if this bill passes, I am willing to be judged, whether it be not a voice of wisdom.

The bill which is now proposed to be passed has this assumed principle for its basis, — that the three branches of this national government, without recurrence to conventions of the people in the States, or to the legislatures of the States, are authorized to admit new partners to a share of the political power in countries out of the

original limits of the United States. Now this assumed
principle I maintain to be altogether without any sanction in the Constitution.   I declare it to be a manifest
and atrocious usurpation of power ; of a nature dissolv-
ing, according to undeniable principles of moral law, the
obligations of our national compact, and leading to all
the awful consequences which flow from such a state of
things.

Concerning this assumed principle, which is the basis
of this bill, this is the general position on which I rest
my argument, — that if the authority now proposed to be
exercised be delegated to the three branches of the government, by virtue of the Constitution, it results either
from its general nature or from its particular provisions.
I shall consider distinctly both these sources, in relation
to this pretended power.

Touching the general nature of the instrument called
the Constitution of the United States, there is no obscurity : it has no fabled descent, like the palladium of
ancient Troy, from the heavens.   Its origin is not con-
fused by the mists of time, or hidden by the darkness
of past, unexplored ages : it is the fabric of our day.
Some now living had a share in its construction : all of
us stood by and saw the rising of the edifice.   There
can be no doubt about its nature.   It is a political compact.   By whom ? and about what ?   The preamble to
the instrument will answer these questions : —

" We, the people of the United States, in order to
form a more perfect union, establish justice, insure domestic tranquillity, provide for the common defence,
promote the general welfare, and secure the blessings
of liberty to ourselves and our posterity, do ordain and

establish this Constitution for the United States of America."

It is we, the people of the United States, for ourselves and our posterity, not for the people of Louisiana, nor for the people of New Orleans, or of Canada. None of these enter into the scope of the instrument: it embraces only "the United States of America." Who these are it may seem strange in this place to inquire., But truly, sir, our imaginations have, of late, been so accustomed to wander after new settlements to the very ends of the earth, that it will not be time ill spent to inquire what this phrase means and what it includes. These are not terms adopted at hazard; they have reference to a state of things existing anterior to the Constitution. When the people of the present United States began to contemplate a severance from their parent State, it was a long time before they fixed definitively the name by which they would be designated. In 1774, they called themselves "the Colonies and Provinces of North America;" in 1775, "the Representatives of the United Colonies of North America;" in the Declaration of Independence, "the Representatives of the United States of America;" and, finally, in the articles of confederation the style of the confederacy is declared to be "the United States of America." It was with reference to the old articles of confederation, and to preserve the identity and established individuality of their character, that the preamble to this Constitution, not content simply with declaring that it is "we the people of the United States" who enter into this compact, adds that it is for "the United States of America." Concerning the territory contemplated by the people of

the United States in these general terms, there can be
no dispute : it is settled by the treaty of peace, and
included within the Atlantic Ocean, the St. Croix, the
lakes, and more precisely, so far as relates to the frontier, having relation to the present argument, within
" a line to be drawn through the middle of the river
Mississippi until it intersect the northernmost part of
the thirty-first degree of north latitude, thence within
a line drawn due east on this degree of latitude to the
river Appalachicola, thence along the middle of this river
to its junction with the Flint river, thence straight to
the head of the St. Mary's river, and thence down the
St. Mary's to the Atlantic Ocean."

I have been thus particular to draw the minds of gentlemen distinctly to the meaning of the terms used in
the preamble ; to the extent which " the United States "
then included ; and to the fact that neither New
Orleans nor Louisiana was within the comprehension
of the terms of this instrument. It is sufficient for the
present branch of my argument to say that there is
nothing in the general nature of this compact from
which the power contemplated to be exercised in this
bill results. On the contrary, as the introduction of a
new associate in political power implies, necessarily, a
new division of power and consequent diminution of
the relative proportion of the former proprietors of it,
there can certainly be nothing more obvious than that,
from the general nature of the instrument, no power can
result to diminish and give away to strangers any proportion of the rights of the original partners. If such
a power exist, it must be found, then, in the particular provisions in the Constitution. The question now

arising is, in which of these provisions is given the power to admit new States, to be created in Territories beyond the limits of the old United States. If it exist anywhere, it is either in the third section of the fourth article of the Constitution or in the treaty-making power. If it result from neither of these, it is not pretended to be found anywhere else.

That part of the third section of the fourth article on which the advocates of this bill rely is the following : " New States may be admitted, by the Congress, into this Union ; but no new State shall be formed or erected within the jurisdiction of any other State, nor any State be formed by the junction of two or more States, or parts of States, without the consent of the legislatures of the States concerned, as well as of the Congress."

I know, Mr. Speaker, that the first clause of this paragraph has been read, with all the superciliousness of a grammarian's triumph, " New States may be admitted, by the Congress, into this Union," accompanied with this most consequential inquiry: " Is not this a new State to be admitted? And is not here an express authority ? " I have no doubt this is a full and satisfactory argument to every one who is content with the mere colors and superficies of things. And if we were now at the bar of some stall-fed justice, the inquiry would insure victory to the maker of it, to the manifest delight of the constables and suitors of his court. But, sir, we are now before the tribunal of the whole American people ; reasoning concerning their liberties, their rights, their Constitution. These are not to be made the victims of the inevitable obscurity of general terms, nor the sport of verbal criticism. The question is con-

cerning the intent of the American people, the proprietors of the old United States, when they agreed to this
article.   Dictionaries and spelling-books are here of no
authority.   Neither Johnson nor Walker nor Webster
nor Dilworth has any voice in this matter.   Sir, the
question concerns the proportion of power reserved by
this Constitution to every State in this Union.   Have
the three branches of this government a right, at will,
to weaken and outweigh the influence respectively secured to each State in this compact, by introducing
at pleasure new partners situate beyond the old limits
of the United States?   The question has not relation
merely to New Orleans.   The great objection is to the
principle of the bill.   If this principle be admitted, the
whole space of Louisiana — greater, it is said, than the
entire extent of the old United States — will be a mighty
theatre in which this government assumes the right of
exercising this unparalleled power.   And it will be —
there is no concealment it is intended to be — exercised.
Nor will it stop until the very name and nature of the
old partners be overwhelmed by new-comers into the
confederacy.   Sir, the question goes to the very root of
the power and influence of the present members of this
Union.   The real intent of this article is, therefore, an
inquiry of most serious import ; and is to be settled only
by a recurrence to the known history and known relations of this people and their Constitution.   These, I
maintain, support this position, that the terms " new
States," in this article, do intend new political sovereignties, to be formed within the original limits of the
United States ; and do not intend new political sovereignties, with territorial annexations, to be created

without the original limits of the United States. I undertake to support both branches of this position to the satisfaction of the people of these United. States. As to any expectation of conviction on this floor, I know the nature of the ground, and how hopeless any arguments are which thwart a concerted course of measures.

I recur, in the first place, to the evidence of history. This furnishes the following leading fact, — that before, and at the time of, the adoption of this Constitution, the creation of new political sovereignties, within the limits of the old United States, was contemplated. Among the records of the old Congress, will be found a resolution, passed as long ago as the 10th of October, 1780, contemplating the cession of unappropriated lands to the United States, accompanied by a provision, " that they shall be disposed of for the common benefit of the United States and be settled and formed into distinct republican States, which shall become members of the federal union, and have the same rights of sovereignty, freedom, and independence as the other States." Afterwards, on the 7th of July, 1786, the subject of " laying out and forming into States " the country lying north-west of the river Ohio came under the consideration of the same body ; and another resolution was passed recommending to the legislature of Virginia to revise their act of cession, so as to permit a more eligible division of that portion of territory derived from her ; " which States," it proceeds to declare, " shall hereafter become members of the federal union, and have the same rights of sovereignty, freedom, and independence as the original States, in conformity with the resolution of Congress of the 10th of October, 1780." All the Territories to which these resolutions had reference were, undeniably, within the ancient limits of the United States. Here, then, is a leading fact, that the article in the Constitution had a condition of things, notorious at the time when it was adopted, upon which it was to act, and to meet the exigency resulting from which such an article was requisite. That is to say, new States, within the limits of the old United States, were contemplated at the time when the foundations of the Constitution were laid. But we have another authority upon this point, which is, in truth, a contemporaneous exposition of this article of the Constitution. I allude to the resolution passed on the 3d of July, 1788, in the words following : " Whereas application has been lately made to Congress by the legislature of Virginia, and the district of Kentucky, for the admission of the said district into the federal union, as a separate member thereof, on the terms contained in the acts of the said legislature, and in the resolutions of the said district, relative to the premises : And whereas Congress, having fully considered the subject, did, on the third day of June last, resolve that it is expedient that the said district be erected into a sovereign and independent State and a separate member of the federal union ; and appointed a committee to report and act accordingly, which committee on the second instant was discharged, it appearing that nine States had adopted the Constitution of the United States, lately submitted to conventions of the people: And whereas a new confederacy is formed among the ratifying States, and there is reason to believe that the State of Virginia, including the said district, did, on the 25th of June last, become a member of the said confederacy: And whereas an act of Congress, in the present state of the government of the country, severing a part of the said State from the other parts thereof, and admitting it into the confederacy, formed by the articles of confederation and perpetual union, as an independent member thereof, may be attended with many inconveniences, while it can have no effect to make the said district a separate member of the federal union formed by the adoption of the said Constitution, and therefore it must be manifestly improper for Congress, assembled under the articles of confederation, to adopt any other measures relative to the premises than those which express their sense that the said district ought to be an independent member of the Union as soon as circumstances shall permit proper measures to be adopted for that purpose, — " *Resolved*, that a copy of the proceedings of Congress, relative to the independency of the district of Kentucky, be transmitted to the legislature of Virginia, and also to Samuel M'Dowell, Esq., late President of the said Convention; and that the said legislature, and the inhabitants of the district aforesaid, be informed that, as the Constitution of the United States is now ratified, Congress think it unadvisable to adopt any further measures for admitting the district of Kentucky into the federal union, as an independent member thereof, under the articles of confederation and perpetual union; but that Congress, thinking it expedient that the said district be made a separate State and member of the Union, as soon after proceedings shall commence under the said Constitution as circumstances shall permit, recommends it to the said legislature, and to the inhabitants of the said district, so to alter their acts and resolutions relative to the premises, as to render them conformable to the provisions made in the said Constitution, to the end that no impediment may be in the way of the speedy accomplishment of this important business."

In this resolution of the old Congress it is expressly declared that the Constitution of the United States having been adopted by nine States, an act of the old Congress could have no effect to make Kentucky a separate member of the Union, and that, although they thought it expedient that it should so be admitted, yet that this could only be done under the provisions made in the new Constitution. It is impossible to have a more direct contemporaneous evidence that the case contemplated in this article was that of Territories within the limits of the old United States; yet the gentleman from North Carolina, Mr. Macon, for whose integrity and independence I have very great respect, told us the other day, that " if this article had not Territories without the limits of the old United States to act upon, it would be wholly without meaning; because the ordinance of the old Congress had secured the right to the States within the old United States, and a provision for that object in the new Constitution was wholly unnecessary." Now, I will appeal to the gentleman's own candor if the very reverse of the conclusion he draws is not the true one, after he has considered the following fact, — that by this ordinance of the old Congress it was declared that the boundaries of the contemplated States, and the terms of their admission, should be, in certain particulars specified in the ordinance, subject to the control of

Congress. Now, as by the new Constitution the old Congress was about to be annihilated, it was absolutely necessary for the very fulfilment of this ordinance that the new Constitution should have this power for the admission of new States within the ancient limits ; so that the ordinance of the old Congress, far from showing the inutility of such a provision for the Territories within the ancient limits, expressly proves the reverse, and is an evidence of its necessity to effect the object of the ordinance itself.

I think there can be no more satisfactory evidence adduced or required of the first part of the position, — that the terms " new States " did intend new political sovereignties within the limits of the old United States. For it is here shown that the creation of such States, within the territorial limits fixed by the treaty of 1783, had been contemplated ; that the old Congress itself expressly asserts that the new Constitution gave the power for that object ; that the nature of the old ordinance required such a power for the purpose of carrying its provisions into effect ; and that it has been, from the time of the adoption of the Federal Constitution unto this hour, applied exclusively to the admission of States within the limits of the old United States, and was never attempted to be extended to any other object. Now, having shown a purpose, at the time of the adoption of the Constitution of the United States, sufficient to occupy the whole scope of the terms of the article, ought not the evidence to be very strong to satisfy the mind that the terms really intended something else besides this obvious purpose ; that it may be fairly extended to the entire circle of the globe, wherever title

can be obtained by purchase or conquest, and that new
partners in the political power may be admitted, at the
mere discretion of this legislature, anywhere that it wills.
A principle, thus monstrous, is asserted in this bill.

But I think it may be made satisfactorily to appear,
not only that the terms, " new States," in this article,
did mean political sovereignties to be formed within the
original limits of the United States, as has just been
shown, but also negatively, that it did not intend new
political sovereignties, with territorial annexations, to
be created without those original limits. This appears
first from the very tenor of the article. All its limitations have respect to the creation of States within
the original limits. Two States shall not be joined ; no
new State shall be erected within the jurisdiction of
any other State, — without the consent of the legislatures of the States concerned as well as of Congress.
Now, had foreign territories been contemplated ; had
the new habits, customs, manners, and language of
other nations been in the idea of the framers of this
Constitution, — would not some limitation have been
devised to guard against the abuse of a power in its
nature so enormous, and so obviously calculated to excite
just jealousy among the States, whose relative weight
would be so essentially affected by such an infusion at
once of a mass of foreigners into their councils and
into all the rights of the country ? The want of all
limitation of such power would be a strong evidence,
were others wanting, that the powers, now about to be
exercised, never entered into the imagination of those
thoughtful and prescient men who constructed the
fabric. But there is another most powerful argument

against the extension of the terms of this article to embrace the right to create States, without the original limits of the United States, deducible from the utter silence of all debates at the period of the adoption of the Federal Constitution, touching the power here proposed to be usurped. If ever there was a time, in which the ingenuity of the greatest men of an age was taxed to find arguments in favor of and against any political measure, it was at the time of the adoption of this Constitution. All the faculties of the human mind were, on the one side and the other, put upon their utmost stretch, to find the real and imaginary blessings or evils likely to result from the proposed measure. Now I call upon the advocates of this bill to point out, in all the debates of that period, in any one publication, in any one pamphlet, in any one newspaper of those times, a single intimation, by friend or foe to the Constitution, approving or censuring it for containing the power here proposed to be usurped, or a single suggestion that it might be extended to such an object as is now proposed. I do not say that no such suggestion was ever made. But this I will say, that I do not believe there is such an one anywhere to be found. Certain I am, I have never been able to meet the shadow of such a suggestion; and I have made no inconsiderable research upon the point. Such may exist; but, until it be produced, we have a right to reason as though it had no existence. No, sir, the people of this country, at that day, had no idea of the territorial avidity of their successors. It was, on the contrary, an argument used against the success of the project, that the territory was too extensive for a republican form of government.

14

But now there are no limits to our ambitious hopes. We are about to cross the Mississippi. The Missouri and Red River are but roads on which our imagination travels to new lands and new States to be raised and admitted (under the power now first usurped) into this Union, among the undiscovered lands in the West. But it has been suggested that the Convention had Canada in view in this article, and the gentleman from North Carolina told this House that a member of the Convention, as I understood him, either now or lately a member of the Senate, informed him that the article had that reference. Sir, I have no doubt the gentleman from North Carolina has had a communication such as he intimates. But, for myself, I have no sort of faith in these convenient recollections, suited to serve a turn, to furnish an apology for a party or give color to a project. I do not deny, on the contrary I believe it very probable, that among the coursings of some discursive and craving fancy, such thoughts might be started ; but that is not the question. Was this an avowed object in the Convention when it formed this article ? Did it enter into the conception of the people when its principles were discussed ? Sir, it did not ; it could not. The very intention would have been a disgrace both to this people and the Convention. What, sir ? Shall it be intimated, shall it for a moment be admitted, that the noblest and purest band of patriots this or any other country ever could boast were engaged in machinating means for the dismemberment of the territories of a power to which they had pledged friendship, and the observance of all the obligations, which grow out of a strict and perfect amity ? The honor of our country forbids and disdains such a suggestion. ·

But there is an argument stronger even than all those which have been produced, to be drawn from the nature of the power here proposed to be exercised. Is it possible that such a power, if it had been intended to be given by the people, should be left dependent upon the effect of general expressions? and such, too, as were obviously applicable to another subject, to a particular exigency contemplated at the time? Sir, what is this power we propose now to usurp? Nothing less than a power changing all the proportions of the weight and influence possessed by the potent sovereignties composing this Union. A stranger is to be introduced to an equal share without their consent. Upon a principle pretended to be deduced from the Constitution this government, after this bill passes, may and will multiply foreign partners in power at its own mere motion, at its irresponsible pleasure; in other words, as local interests, party passions, or ambitious views, may suggest. It is a power that from its nature never could be delegated, never was delegated; and, as it breaks down all the proportions of power guaranteed by the Constitution to the States, upon which their essential security depends, utterly annihilates the moral force of this political contract. Would this people, so wisely vigilant concerning their rights, have transferred to. Congress a power to balance at its will the political weight of any one State, much more of all the States, by authorizing it to create new States at its pleasure in foreign countries, not pretended to be within the scope of the Constitution or the conception of the people at the time of passing it? This is not so much a question concerning the exercise of sovereignty as it is who shall be sovereign; whether

the proprietors of the good old United States shall manage their own affairs in their own way, or whether they
and their Constitution and their political rights shall be
trampled under foot by foreigners, introduced through
a breach of the Constitution. The proportion of the
political weight of each sovereign State constituting
this Union depends upon the number of the States
which have a voice under the compact. This number
the Constitution permits us to multiply at pleasure
within the limits of the original United States, observing
only the expressed limitations in the Constitution. But
when, in order to increase your power of augmenting
this number, you pass the old limits, you are guilty of a
violation of the Constitution in a fundamental point,
and in one also which is totally inconsistent with the
intent of the contract and the safety of the States
which established the association. What is the practical difference to the old partners whether they hold
their liberties at the will of a master, or whether, by
admitting exterior States on an equal footing with the
original States, arbiters are constituted, who, by avail-
ing themselves of the contrariety of interests and views
which in such a confederacy necessarily will arise, hold
the balance among the parties which exist and govern
us by throwing themselves into the scale most conformable to their purposes ? In both cases there is an effective despotism. But the last is the more galling, as we
carry the chain in the name and with the gait of freemen.

I have thus shown, and whether fairly I am willing to
be judged by the sound discretion of the American people, that the power proposed to be usurped in this bill

results neither from the general nature nor the particular provisions of the Federal Constitution, and that it is a palpable violation of it in a fundamental point, whence flow all the consequences I have intimated.

But says the gentleman from Tennessee (Mr. Rhea), " These people have been seven years citizens of the United States." I deny it, sir. As citizens of New Orleans or of Louisiana they never have been, and by the mode proposed they never will be, citizens of the United States. They may be girt upon us for a moment, but no real cement can grow from such an association. What the real situation of the inhabitants of those foreign countries is, I shall have occasion to show presently. But says the same gentleman, "If I have a farm, have not I a right to purchase another farm in my neighborhood, and settle my sons upon it, and in time admit them to a share in the management of my household?" Doubtless, sir. But are these cases parallel? Are the three branches of this government owners of this farm called the United States? I desire to thank heaven they are not. I hold my life, liberty, and property, and the people of the State from which I have the honor to be a representative hold theirs, by a better tenure than any this national government can give. Sir, I know your virtue; and I thank the Great Giver of every good gift that neither the gentleman from Tennessee nor his comrades, nor any nor all the members of this House, nor of the other branch of the legislature, nor the good gentleman who lives in the palace yonder, nor all combined, can touch these my essential rights, and those of my friends and constituents, except in a limited and prescribed form. No, sir:

we hold these by the laws, customs, and principles of the Commonwealth of Massachusetts. Behind her ample shield we find refuge and feel safety. I beg gentlemen not to act upon the principle that the Commonwealth of Massachusetts is their farm.

But the gentleman adds, " What shall we do if we do not admit the people of Louisiana into our Union ? Our children are settling that country." Sir, it is no concern of mine what he does. Because his children have run wild and uncovered into the woods, is that a reason for him to break into my house or the houses of my friends to filch our children's clothes in order to cover his children's nakedness ? This Constitution never was and never can be strained to lap over all the wilderness of the West without essentially affecting both the rights and convenience of its real proprietors. It was never constructed to form a covering for the inhabitants of the Missouri and the Red River country ; and whenever it is attempted to be stretched over them it will rend asunder. I have done with this part of my argument. It rests upon this fundamental principle, that the proportion of political power, subject only to the internal modifications permitted by the Constitution, is an unalienable, essential, intangible right. When it is touched, the fabric is annihilated ; for on the preservation of these proportions depend our rights and liberties.

If we recur to the known relations existing among the States at the time of the adoption of this Constitution, the same conclusion will result. The various interests, habits, manners, prejudices, education, situation, and views, which excited jealousies and anxieties in the breasts of some of our most distinguished citizens touching the result of the proposed Constitution, were potent obstacles to its adoption. The immortal leader of our Revolution, in his letter to the President of the old Congress, written as President of the Convention which formed this compact, thus speaks on this subject : " It is at all times difficult to draw with precision the line between those rights which must be surrendered and those which may be reserved ; and, on the present occasion, this difficulty was increased by a difference among the several States as to their situation, extent, habits, and particular interests." The debates of that period will show that the effect of the slave votes upon the political influence of this part of the country, and the anticipated variation of the weight of power to the West, were subjects of great and just jealousy to some of the best patriots in the Northern and Eastern States. Suppose, then, that it had been distinctly foreseen that, in addition to the effect of this weight, the whole population of a world beyond the Mississippi was to be brought into this and the other branch of the legislature to form our laws, control our rights, and decide our destiny. Sir, can it be pretended that the patriots of that day would for one moment have listened to it? They were not madmen. They had not taken degrees at the hospital of idiocy. They knew the nature of man, and the effect of his combinations in political societies. They knew that when the weight of particular sections of a confederacy was greatly unequal, the resulting power would be abused ; that it was not in the nature of man to exercise it with moderation. The very extravagance of the intended use is a conclusive evidence against the possibility of the grant of such a power as is here proposed. Why, sir, I have already heard of six States, and some say there will be at no great distance of time more. I have also heard that the mouth of the Ohio will be far to the east of the centre of the contemplated empire. If the bill is passed, the principle is recognized. All the rest are mere questions of expediency. It is impossible such a power could be granted. It was not for these men that our fathers fought. It was not for them this Constitution was adopted. You have no authority to throw the rights and liberties and property of this people into " hotch-pot " with the wild men on the Missouri, nor with the mixed, though more respectable, race of Anglo-Hispano-Gallo-Americans who bask on the sands in the mouth of the Mississippi. I make no objection to these from their want of moral qualities or political light. The inhabitants of New Orleans are, I suppose, like those of all other countries, — some good, some bad, some indifferent.

As then the power in this bill proposed to be usurped is neither to be drawn from the general nature of the instrument nor from the clause just examined, it follows that, if it exist anywhere, it must result from the treaty-making power. This the gentleman from Tennessee (Mr. Rhea) asserts, but the gentleman from North Carolina (Mr. Macon) denies, and very justly; for what a monstrous position is this, that the treaty-making power has the competency to change the fundamental relations of the Constitution itself! that a power under the Constitution should have the ability to change and annihilate the instrument from which it derives all its power! and if the treaty-making power can introduce new partners to the political rights of the States, there is no length, however extravagant or inconsistent with the end, to which it may not be wrested. The present President of the United States, when a member of the Virginia Convention for adopting the Constitution, expressly declares that the treaty-making power has limitations; and he states this as one, " that it cannot alienate any essential right." Now is not here an essential right to be alienated ? — the right to that proportion of political power which the Constitution has secured to every State, modified only by such internal increase of States as the existing limits of the territories at the time of the adoption of the Constitution permitted. The debates of that period chiefly turned upon the competency of this power to bargain away any of the old States. It was agreed, at that time, that by this power old States, within the ancient limits, could not be sold from us; and I maintain that by it new States, without the ancient limits, cannot be saddled upon us. It was agreed, at that time, that the treaty-making power " could not cut off a limb ;" and I maintain that neither has it the competency to clap a hump upon our shoulders. The fair proportions devised by the Constitution are in both cases marred, and the fate and felicity of the political being, in material particulars related to the essence of his constitution, affected. It was never pretended, by the most enthusiastic advocates for the extent of the treaty-making power, that it exceeded that of the king of Great Britain. Yet I ask, suppose that monarch should make a treaty stipulating that Hanover or Hindostan should have a right of representation on the floor of Parliament, would such a treaty be binding? No, sir; not, as I believe, if a House of Commons and of Lords could be found venal enough to agree to it. But although, in that country, the three branches of its legislature are called omnipotent, and the people might not deem themselves justified in resistance, yet here there is no apology of this kind. The limits of our power are distinctly marked; and, when the three branches of this government usurp upon this Constitution in particulars vital to the liberties of this people, the deed is at their peril.

I have done with the constitutional argument. Whether I have been able to convince any member of this House, I am ignorant: I had almost said indifferent; but this I will not say, because I am indeed deeply anxious to prevent the passage of this bill. Of this I am certain, however, that when the dissensions of this day are passed away; when party spirit shall no longer prevent the people of the United States from looking at the principle assumed in it, independent of gross and deceptive attachments and antipathies, — the ground here defended will be acknowledged as a high constitutional bulwark, and that the principles here advanced will be appreciated.

I will add one word touching the situation of New Orleans. The provision of the treaty of 1803 which stipulates that it shall be " admitted as soon as possible " does not therefore imply a violation of the Constitution. There are ways in which this may constitutionally be effected, — by an amendment of the Constitution, or by reference to Conventions of the people in the States. And I do suppose that, in relation to the objects of the

present bill (the people of New Orleans), no great difficulty would arise. Considered as an important accommodation to the Western States, there would be no
violent objection to the measure. But this would not
answer all the projects to which the principle of this
bill, when once admitted, leads, and is intended to be
applied. The whole extent of Louisiana is to be cut up
into independent States, to counterbalance and to paralyze whatever there is of influence in other quarters
of the Union, — such a power I am well aware that the
people of the States would never grant you. And
therefore, if you get it, the only way is by the mode
adopted in this bill, — by usurpation.

The objection here urged is not a new one. I refer
with great delicacy to the course pursued by any member of the other branch of the legislature; yet I have
it, from such authority that I have an entire belief of
the fact, that our present minister in Russia,* then a
member of that body when the Louisiana treaty was
under the consideration of the Senate, although he was
in favor of the treaty, yet expressed great doubts, on
the ground of constitutionality, in relation to our control over the destinies of that people, and the manner
and the principles on which they could be admitted
into the Union. And it does appear that he made two
several motions in that body, having for their object,
as avowed and as gathered from their nature, an alteration in the Constitution to enable us to comply with
the stipulations of that Convention.

I will add only a few words, in relation to the moral

---

* Mr. John Quincy Adams.

and political consequences of usurping this power. I
have said that it would be a virtual dissolution of the
Union; and gentlemen express great sensibility at the
expression. But the true source of terror is not the
declaration I have made, but the deed you propose. Is
there a moral principle of public law better settled, or
more conformable to the plainest suggestions of reason,
than that the violation of a contract by one of the parties
may be considered as exempting the other from its
obligations? Suppose, in private life, thirteen form a
partnership, and ten of them undertake to admit a new
partner without the concurrence of the other three,
would it not be at their option to abandon the partnership after so palpable an infringement of their rights?
How much more in the political partnership, where the
admission of new associates, without previous authority,
is so pregnant with obvious dangers and evils! Again:
it is settled as a principle of morality, among writers on
public law, that no person can be obliged beyond his
intent at the time of the contract. Now who believes,
who dare assert, that it was the intention of the people,
when they adopted this Constitution, to assign event-
ually to New Orleans and Louisiana a portion of their
political power, and to invest all the people those
extensive regions might hereafter contain with an
authority over themselves and their descendants?
When you throw the weight of Louisiana into the scale,
you destroy the political equipoise contemplated at the
time of forming the contract. Can any man venture to
affirm that the people did intend such a comprehension
as you now by construction give it? or can it be concealed that, beyond its fair and acknowledged intent,

such a compact has no moral force? If gentlemen are
so alarmed at the bare mention of the consequences, let
them abandon a measure which, sooner or later, will
produce them. How long before the seeds of discontent
will ripen no man can foretell; but it is the part of
wisdom not to multiply or scatter them. Do you suppose the people of the Northern and Atlantic States
will or ought to look on with patience and see Representatives and Senators, from the Red River and Missouri, pouring themselves upon this and the other floor,
managing the concerns of a sea-board fifteen hundred
miles at least from their residence, and having a pre-
ponderancy in councils into which, constitutionally,
they could never have been admitted? I have no hesitation upon this point. They neither will see it, nor
ought to see it, with content. It is the part of a wise
man to foresee danger and to hide himself. This great
usurpation, which creeps into this House under the
plausible appearance of giving content to that important
point, New Orleans, starts up a gigantic power to control
the nation. Upon the actual condition of things, there
is, there can be, no need of concealment. It is apparent
to the blindest vision. By the course of nature and
conformable to the acknowledged principles of the Constitution, the sceptre of power in this country is passing
towards the North-west. Sir, there is to this no objection. The right belongs to that quarter of the country:
enjoy it. It is yours. Use the powers granted, as you
please; but take care, in your haste after effectual
dominion, not to overload the scale by heaping it with
these new acquisitions. Grasp not too eagerly at your
purpose. In your speed after uncontrolled sway,

trample not down this Constitution.   Already the old
States sink in the estimation of members, when brought
into comparison with these new countries.   We have
been told that " New Orleans was the most important
point in the Union."   A place, out of the Union, the
most important place within it!   We have been asked
" what are some of the small States, when compared
with the Mississippi Territory ? "   The gentleman from
that territory (Mr. Poindexter) spoke the other day of
the Mississippi as "of a high road between "— Good
heavens! between what, Mr. Speaker?   Why, " The
Eastern and Western States."   So that all the north-
western territories, all the countries once the extreme
western boundary of our Union, are hereafter to be
denominated Eastern States !

[Mr. Poindexter explained.   He said that he had not
said that the Mississippi was to be the boundary between
the Eastern and Western States.   He had merely
thrown out a hint that, in erecting new States, it might
be a good high road between the States on its waters.
His idea had not extended beyond the new States on
the waters of the Mississippi.]

I make no great point of this matter.   The gentleman
will find in the " National Intelligencer " the terms to
which I refer.   There will be seen, I presume, what he
has said, and what he has not said.   The argument is
not affected by the explanation.   New States are intended to be formed beyond the Mississippi.   There is
no limit to men's imaginations, on this subject, short of
California and Columbia river.   When I said that the
bill would justify a revolution and would produce it, I
spoke of its principle and its practical consequences.

To this principle and those consequences I would call the attention of this House and nation. If it be about to introduce a condition of things absolutely insupportable, it becomes wise and honest men to anticipate the evil, and to warn and prepare the people against the event. I have no hesitation on the subject. The extension of this principle to the States contemplated beyond the Mississippi cannot, will not, and ought not to be borne. And the sooner the people contemplate the unavoidable result the better, — the more chance that convulsions may be prevented, the more hope that the evils may be palliated or removed.

Mr. Speaker, what is this liberty of which so much is said? Is it to walk about this earth, to breathe this air, and to partake the common blessings of God's providence? The beasts of the field and the birds of the air unite with us in such privileges as these. But man boasts a purer and more ethereal temperature. His mind grasps in its view the past and future, as well as the present. We live not for ourselves alone. That which we call liberty is that principle on which the essential security of our political condition depends. It results from the limitations of our political system prescribed in the Constitution. These limitations, so long as they are faithfully observed, maintain order, peace, and safety. When they are violated in essential particulars, all the concurrent spheres of authority rush against each other; and disorder, derangement, and convulsion are, sooner or later, the necessary consequences.

With respect to this love of our Union, concerning which so much sensibility is expressed, I have no fear about analyzing its nature. There is in it nothing of mystery. It depends upon the qualities of that Union, and it results from its effects upon our and our country's happiness. It is valued for " that sober certainty of waking bliss " which it enables us to realize. It grows out of the affections ; and has not, and cannot be made to have, any thing universal in its nature. Sir, I confess it, the first public love of my heart is the Commonwealth of Massachusetts. There is my fireside ; there are the tombs of my ancestors.

> " Low lies that land, yet blest with fruitful stores,
>   Strong are her sons, though rocky are her shores ;
>   And none, ah ! none, so lovely to my sight,
>   Of all the lands which heaven o'erspreads with light."

The love of this Union grows out of this attachment to my native soil, and is rooted in it. I cherish it, because it affords the best external hope of her peace, her prosperity, her independence. I oppose this bill from no animosity to the people of New Orleans, but from the deep conviction that it contains a principle incompatible with the liberties and safety of my country. I have no concealment of my opinion. The bill, if it passes, is a death-blow to the Constitution. It may afterwards linger ; but lingering, its fate will, at no very distant period, be consummated.

SPEECH

ON THE INFLUENCE OF PLACE AND PATRONAGE.

Jan. 30, 1811.

15

SPEECH

ON THE INFLUENCE OF PLACE AND PATRONAGE.

JAN. 30, 1811.

[THE following speech was one of the earliest protests in our history against the abuse of making the offices under government a fund for buying political support. The Marcy heresy, that "to the victors belong the spoils," had not yet been broached; and compared with the flood of corruption, the gates of which were opened under the disgraceful administration of General Jackson, and which have not yet been closed, the stream which flowed from the White House sixty years since was but a rill. But little things seemed great in those days of small things, and Mr. Quincy was moved to utter the following words of admonition and reproof, as a relief to his own mind rather than with any sanguine hope of effecting a reformation. Though its assaults and its innuendoes could not have been well-pleasing to the supporters of the administration, it was listened to with apparent good-humor, and its hits met with abundant laughter. Mr. Macon, of North Carolina, having moved that an amendment to the Constitution be submitted to the people, providing that no Senator or Representative should be appointed to any office under government until the presidential term under which he had served as such should have expired, Mr. Quincy moved as an amendment that "no person standing to any Senator or Representative in the relation of father, brother, or son, by blood or marriage, shall be appointed to any civil office under the United States, or shall receive any place, agency, contract, or

emolument from or under any department or officer thereof."
After his speech was finished, Mr. Wright, of Maryland, moved,
by way of *reductio ad absurdum,* that "every Senator and Representative, on taking his seat, should furnish a table of his
genealogy," which he afterwards modified, on the suggestion
that a Senator or Representative might marry, and thus change
his connections, so as to read, " Each member of the Senate and
House, when he takes his seat, shall file a list of his relatives
precluded by said resolution." It need hardly be told that not
only the amendments but the Self-denying Ordinance itself failed
of the necessary majority. This speech was well approved by
the Federalists, and Mr. Quincy received many assurances of
approval of it. President John Adams wrote him a letter
couched in terms of admiration, which even filial piety cannot
regard as otherwise than excessive, not to say hyperbolical. He
writes, "I owe you thanks for your speech on Place and Patronage ; the moral and patriotic sentiments are noble and exalted,
the eloquence masterly, and the satire inimitable. There are
not in Juvenal nor in Swift any images more exquisitely ridicu-
lous."—ED.]

Mr. CHAIRMAN,—The amendment to the Constitution proposed by the gentleman from North Carolina is
of the nature of a remedy for an evil. The proposition
which I have the honor to submit is similar in principle,
but embraces a wider sphere of action, and is offered as
a medicament of a higher power. His amendment has
for its object to purify the legislature of that corruption
which springs from the hope of office for ourselves.
My proposition has for its object to purify the legislature
of that corruption which springs from the attainment
of office for our relations ; and if the House will take
the trouble to analyze the respective natures of these
two evils, it will find that the evil to which my proposition refers is higher in nature and more intense in

degree than that to which the amendment of the gentleman from North Carolina has reference ; that is to say,
the present attainment of office for our relations, for
those near and dear to us, who are parts of our blood,
and, if our natures be generous, parts of ourselves,
is an application to the principle of human action, as
much more strong and alluring than the distant hope of
office for ourselves, as fruition is a nearer approximation
to bliss than expectation, or as payment in hand is
better than payment in promise.

I shall offer a few considerations in support of my
proposition, not only by way of elucidation to this
House, but also for the purpose of attracting the attention of the public to the subject ; for I am well aware
that, let it be discussed when it will, and under what
administration it will, it cannot fail to be in this and the
other branch of the legislature a bitter pill ; and, unless
it have the aid of external pressure, it will stick in the
passage.

I know the nature of the subject, and am aware that
it is very delicate and very critical. Why, sir, it relates
to nothing less than our blood and our purses, — objects,
of all others, the most squeamishly sensitive, and the
most jealous of other people's interference. It shall be
my endeavor, however, to handle the topic with as much
caution as possible ; and, in order to avoid all appearance
of party or personality, I shall speak concerning things
past and things future, without particular notice of
things present.

In the first place, I would remark that our general
mode of speaking, both on this floor and in common
conversation, concerning this power of distributing

offices, is, in my judgment, not strictly accurate in itself, and may be questioned as unjust to the President of the United States. It is denominated executive influence; by way of analogy and in conformity perhaps to the practice in Great Britain, where the Crown, being proprietor of offices, distributes them at will among favorites. But the state of things is different in this country. Here the executive has no proprietary interest in the offices which he distributes. He does not create them; he does not, except in a few instances, even designate the amount of emolument. All these, in fact, proceed from the legislature. We are the creators; he is the channel for communicating them to their objects: so that if the members of this and the other branch of the legislature become venal in this country, they are, to say the least, half workers in their own corruption. A mode of expression ought not, therefore, to be used tending to throw the guilt exclusively on another branch of the government. Another phrase is more just and appropriate. Sir, it ought to be called pecuniary influence, — the love of money wrapped up in very thin covers and disguises, called offices for ourselves and offices for our relations.

I shall consider the principle of this amendment and proposition in relation to the Constitution, its nature and necessity.

If we look into the Constitution, we shall find no part more palpably defective than its provision against the effects of that executive influence, as it is called, resulting from the power of distributing offices at pleasure among the members of both branches of the legislature and their relations. There is, I think, but one provision upon the subject. This is contained in the following clause of the last paragraph of the sixth section of the first article: " No senator or representative shall, during the time for which he was elected, be appointed to any civil office under the authority of the United States, which shall have been created, or the emoluments whereof shall have been increased, during such time." This provision, I say, considered as a security against that corruption which springs from the distribution of offices, is palpably defective. In relation to its objects it is limited, and in its means wants efficiency. What are its objects? It aims only to prevent multiplication of offices and increase of their emolument; so that, provided we do not create new offices, nor increase the old emolument, the craving spirit of avarice has free range to solicit and corrupt both branches of the legislature. All the numerous allurements of existing offices, all the rich reward of established salaries, are permitted to play their bewitching fascinations before our eyes. So long as a man does not attempt to take the fruit of seed of his own sowing, he may botanize at his pleasure in this great executive garden ; and whether he seek flower or fruit he may, to the full, please his fancy or satiate his appetite. And if we consider the means, it will be found that they are inadequate. There is but one limitation . . . " during the time for which he was elected." What is this, considered as security? It is scarcely less than totally inefficient. Notwithstanding this provision a man may,— I say may, Mr. Chairman, for I would not be understood to affirm that any such creature now exists, or has ever heretofore appeared in this or the other branch of the legislature ; but I speak of the possibility of that gross and debasing corruption, such as has appeared in other countries, and may, therefore, hereafter appear in this, — a man may be a mere spaniel to the executive : he may fetch and carry, run upon all his errands, and, at his whistle, roll himself over on these floors, without regard to either coat or conscience ; and on the last day of the term for which he was elected, when, perhaps, he has been ejected from the people's favor as foul and odious, he may, in spite of this provision, be instrumental in creating an office, or increasing an emolument, of which the very next day he shall take the profits. Is not such a provision, considered as a security against corruption from the distribution of offices, like tantalism to this people? I would not, however, be thought to hold at a mean rate this part of our Constitution. Notwithstanding its deficiency, it is precious; because it recognizes the possibility of the existence of this principle of corruption in this and the other branch of the legislature ; because it is a standing and a solemn warning against its effects. It gives us ground to stand upon, and, through the instrumentality of the power of amendment, may enable this people to wrench out of this soil by the roots this foul and growing pollution.

If we compare the principle of this amendment and my proposition with the principles of the Constitution, we shall find that it no less harmonizes with them than it does with this provision of the instrument. If there be a principle universally allowed by men of all parties to be the basis of liberty, with the existence of which it is admitted on all hands that the essence of freedom is identified, it is, that the three great departments of power — the legislative, executive, and judicial — ought to be separate and distinct.   The consolidation of these three powers into one has been denominated " the definition of despotism ; " and in proportion as these powers approximate to consolidation, the spirit of despotism steals over us.   At the time of the adoption of this instrument, it was an objection raised against it by some of its most enlightened opposers, that its tendency was to such a consolidation, and on this account they strove to rouse the spirit of liberty ; but their anticipations had chiefly reference to the forms of the Constitution, and particularly to that qualified control which the executive has over the acts of the legislature.   They anticipated not at all, or at least very obscurely, that consolidation which has grown and is strengthening under the influence of the office-distributing power vested in the executive : a consolidation perceptible to all, and which is the more fixed and inseparable, inasmuch as the cement is constituted of the strongest of all amalgams, — that of the precious metals.   This state of things is not the less to be deprecated, on account of the fact that the forms of the Constitution are preserved while its spirit is perishing.   The members of both branches may meet, deliberate, and act, but the spirit of independence is gone whenever the action of the legislature is identified with the will of the executive by the potent influence of the office-hoping and the office-holding charm.

With respect to the nature of this influence, I remark that a misconception seems to be entertained concerning it.   The bare suggestion of its existence is almost thought to be indecorous, because of the gross and palpable corruption in which it is supposed to consist. It is thought to imply a sort of precontract between the executive and his selected favorites, — so many votes for so many offices, or such an office for such a term of Swiss service. Sir, nothing of this kind is pretended. Such sale of conscience and duty in open market is not reconcilable with the present state of civilized society. And they are mightily offended if there be any suggestion, ever so remote, of pollution, or any hint that they have been about any thing else, in their transactions with the executive, than pursuing the pure love of glory and their country. But the corruption of which I speak, and which is the object of both the amendment and proposition, is of a nature neither very gross nor very barefaced. Yet on these accounts it is not the less to be deprecated. On the contrary, from its very insidiousness and its appearing so often almost in the garb of a virtue ought it to be watched and restricted.

Such is its nature that it corrupts the very fountain of action. It springs up out of the human heart and the condition of things, so that it is almost impossible that it should not exist, or that it should be altogether resisted. It has its origin in that love of place which is so inherent in the human heart that it may be called almost an universal and instinctive passion. It cannot be otherwise; for so long as the love of honor and the love of profit are natural to man, so long the love of place, which includes either the one or the other or both, must be a very general and prevalent impulse. It cannot, therefore, but be true as a general principle, and it casts no reflection to admit that all members of Congress may love offices at least as well as their neighbors. Now, with the love of place there is another principle concurrent in relation to members of Congress, which is the result of our political condition, and is this : that those most desirous of places in the executive gift will not expect to be gratified except through their support of the executive. In referring to this principle as the result of our political condition, I mean to cast no particular reflection on our present chief magistrate. It grows out of the nature of political combinations. But, with some highly honorable exceptions, it has been true in all past, and will be true in all future administrations, that the general way for members of Congress to gain offices for themselves or their relations is to coincide in opinion, and vote with the executive. Out of the union of these two principles, the love of office and the general impression that coincidence with the executive is an essential condition for obtaining office, grows that corruption of the very fountain of action, the purification of which is the aim of both the amendment and my proposition under consideration. It exists without any precontract with the executive. He knows our wants, without any formal specification from us; and we know his terms, without any previous statement from him. The parties proceed together, mutually gratifying and gratified as occasions offer, and the harmonies of the happy part of the legislature and of the executive are complete ; and were it not that there is a third party concerned, called the people of the United States, nothing would seem more pleasant or unexceptionable than this partnership in official felicity. But so it is, in truth, that the interests and liberties of the people, which we are sent here to consult, will not only be sometimes neglected, but at others absolutely sacrificed, while the constituted guardians are gaping after offices for themselves, or hunting them up for their relations. The nature of the corruption is such as not only easily to be concealed from the world, but also in a great measure from the individual himself. And so long as that free access, which is at present permitted by the Constitution, is unrestrained, it will continue, and may increase. On every question which arises and has relation to executive measures, in addition to all the other considerations of honor, policy, justice, propriety, and the like, this also is prepared to be thrown into the scale, — that if a man means to gain office he must coincide with the executive. It is not possible for any man to decide what degree of influence this consideration has upon another, and it is nearly, if not quite, as difficult for him to decide what degree of influence it may have upon himself. For let any man reflect upon the springs of any particular course of action, which various, concurrent, complex motives have induced him to adopt, and he will find it very difficult to apportion to each of the concurring motives the precise degree of influence which belongs to it. And he will also find that, if there be in the group one motive base, and consequently bashful of the light, it will shrink away into the deepest recesses of the heart, and there cover itself over with such an accumulation of plausible, specious motives, that it is beyond the power of poor human nature, in the ordinary strength of its moral sense, always to discover it. From the liability of having the source of our public actions corrupted by the infusion of such

a taint, every honest mind will be solicitous to be delivered ; for, whether the office which allures our fancy be
for ourselves or for our relatives, the result is the same.
No man can stand up wholly independent of the hand
by which he hopes to be fed, or which is in the act of
feeding his children and relatives. Nor can any man,
however honest or scrupulous, placed in such situation, be positively certain as to his own motive, or know
whether in such cases his polarity with the executive
be the result of the intrinsic nature and reason of things,
or whether it be the effect of the influence of those
metallic strata which unite that executive with the
centre of his best affections.

With respect to the degree in which this corruption
has heretofore or may hereafter exist, it is impossible
precisely to estimate ; because the offices in the gift of
the executive and the departments are so numerous, are
extended over so wide a surface, — being for the whole
United States, — and the relations of members of Congress are so little known to each other and the world, that
it is not to be expected that we, much less that the people,
should be able to trace this influence in all its ramifications. But one thing is certain, that it exceeds popular
estimation as much as it evades legislative scrutiny.
Why, sir, there is annually distributed from the great
departments an amount not less than five and a half
millions of dollars, and from the post-office establishment not less than four and a half millions, making the
annual aggregate of ten millions of dollars. All this
abundant reservoir is distributable annually to its objects,
in streams of various magnitudes and in every direction,
at the executive will. Now, we stand at the very spot

when this luscious fountain overflows in all its exuber-
ance. Having the power, can we promise that we shall
refrain from turning aside to ourselves and our relatives
at least a full portion of these pecuniary bounties? Is
it in human nature generally to practise so much stoical
self-denial as a contrary conduct would imply? I have
said that it was impossible to prove the full extent of
the accommodation which we and our relatives may
obtain in one shape and another out of the treasury, so
long as such a latitude is given to our capacity to receive; yet, every now and then, some evidence occurs
tending to give a glimpse of the amount in which the
transfer of public money may be made to run in particular directions. At this moment there lies upon our
tables an account of the navy agent at Baltimore, who,
as it appears, under the directions of the then Secretary
of the Navy, did purchase, in about eighteen months, of
a single mercantile house in that city, bills of exchange to
the amount of two hundred and forty thousand dollars,
the head of which mercantile house was and is a senator
of the United States, and the brother of that Secretary
of the Navy. In referring to this subject, I beg to be
understood as giving no opinion on that transaction, or
as representing it as exceptionable in its nature. I
adduce it with no other design than to show the extent
to which relations may, if they please, accommodate one
another, so long as no constitutional restrictions exist,
and the impossibility of estimating the amount and of
pursuing the evil into all its ramifications.

Upon this subject of offices, my sentiments may, perhaps, be too refined for the present condition of human
nature. And I am aware, in what I am about to say,

that I may run athwart political friends as well as
political foes. Such considerations as these shall not,
however, deter me from introducing just and high notions of their duties to the consideration of the members of the legislature.   I hold, sir, the acceptance of
an office of mere emolument, or which is principally
emolument, by a member of Congress, from the executive, as unworthy his station, and incompatible with
that high sense of irreproachable character which it is
one of the choicest terrestrial boons of virtue to attain.
For while the attainment of office is to members of Congress the consequence, solely, of coincidence with the
executive, he who has the office carries on his forehead
the mark of having fulfilled the condition.   And, although his self-love may denominate his attainment of
the office to be the reward of merit, the world, which
usually judges acutely on these matters, will denominate it the reward of service.   And in such cases,
ninety-nine times in the hundred, the world will be
right.   An exception to this rule may, perhaps, exist in
the cases of offices of high responsibility, to which a
member of Congress may be called, on account of distinguished and peculiar qualifications; in which the voice
of the executive is, in truth, what it ought always to be,
the voice of his country.   Such cases are so rare that,
when they exist, they make a law for themselves.   They
are exceptions which prove, rather than invalidate, the
rule.   For us, it is honor enough to be thus intrusted
with the high concerns of this people; to be thus debating; thus maintaining their liberties, or striving to
improve their condition.   Let us put it out of our power,
and remove from us the temptation, to grub in the low
pursuits of avarice and base ambition.

Such is the opinion which, in my judgment, ought to be entertained of the mere acceptance of office by members of Congress. But as to that other class of persons, who are open, notorious solicitors of office, they give occasion to reflections of a very different nature. This class of persons, in all times past, have appeared, and (for I say nothing of times present), in all times future, will appear, on this and the other floor of Congress, — creatures who, under pretence of serving the people, are in fact serving themselves, — creatures who, while their distant constituents, good easy men, industrious, frugal, and unsuspicious, dream in visions that they are laboring for their country's welfare, are in truth spending their time mousing at the doors of the palace or the crannies of the departments, and laying low snares to catch, for themselves and their relations, every stray office that flits by them. For such men, chosen into this high and responsible trust, to whom have been confided the precious destinies of this people, and who thus openly abandon their duties, and set their places and their consciences to sale, in defiance of the multiplied strong and tender ties by which they are bound to their country, I have no language to express my contempt. I never have seen, and I never shall see, any of these notorious solicitors of office for themselves or their relations, standing on this or the other floor, bawling and bullying, or coming down with dead votes in support of executive measures, but I think I see a hackney, laboring for hire in a most degrading service, — a poor earth-spirited animal, trudging in his traces, with much attrition of the sides and induration of the membranes, encouraged by this special certainty, that, at the end of his journey, he shall have measured out to him his proportion of provender.

But I have heard that the bare suggestion of such corruption was a libel upon this House, and upon this people. I have heard that we were, in this country, so virtuous that we were above the influence of these allurements; that beyond the Atlantic, in old governments, such things might be suspected, but that here we were too pure for such guilt, too innocent for such suspicions. Mr. Chairman, I shall not hesitate, in spite of such popular declamation, to believe and follow the evidence of my senses and the concurrent testimonies of contemporaneous beholders. I shall not, in my estimation of character, degrade this people below, nor exalt them far above, the ordinary condition of cultivated humanity. And of this be assured, that every system of conduct, or course of policy, which has for its basis an excess of virtue in this country beyond what human nature exhibits in its improved state elsewhere, will be found, on trial, fallacious. Is there on this earth any collection of men in which exists a more intrinsic, hearty, and desperate love of office or place, particularly of fat places? Is there any country more infested than this with the vermin that breed in the corruptions of power? Is there any in which place and official emolument more certainly follow distinguished servility at elections, or base scurrility in the press? And as to eagerness for the reward, what is the fact? Let, now, one of your great office-holders, a collector of the customs, a marshal, a commissioner of loans, a postmaster in one of your cities, or any officer, agent, or factor for your territories or public lands, or person holding a place of

16

minor distinction, but of considerable profit, be called upon to pay the last great debt of nature. The poor man shall hardly be dead, he shall not be cold, long before the corpse is in the coffin, the mail shall be crowded, to repletion, with letters and certificates, and recommendations and representations, and every species of sturdy, sycophantic solicitation, by which obtrusive mendicity seeks charity or invites compassion. Why, sir, we hear the clamor of the craving animals, at the treasury trough, here in this capital. Such running, such jostling, such wriggling, such clambering over one another's backs, such squealing because the tub is so narrow and the company so crowded! No, sir, let us not talk of stoical apathy towards the things of the national treasury, either in this people or in their Representatives or Senators.

But it will be asked, for it has been asked, Shall the executive be suspected of corrupting the national legislature? Is he not virtuous? Without making personal distinctions or references, for the sake of argument it may be admitted that all executives for the time being are virtuous, — reasonably virtuous, Mr. Chairman, — flesh and blood notwithstanding. And without meaning, in this place, to cast any particular reflections upon this or upon any other executive, this I will say, that if no additional guards are provided, and now after the spirit of party has brought into so full activity the spirit of patronage, there never will be a President of these United States, elected by means now in use, who, if he deals honestly with himself, will not be able, on quitting, to address his presidential chair as John Falstaff addressed Prince Hal: "Before I knew thee, I knew

nothing, and now I am but little better than one of
the wicked." The possession of that station, under the
reign of party, will make a man so acquainted with the
corrupt principles of human conduct, he will behold our
nature in so hungry and shivering and craving a state,
and be compelled so constantly to observe the solid
rewards daily demanded by way of compensation for
outrageous patriotism, that, if he escape out of that
atmosphere without partaking of its corruption, he
must be below or above the ordinary condition of mortal nature. Is it possible, sir, that he should remain
altogether uninfected? What is the fact? The Constitution prohibits the members of this and of the other
branch of the legislature from being electors of the
President of the United States. Yet what is done?
The practice of late. is so prevalent as to have grown
almost into a sanctioned usage party. Prior to the presidential term of four years, members of Congress, having
received the privileged ticket of admission, assemble
themselves, in a sort of electoral college, on the floor of
the Senate or of the House of Representatives. They
select a candidate for the presidency. To their voice,
to their influence, he is indebted for his elevation. So
long as this condition of things continues, what ordinary
executive will refuse to accommodate those who, in so
distinguished a manner, have accommodated him? Is
there a better reason, in the world, why a man should
give you, Mr. Chairman, an office worth two or three
thousand dollars a year, for which you are qualified,
and which he could give as well as not, than this, that
you had been greatly instrumental in giving him one,
worth five and twenty thousand, for which he was

equally qualified? It is in vain to conceal it. So long as the present condition of things continues, it may reasonably be expected that there shall take place regularly, between the President of the United States and a portion of both Houses of Congress, an interchange, strictly speaking, of good offices.

The principle for which I contend, and which is the basis both of the original amendment and of my proposition, is this: Put it out of the power of the executive to seem to pay any of the members of Congress, by putting it out of their power to receive. " Avoid the appearance of evil." We have been taught to pray, " Lead us not into temptation." They who rightly estimate their duties may find in public life no less necessity than in private life frequently to repeat this aspiration.

SPEECH

ON THE PROPOSITION TO REVIVE AND ENFORCE
THE NON-INTERCOURSE LAW AGAINST GREAT
BRITAIN.

FEB. 25, 1811.

SPEECH

ON THE PROPOSITION TO REVIVE AND ENFORCE THE
NON-INTERCOURSE LAW AGAINST GREAT BRITAIN.

FEB. 25, 1811.

[THE non-intercourse with England and France which had
been enacted at the time of the repeal of the embargo, expired
by its own limitation in May, 1810. It was then enacted that
in case either of the belligerent powers should revoke their acts
hostile to American neutrality, the fact should be announced by
proclamation, and, unless the other belligerent should do the
same within three months, the non-intercourse should revive as
to the contumacious nation. Bonaparte, professing to be satisfied with the act of May, informed General Armstrong, the
American minister, that he had revoked the Berlin and Milan
decrees, and that the revocation would take effect on the 1st of
November, provided England did the same by her Orders in
Council. Mr. Madison, in his eagerness to escape from the
political perplexities in which he was involved, issued his proclamation on the 2d of November, declaring the non-intercourse
at an end, without waiting to see whether England would or
would not revoke her Orders in Council, which was the condition precedent of Bonaparte's revocation of his decrees. It so
happened that England would do nothing of the kind, so that
Mr. Madison had the mortification of informing the nation of
this fact by proclamation of the date of Feb. 2, 1811. As
there was some doubt as to whether non-intercourse with England could be legally revived under the law of May, inasmuch
as the proclamation of November had been issued without wait-

ing for the action of England in the premises, it was thought
best to re-enact non-intercourse as to her. It was on this bill that
Mr. Quincy made the following speech. Bonaparte, it may
be well to say, had not merely seized and confiscated all the
American ships and cargoes he could lay his hands on during the non-intercourse of 1809, but continued to do so even
after the President's proclamation of November had arrived in
France; while he utterly refused to make compensation for any
of his seizures. This, he vouchsafed to explain, was merely done
to insure our enforcement of the non-intercourse with England.
— ED.]

MR. SPEAKER, — The amendments contained in the
sections under consideration contemplate the continuance and enforcement of the non-intercourse law.
This proposition presents a great, an elevated, and
essential topic of discussion, due to the occasion and
claimed by this people, which comprehend within the
sphere and analogies of just argument the chief of those
questions, the decision of which at this day involves the
peace, the happiness, and honor of this nation. Whatever has a tendency to show that, if the system of non-
intercourse exist, it ought not to be continued, or that, if
it do not exist, it ought not to be revived; whatever has
a tendency to prove that we are under no obligation to
persist in it, or under an obligation to abandon it, — is
now within the fair range of debate.

After long delay and much coy demeanor, the administration of this country have condescended to develop
their policy. Though they have not spoken to our
mortal ears with their fleshly tongues, yet they have
whispered their purposes through the constituted organs
of this House; and these are the features of the policy

which they recommend : It is proposed to grant particular and individual relief from anticipated oppressions
of the commercial restrictive system ; it is proposed to
perpetuate that system indefinitely, and leave our citizens still longer subject to its embarrassments, its uncertainty, and its terrors. The chairman of our Committee
of Foreign Relations [Mr. Eppes], at the time he introduced these amendments to the House, exhibited the
true character of this policy, when he told us that it was
" modelled upon the principle not to turn over to the
judiciary the decision of the existence of the non-intercourse law, but to make it the subject of legislative
declaration." In other words, it is found that the
majority of this House have too much policy to deny,
and too much principle to assert, that the fact on which,
and on which alone, the President of the United States
was authorized to issue his proclamation of the 2d of
November last has occurred. A scheme has, therefore,
been devised by which, without any embarrassment on
this intricate point, the continuance and enforcement of
non-intercourse may be insured, and toils, acceptable
to France, woven by the hands of our own administration, spread over almost the only remaining avenue of
our commercial hope.

The proposition contained in these amendments has
relation to the most momentous and most elevated of
our legislative obligations. We are not now about to
discuss the policy by which a princely pirate may be
persuaded to relinquish his plunder ; nor yet the expectation entertained of relaxation in her belligerent system
of a haughty and perhaps jealous rival ; nor yet the faith
which we owe to a treacherous tyrant ; nor yet the fond

but frail hopes of favors from a British regency, melting into our arms in the honeymoon of power. The obligations which claim our observance are of a nature much more tender and imperious, — the obligations which, as representatives, we owe to our constituents; the allegiance by which we are bound to the American people; the obedience which is due to that solemn faith by which we are pledged to protect their peace, their prosperity, and their honor. All these high considerations are materially connected with this policy.

It is not my intention, Mr. Speaker, to dilate on the general nature and effects of this commercial restrictive system. It is no longer a matter of speculation. We have no need to resort for illustration of its nature to the twilight lustre of history, nor yet to the vibrating brightness of the human intellect. We have experience of its effects. They are above, around, and beneath us. They paralyze the enterprise of your cities; they sicken the industry of your fields; they deprive the laborer and the mechanic of his employment; they subtract from the husbandman and planter the just reward for that product which he has moistened with the sweat of his brow; they crush individuals in the ruins of their most flattering hopes, and shake the deep-rooted fabric of general prosperity.

It will, however, be necessary to say a word on the general nature of this system, not so much for the purpose of elucidating, as to clear the way, and give distinctness to the course of my argument. It will also be useful to deprive the advocates of this system of those colors and popular lures to which they resort on a subject in no way connected with the objects with which they associate it.

My argument proceeds upon the assumption of the irrelevancy of four topics usually adduced in support of the system contained in the law of May, 1810, and of March, 1809, commonly called the Non-intercourse System. I take for granted that it is not advantageous; in other words, that it is injurious; that it is not fiscal in its nature, nor protective of manufactures, nor competent to coerce either belligerent. That it is injurious is certain, not only because it is deprecated by that part of the community which it directly affects, but because no man advocates it as a permanent system, and every one declares his desire to be rid of it. Fiscal it cannot be, because it prohibits commerce and consequently revenue, and, by the high price and great demand for foreign articles which it produces, encourages smuggling. Protective of manufactures it cannot be, because it is indiscriminate in its provisions and uncertain in its duration; and this uncertainty depends, not on our legislative discretion, but on the caprice of foreign powers, — our enemies or rivals. No commercial system which is indiscriminate in its restrictions can be generally protective to manufactures. It may give a forced vivacity to a few particular manufactures; but in all countries some, and in this almost all, manufactures depend either for instruments or materials on foreign supply. But, if this were not the case, a system whose continuance depended upon the will or the ever-varying policy of foreign nations can never offer such an inducement to the capitalist as will encourage him to make extensive investments in establishments resting on such precarious foundations. As to the incompetency of this system to coerce either belligerent, I take that for granted, because

no man, as far as I recollect, ever pretended it ; at least,
no man ever did show, by any analysis or detailed
examination of its relative effects on us and either belligerent, that it would necessarily coerce either out of that
policy which it was proposed to counteract. Embargo
had its friends. There were those who had a confidence
in its success; but who was ever the friend of non-
intercourse ? Who ever pretended to believe in its
efficacy ? The embargo had a known origin, and the
features of its character were distinct. But " where
and what was this execrable shape, if shape it may be
called, which shape has none ? " We all know that the
non-intercourse was not the product of any prospective
intelligence. It was the result of the casual concurrence
of chaotic opinions. It was agreed upon because the
majority could agree upon nothing else. They who
introduced it abjured it ; they who advocated it did not
wish, and scarcely knew, its use. And now that it is
said to be extended over us, no man in this nation, who
values his reputation, will take his Bible oath that it is
in effectual and legal operation. There is an old riddle
on a coffin, which, I presume, we all learnt when we
were boys, that is as perfect a representation of the
origin, progress, and present state of this thing, called
non-intercourse, as is possible to be conceived.

> " There was a man bespoke a thing,
> Which when the maker home did bring,
> That same maker did refuse it ;
> The man that spoke for it did not use it,
> And he who had it did not know
> Whether he had it, — yea or no."

True it is that if this non-intercourse shall ever be, in
reality, extended over us, the similitude will fail in a

material point. The poor tenant of the coffin is ignorant of his state; but the poor people of the United
States will be literally buried alive in non-intercourse,
and realize the grave closing on themselves and their
hopes with a full and cruel consciousness of all the
horrors of their condition.

For these reasons I put all such commonplace topics
out of the field of debate. This, then, is the state of
my argument, that as this non-intercourse system is not
fiscal, nor protective of manufactures, nor competent to
coerce, and is injurious, it ought to be abandoned, unless
we are bound to persist in it by imperious obligations.
My object will be to show that no such obligations
exist; that the present is a favorable opportunity, not to
be suffered to escape, totally to relinquish it; that it is
time to manage our own commercial concerns according
to our own interests, and no longer put them into the
keeping of those who hate or those who envy their
prosperity; that we are the constituted shepherds, and
ought no more to transfer our custody to the wolves.

It is agreed on all sides that it is desirable to abandon
this commercial restrictive system; but the advocates of
the measures now proposed say that we cannot abandon
it, because our faith is plighted. Yes, sir, our faith is
plighted, and that, too, to that scrupulous gentleman,
Napoleon, a gentleman so distinguished for his own
regard of faith, for his kindness and mercies towards us,
for angelic whiteness of moral character, for overweening affection for the American people and their prosperity. Truly, sir, it is not to be questioned but that
our faith should be a perfect work towards this paragon
of purity. On account of our faith plighted to him, it
is proposed to continue this non-intercourse.

But, Mr. Speaker, we may be allowed, I presume, to inquire whether any such faith be plighted. I trust we are yet freemen. We are not yet so far sunk in servility that we are forbidden to examine into the grounds of our national obligations. Under a belief that this is permitted, I shall enter upon the task, and inquire whence they arise, and what is their nature.

Whence they arise is agreed. Our obligations result, if any exist, under the act of May 1, 1810, called "An Act concerning the commercial intercourse between the United States and Great Britain and France and their dependencies, and for other purposes." It remains, therefore, to inquire into the character of this act, and the obligations arising under its provisions.

Before, however, I proceed, I would premise that while I am doubtful whether I shall obtain, I am sure that the nature of my argument deserves, the favor and prepossession for its success of every member in the House. My object is to show that the obligation which we owe to the people of the United States is a free and unrestricted commerce. The object of those who advocate these measures is to show that the obligation we owe to Napoleon Bonaparte is a commerce restricted and enslaved. Now, as much as our allegiance is due more to the people of the United States than it is to Napoleon Bonaparte, just so much ought my argument to be received by an American Congress with more favor and prepossession than the argument of those who advocate these measures. It is my intention to make my course of reasoning as precise and distinct as possible, because I invite scrutiny. I contend for my country according to my conscientious conceptions of its best interests. If there be fallacy, detect it. My invitation is given to generous disputants. As to your stump orators, who utter low invective, and mistake it for wit, and gross personality, and pass it off for argument, I descend not to their level, nor recognize their power to injure, nor even to offend.

Whatever obligations are incumbent upon this nation in consequence of the act of the 1st of May, 1810, they result from the following section : " *And be it further enacted*, That in case either Great Britain or France shall, before the third day of March next, so revoke or modify her edicts as that they shall cease to violate the neutral commerce of the United States, which fact the President of the United States shall declare by proclamation, and if the other nation shall not within three months thereafter so revoke or modify her edicts in like manner, then the third, fourth, fifth, sixth, seventh, eighth, ninth, tenth, and eighteenth sections of the act entitled ' An Act to interdict the commercial intercourse between the United States and Great Britain and France and their dependencies, and for other purposes,' shall, from and after the expiration of three months from the date of the proclamation aforesaid, be revived and have full force and effect, so far as relates to the dominions, colonies, and dependencies of the nation thus refusing or neglecting to revoke or modify her edicts in manner aforesaid. And the restrictions imposed by this act shall, from the date of such proclamation, cease and be discontinued in relation to the nation revoking or modifying her decrees in the manner aforesaid."

Divested of technical expression, this is the abstract form of this section : It provides that a new commercial condition shall result on the occurrence of a specified fact, which fact the President shall declare. On this state of the subject, I observe that nothing in the act indicates whether the object of the United States in providing for this eventual commercial condition was its own benefit, convenience, or pleasure, or whether it was in the nature of a proffer to foreign nations. It will, however, be agreed on all sides that the object was either the one or the other. If the object were our own benefit, convenience, or pleasure, it will not be . pretended that we are under any obligation to continue the system ; for that which was adopted solely for either of these ends may, whenever our views concerning them vary, be abandoned, it being the concern of no other. But it is said that the act was, in truth, a proffer to the two belligerents of commerce to the obsequious nation, prohibition of commerce to the contumacious nation. If this were the case, I shall agree, for the sake of argument, that it ought to be fulfilled to the full extent of the terms. But, inasmuch as there is in the terms of the act no indication of such a proffer, it follows that its nature must arise from the circumstances of the case, and that the whole of the obligation, whatever it is, grows out of an honorable understanding, and nothing else. As such, I admit, it should be honorably fulfilled. The nature of this proffer is that of a *proposition upon terms*. Now, what I say is, and it is the foundation of my argument, that whoever claims an honorable compliance with such a proposition must be able to show on his part an honorable acceptance and fulfilment of the terms. The terms our act proposed were an act to be done, an effect to be produced. The act to be done

was the revocation or modification of the edicts. The
effect to be produced was, that this revocation or modification should be such as that these edicts should " cease
to violate our neutral commerce." Now the questions
which result are, Has the act been done ? If done, has
it been so done as to amount to an honorable fulfilment
or acceptance of our terms ? The examination of these
two points will explain the real situation of these United
States, and the actual state of their obligations.

In considering the question whether the fact of revocation or modification has occurred, it is unfortunate
that it does involve, at least in popular estimation, the
propriety of the proclamation, issued on the 2d of November last by the President of the United States. I
regret as much as any one that such is the state of
things that the question whether a foreign despot has
done a particular act seems necessarily to be connected
with the question concerning the prudence or perspicac-
ity with which our own Chief Magistrate has done another act. I say in popular estimation these subjects
seem so connected. I do not think that, in the estimation of wise and reflecting men, they are necessarily
thus connected ; for the fact might not have occurred
precisely in the form contemplated by the act of May,
1810 ; and yet the President of the United States, in
issuing his proclamation, might be either justifiable or
excusable. It might be justifiable. A power intrusted
to a politician, to be used on the occurrence of a particular event, for the purpose of obtaining a particular
end, he may sometimes be justifiable in using in a case
which may not be precisely that originally contemplated.
It may be effectually, though not formally, the same.

17

It may be equally efficient in attaining the end. In such case a politician never will, and perhaps ought not to, hesitate at taking the responsibility which arises from doing the act in a case not coming within the verbal scope of his authority. Thus, in the present instance, the President of the United States might have deemed the terms, in the letter of the Duke of Cadore, such as gave a reasonable expectation of acceptance on the part of Great Britain. He has taken the responsibility ; he has been deceived. Neither Great Britain accepts the terms, nor France performs her engagements. The proclamation might thus have been wise, though unfortunate in its result ; and as to excuse will it be said that there is nothing of the sort in this case ? Why, sir, our administration saw France by Napoleon's confession, over head and ears in love with the American people. At such a sight as this was it to be expected of flesh and blood that they should hesitate to plunge into a sea of bliss, and indulge in joy with such an amorous cyprian ?

But whether the fact has occurred on which alone this proclamation could have legally issued is a material inquiry, and cannot be evaded, let it reach where or whom it will ; for with this is connected the essential condition of this country ; on this depends the multiplied rights of our fellow-citizens, whose property has been, or may be, seized or confiscated under this law ; and hence result our obligations, if any, as is pretended, exist. It is important here to observe that, according to the terms of the act of May 1, 1810, the law of March 1, 1809, revives on the occurrence of the fact required, and not on the proclamation issued. If the fact had not occurred, the proclamation is a dead letter, and no subsequent performance of the required fact by either belligerent can retroact so as to give validity to the previous proclamation. The course required by the act of the 1st of May, 1810, unquestionably is, that the fact required to be done should be precedent, in point of time, to the right accruing to issue the proclamation; and of consequence that by no construction can any subsequent performance of the fact required operate backward to support a proclamation issued previous to the occurrence of that fact. Whenever this fact is really done, a new proclamation is required to comply with the provisions of the act, and to give efficacy to them. I am the more particular, in referring to this necessary construction resulting from the terms of the act of the 1st of May last, because it is very obvious that a different opinion did, until very lately, and probably does now, prevail on this floor. We all recollect what a state of depression the conduct of Bonaparte, in seizing our vessels subsequent to the 1st of November, produced as soon as it was known in this House, and what a sudden joy was lighted up in it when the news of the arrival of a French minister was communicated. Great hopes were entertained and expressed that he would bring some formal revocation of his edicts or disavowal of the seizures, which might retroact and support the proclamation. It was confidently expected that some explanation, at least, of these outrages would be contained in his portmanteau; that, under his powder-puff or in his snuff-box, some dust would be found to throw into the eyes of the American people, which might so far blind the sense as to induce them to acquiesce in the

enforcement of the non-intercourse, without any very
scrupulous scrutiny into the performance of the conditions by Bonaparte. But, alas, sir! the minister is as
parsimonious as his master is voracious. He has not
condescended to extend one particle, not one pinch, of
comfort to the administration. From any thing in the
messages of our President, it would not be so much as
known that such a blessed vision as was this new envoy
had saluted his eyes. His communications preserve an
ominous silence on the topic. Administration, after all
their hopes, have been compelled to resort to the old
specific, and have caused to be tipped up on our tables a
cart-load of sand, grit, and sawdust, from our meta-
physical mechanic, who see-saws at St. James as they
pull the wire here in Washington. Yes, sir: a letter,
written on the tenth day of December last by our minister in London, is seriously introduced, to prove by abstract reasoning that the Berlin and Milan decrees had
ceased to exist on the first of the preceding November,
of whose existence, as late as the 25th of last December,
we have, as far as the nature of things permit, ocular,
auricular, and tangible demonstration. And the people
of this country are invited to believe the logic of Mr.
Pinkney, in the face of the fact of a continued seizure
of all the vessels which came within the grasp of the
French custom-house, from the 1st of November down
to the date of our last accounts; and in defiance of the
declaration of our *chargé-d'affaires*, made on the 10th
of December, that "it will not be pretended that the
decrees have, in fact, been revoked;" and in utter dis-
credit of the allegation of the Duke of Massa, made
on the 25th of the same month, which in effect declares

the Berlin and Milan decrees exist, by declaring " that they shall remain suspended." After such evidence as this the question whether a revocation or modification of the edicts of France has so occurred " as that they cease to violate the neutral commerce of the United States " does no longer depend upon the subtleties of syllogistic skill, nor is to be disproved by any power of logical illation. It is an affair of sense and feeling. And our citizens — whose property has been since the 1st of November uniformly seized, and of which they are avowedly to be deprived three months, and which is then only to be returned to them on the condition of good behavior — may as soon be made to believe by the teaching philosophy that their rights are not violated, as a wretch writhing under the lash of the executioner might be made by a course of reasoning to believe that the natural state of his flesh was not violated, and that his shoulders, out of which blood was flowing at every stroke, were in the quiet enjoyment of cuticular ease.

Whether the revocation expressed in the letter of the Duke of Cadore was absolute or conditional, or whether the conditions were precedent or subsequent, in the present state of our evidence it seems scarcely important to inquire. Yet the construction of that celebrated passage in his letter of the 5th of August has been, as far as I have ever seen, given so much in the manner of lawyers and so little in that of statesmen, that it deserves a short elucidation. All the illustration of that letter in the documents is drawn from the form and the force of its technical expressions, — how much the words, " it being understood that," in their particular position, are worth ; and whether they have the effect of a condition precedent or of a condition subsequent. A statesman will look at the terms contained in that letter in a different aspect, — not for the purpose of ascertaining how much a court of law might be able to make of them, but to discern in what position of language the writer intended to intrench himself, and to penetrate his real policy, notwithstanding the veil in which he chose to envelop it. He will consider the letter in connection with the general course of French policy, and the particular circumstances which produced it. By these lights, it is scarcely possible to mistake the character and true construction of these expressions. Upon recurring to the Berlin and Milan decrees, it will be found that they contain a solemn pledge that " they shall continue to be vigorously in force, as long as that (the English) government does not return to the principle of the law of nations." Their determination to support this pledge the French government has uniformly and undeviatingly declared. They have told us constantly that they required a previous revocation on the part of Great Britain as the condition of their rescinding those edicts. The question, who should first revoke their edicts, had come to be, notoriously, a sort of point of honor between the two belligerents. Perfectly acquainted with this state of things, we have been perpetually negotiating between the one and the other, and contending with each that it was his duty previously to revoke. At length, the French government — either tired with our solicitations, or, more probably, seeing their own advantage in our anxiety to get rid of these decrees, which yet, as an essential part of its continental system of total commercial exclusion, it never intended to abandon — devised this scheme of policy, which has been the source of so much contest, and has puzzled all the metaphysicians in England and the United States. Cadore is directed to say to Mr. Armstrong, " In this new state of things, I am authorized to declare to you sir, that the decrees of Berlin and Milan are revoked, and that, after the 1st of November, they will cease to have effect ; it being understood that, in consequence of this declaration, the English shall revoke their Orders in Council, and renounce the new principles of blockade which they have wished to establish ; or that the United States, conformably to the act you have just communicated, shall cause their rights to be respected by the English." In this curious gallimaufry of time present and time future, of doing and refraining to do, of declaration and understanding, of English duties and American duties, it is easy to trace the design and see its adaptation to the past and present policy of the French Emperor. The time present was used, because the act of the United States required that previously to proclamation the edicts " shall be " revoked. And this is the mighty mystery of time present being used in expressing an act intended to be done in time future. For if, as the order of time and the state of intention indicated, time future had been used, and the letter of Cadore had said the decrees shall be revoked on the 1st of November next, then the proclamation could not be issued, because the President would be obliged to wait to have evidence that the act had been effectually done. Now, as the French Emperor never intended that it should be effectuated, and yet meant to have all the advantage of an effectual deed without performing it, this notable scheme was invented. And, by French *finesse* and American acquiescence, a thing is considered as effectually done if the declaration that it is done be made in language of time present, notwithstanding the time of performance is in the same breath declared to be in time future. Having thus secured the concurrence of the American administration, the next part of the scheme was so to arrange the expression that either the British government should not accede, or, if it did accede, that it should secure to France the point of honor, — a previous revocation by the British; and, if they did not accede, that there should be a color for seizures and sequestrations, and thus still farther to bind the Americans over to their good behavior. All this is attained by this well-devised expression, " It being understood that, in consequence of this declaration, the English shall revoke." Now Great Britain either would accede to the terms, or she would not. If she did, and did it, as the terms required. in consequence of this declaration, then it must be done previous to the 1st of November, and then the point of honor was saved to France; so that thus France by a revocation verbally present, effectually future, would attain an effectual, previous revocation from the English. But if, as France expected, Great Britain would not trust in such paper security, and therefore not revoke previously to the 1st of November, then an apology might be found for France to justify her in refusing to effectuate that present, future, absolute, conditional revocation. And if ever the Duke of Cadore shall condescend, which, it is probable he never will, to reason with our government on the subject, he may tell them that they knew that the French Emperor had issued those decrees, upon the pledge that they were to continue until the British abandoned their maritime principles; that he told us, over and over and over again, that previous revocation by the British was absolutely required; that for the purpose of putting to trial the sincerity of the British, he had indeed declared that the French decrees "are revoked" on the first day of November ensuing, but then it was on the expressed condition that in consequence of that declaration, — not of the revocation, but of that declaration, — the British were to revoke, and, if they did not, the "understanding" was not realized, and his rights of enforcing his system remained to him. And I confess I do not well see what answer can be made to such an argument. Let us examine the case in common life. You, Mr. Speaker, have two separate tracts of land, each lying behind the farms of A and B, so that you cannot get to one of the tracts without going over the farm of A, nor to the other tract without going over the farm of B. For some cause or other, both A and B have a mutual interest that you should enjoy the right of passage to your tract over the farm of each respectively. A and B get into quarrels and wish to involve you in the dispute. You keep aloof, but are perpetually negotiating with each for your old right of passage-way, and telling each that it is owing to him that the other prohibits your enjoyment of it. At last A says, "Come. We will put this B to trial. I, on this fifth day of August, declare my prohibitions of passage-way are revoked, and after the first day of November my prohibitions shall cease to have effect; but it is understood that B,

in consequence of this declaration, shall also revoke his
prohibition of passage-way." If B refuses, does A,
under the circumstances of such a declaration, violate
any obligation should he refuse to permit the passage ?
Might not A urge, with great color and force of argument, that this arrangement was the effect of your
solicitation and assurance that B would be tempted
by such a proffer, and that the revocation of B was required, by the terms, to be the consequence of A's declaration, for the very purpose of indicating that it must
be anterior to the fact of A's effectual revocation. But,
let this be as it will, suppose that you, on the 1st of
November, in consequence of A's assurances, had sent
your servants and teams to bring home your products,
and A should seize your oxen and teams and products,
and drive your servants, after having stripped them,
from his farm, and should tell you that he should keep
this, and all other property of yours on which he can
lay his hands, for three months, and then he should
restore it to you or not as he saw fit, according to his
opinion of your good behavior, — I ask if, in any sense,
you could truly say that on the first day of November
the prohibitions or edicts of A were so revoked that
they ceased to violate your liberty of passage. Sir,
when viewed in relation to common life, the idea is
so absurd that it would be absolutely insulting to ask
the question. I refer the decision of so simple a case
to the sound sense of the American people, and not to
that of 'scurvy politicians, who seem to see the things
they do not.' In a condensed form my argument is this.
From a revocation merely verbal, no obligations result.
By the terms of our act the revocation must be effectual,

" so as the edict shall cease to violate our rights." Now
the simple question is, whether an uniform seizure, since
the 1st of November, under those edicts (for none other
are pretended) of all their property, and holding it for
three months to see how they will behave, be or- be
not a violation of the rights of the American people.
In relation to the revival by a formal declaration of the
non-intercourse system, as is proposed in one of these
sections, I offer this argument. Either the fact on
which the President's proclamation could alone have
been issued has occurred, or it has not. If it have
occurred, then the law of March, 1809, is revived, and
this provision for its revival by a declarative law is
unnecessary. If it have not occurred, then there is no
obligation to revive it, for alone on the occurrence of
the specified fact does our obligation depend. In such
case the revival by declaration is a mere gratuity to
Napoleon. This is, in fact, the true character of the
law. As to the provisions for relief of our merchants
against anticipated seizure, I hold them scarcely deserv-
ing consideration. Heaven be praised! we have independent tribunals and intelligent juries. Our judges
are not corrupt, and our yeomanry will not be swayed,
in their decisions, by the hope of presidential favors,
nor be guided by party influence. The harpies of your
custom-house dare as soon eat off their own claws, as
thrust them in the present state of the law of March,
1809, into the fatness of their fellow-citizens. The
timorous and light-shunning herd of spies and informers
have too much instinct to pounce on such a prey.

But, in order to cause any obligation to result under
the law of May 1, 1810, it is necessary, not only that

the fact required be done, and the effect required produced, but also the terms of that act must be accepted.
The proffer we made, if such be the character of that
act, was only to revive the non-intercourse law against
the contumacious belligerent, after three months had
expired from the date of the proclamation.   Now it is
remarkable that, so far from accepting the terms of the
proposition contained in our act as the extent of our
obligations, Bonaparte expressly tells us that he understands that they mean something else ; and something,
too, that no man in this House will dare to aver they
really intend.   It is also remarkable that the terms of
this celebrated letter from the Duke of Cadore, of the
5th of August, which have been represented as a relaxation in the rigor of the French Emperor's policy, are in
fact something worse than the original terms of the
Milan decree, and that, instead of having obtained a
boon from a friend in this boasted letter, our administration have only caught a gripe from a Tartar.   By the
terms of the Milan decree, it was to " cease with respect
to all nations who compelled the English to respect their
flag."   By the terms of the letter of Cadore, it was to
cease on condition that the United States " cause their
rights to be respected."   Now, as much as an obligation
of an indefinite extent is worse than a definite obligation, just so much worse are the terms of the letter of
Cadore than the original terms of the Milan decree.
Mr. Speaker, let us not be deceived concerning the policy
of the French Emperor.   It is stern, unrelenting, and
unrelaxing.   So far from any deviation from his original
system being indicated in this letter of the Duke of Cadore,
a strict adherence to it is formally and carefully expressed.

Ever since the commencement of "his continental system," as it is called, the policy of Napoleon has uniformly been to oblige the United States to effectual co-operation in that system. As early as the 7th of October, 1807, his minister, Champagny, wrote to General Armstrong that the interests of all maritime powers were common to unite in support of their rights against England. After this followed the embargo which co-operated effectually, at the very critical moment, in his great plan of continental commercial restriction. On the 24th of the ensuing November, he resorts to the same language, " In violating the rights of all nations, England has united them all by a common interest. and it is for them to have recourse to force against her." He then proceeds to invite the United States to take with the whole continent the part of guaranteeing itself from her injustice," and "in forcing her to a peace." On the 15th of January, 1808, he is somewhat more pointed and positive as to our efficient concurrence in his plan of policy. For his minister, Champagny, then tells us that " his Majesty has no doubt of a declaration of war against England by the United States," and he then proceeds to take the trouble of declaring war out of our hands, and volunteers his services gratuitously to declare it in our name and behalf. " War exists, then, in fact between England and the United States ; and his Majesty considers it as declared from the day on which England published her decrees." And, in order to make assurance doubly sure, he sequesters our vessels in his ports " until a decision may be had on the dispositions to be expressed by the United States " on his proposition of considering themselves " associated in the

cause of all the powers" against England. Now in all
this there is no deception, and can be no mistake, as to
the purpose of his policy. He tells us, as plain as language can speak, that " by causing our rights to be respected," he means war, on his side, against Great
Britain ; that " our interests are common ; " that he considers us already " associates in the war ; " and that he
sequesters our property by way of security for our dispositions. This is his old policy. I pray some gentleman on the other side of the House to point out in what
it differs from the new. The letter of Cadore on the
5th of August tells us it is expected that we " cause
our rights to be respected in conformity to our act,"
and the same letter also tells us what he understands to
be the meaning of our act, — " In short Congress en-
gages to oppose itself to that one of the belligerent
powers which shall refuse to acknowledge the rights of
neutrals." In other words, " by causing our rights to
be respected " he means war on his side against Great
Britain. In perfect conformity with this uniform, unde-
viating policy, his minister, Turreau, tells our government, in his letter of the 28th of November last, that
" the modifications to be given to the present absolute
exclusion of our products will not depend upon the
chance of events, but will be the result of measures,
firm and pursued with perseverance, which the two
governments will continue to adopt, to withdraw, from
the monopoly and from the vexations of the common
enemy, a commerce loyal and necessary to France, as
well as the United States." And to the end that no
one feature of his policy should be changed, or even
appear to be relaxed, his Excellency the Duke of Massa,

and his Excellency the Duke of Gaëtta, in their respective letters of the 25th of December, declare that the property taken shall be "only sequestered until the United States have fulfilled their engagements to cause their rights to be respected." Now, Mr. Speaker, is there a man in this House bold enough to maintain, or with capacity enough to point out, any material variation between the policy of France to this country subsequent to the Cadore letter of the 5th of August, and its policy anterior to that period. The character of the policy is one and indivisible. Bonaparte has not yielded one inch to our administration. Now, as he has neither performed the act required by the law of May, 1810; nor produced the effect; nor accepted the terms it proposed, — whence arise our obligations? How is our faith plighted? In what way are we bound again to launch our country into this dark sea of restrictions, surrounded on all sides with perils and penalties?

The true nature of this Cadore policy is alone to be discovered in the character of his master. Napoleon is an universal genius. "He can exchange shapes with Proteus to advantage." He hesitates at no means, and commands every skill. He toys with the weak; he tampers with the mean; he browbeats the haughty; with the cunning, he is a serpent; for the courageous, he has teeth and talons; for the cowering, he has hoofs. He found our administration a pen-and-ink gentry, — parchment politicians; and he has laid, for these ephemeral essences, a paper fly-trap dipped in French honey. Hercules, finding that he could not reach our administration with his club, and that they were out of their wits at the sight of his lion's skin, has condescended to meet them in petticoats, and conquer them, spinning at their own distaff.

As to those who, after the evidence now in our hands, deny that the decrees exist, I can no more reason with them than with those who should deny the sun to be in the firmament at noon-day. The decrees revoked! The formal statute act of a despot revoked by the breath of his servile minister, uttered on conditions not performed by Great Britain; and claiming terms, not intended to be performed by us! The fatness of our commerce secure, when every wind of heaven is burdened with the sighs of our suffering seamen, and the coast of the whole continent heaped with the plunder of our merchants! The den of the tiger safe, yet the tracks of those who enter it are innumerable, and not a trace is to be seen of a returning footstep! The den of the tiger safe, while the cry of the mangled victims are heard through the adamantine walls of his cave, — cries which despair and anguish utter, and which despotism itself cannot stifle!

No, Mr. Speaker, let us speak the truth. The act now proposed is required by no obligation. It is wholly gratuitous. Call it, then, by its proper name, — the first fruit of French allegiance; a token of transatlantic submission: any thing except an act of an American Congress, the representatives of freemen.

The present is the most favorable moment for the abandonment of these restrictions, unless a settled co-operation with the French continental system be determined. We have tendered the provisions of this act to both belligerents. Both have accepted. Both, as principals or by their agents, have deceived us.

We talk of the edicts of George the Third and of Napoleon. Yet those of the President of the United States, under your law, are far more detestable to your merchants. Their edicts plunder the rich: his make those who are poor still poorer. Their decrees attack the extremities: his proclamation fixes upon the vitals, and checks the action of the seat of commercial life.

I know that great hopes are entertained of relief from the proposed law by the prospect of a British regency. Between a mad monarch and a simpering successor, it is expected that the whole system of that nation will be abandoned. Let gentlemen beware, and not calculate too certainly on the fulfilment by men in power of professions made out of it. The majority need not go out of our own country, nor beyond their own practice, to be convinced how easily in such cases proud promises may eventuate in meagre performance.

The whole bearing of my argument is to this point. It is time to take our own rights into our own keeping. It is time, if we will not protect, to refrain from hampering by our own acts, the commerce of our country. Put your merchants no longer under the guardianship and caprice of foreign powers. Punish not, at the instigation of foreigners, your own citizens for following their righteous callings. We owe nothing to France. We owe nothing to Great Britain. We owe every thing to the American people. Let us show ourselves really independent; and look to a grateful, a powerful, and then united, people for support against every aggressor.

18

SPEECH

ON THE PAY OF NON-COMMISSIONED OFFICERS.

Jan. 5, 1813.

SPEECH

ON THE PAY OF NON-COMMISSIONED OFFICERS.

JAN. 5, 1813.

[THIS speech would be more correctly entitled one on the Enlistment of Minors, — one clause of the bill authorizing the enlistment of minors and apprentices without the previous consent of parents, masters, and guardians. It greatly exasperated the administration members, and called down on Mr. Quincy's head the bitterest personalities and the most furious rage that had ever yet been visited upon him. It was denounced as "a foul and atrocious libel" and an "atrocious falsehood." None of these things, however, moved his constant soul; and he had the satisfaction of knowing that the objectionable clause was struck out by the Senate, after it had passed the House, mainly through the influence of this speech. Only four Senators voted for it. — ED.]

MR. SPEAKER, — I am sensible that I owe an apology for addressing you at so early a period of the session, and so soon after taking my seat, if not to the House, at least to my particular constituents. It is well known to them, at least to very many of them, for I have taken no pains to conceal the intention, that I came to this session of Congress, with a settled determination to take no part in the deliberations of the House. I had adopted this resolution, not so much from a sense of self-respect as of public duty. Seven years' experience in the business of this House has convinced me that from this side of the House all argument is hopeless; that, whatever a majority has determined to do, it will do, in spite of any moral suggestion or any illustration made in this quarter. Whether it be from the nature of man, or whether it be from the particular provisions of our Constitution, I know not, but the experience of my political life has perfectly convinced me of this fact, that the will of the cabinet is the law of the land. Under these impressions, I have felt it my duty not to deceive my constituents, and had therefore resolved by no act or expression of mine in any way to countenance the belief that any representation I could make on this floor could be useful to them, or that I could serve them any farther than by a silent vote. Even now, sir, it is not my intention to enter into this discussion. I shall present you my thoughts, rather by way of protest than of argument. And I shall not trouble myself afterwards with any cavils that may be made; neither by whom, nor in what manner.

I should not have deviated from the resolution of which I have spoken, were it not for what appears to me the atrocity of the principle and the magnitude of the mischief contained in the provisions of this bill. When I speak of the principle as atrocious, I beg distinctly to be understood as not impeaching the motives of any gentlemen, or representing them as advocating an atrocious principle. I speak only of the manner in which the object presents itself to my moral view.

It is the principle contained in the third section of the bill of which I speak. That section provides that

" every person above the age of eighteen years, who shall be enlisted by any officer, shall be held in the service of the United States during the period of such enlistment, any thing in any act to the contrary notwithstanding." The nature of this provision is apparent; its tendency is not denied. It is to seduce minors of all descriptions — be they wards, apprentices, or children — from the service of their guardians, masters, and parents. On this principle I rest my objection to the bill. I meddle not with the nature of the war. Nor is it because I am hostile to this war, both in its principle and its conduct, that I at present make any objection to the provisions of the bill. I say nothing against its waste of public money. If eight dollars a month for the private be not enough, take sixteen dollars. If that be not enough, take twenty. Economy is not my difficulty. Nor do I think much of that objection of which my honorable friend from Pennsylvania (Mr. Milnor) seemed to think a great deal, — the liberation of debtors from their obligations. So far as relates to the present argument, without any objection from me, you may take what temptations you please, and apply them to the ordinary haunts for enlistment, — clear the jails; exhaust the brothel; make a desert of the tippling shop; lay what snares you please for overgrown vice, for lunacy which is of full age and idiocy out of its time. But here stop. Touch not private right; regard the sacred ties of guardian and master; corrupt not our youth; listen to the necessities of our mechanics and manufacturers; have compassion for the tears of parents.

In order to give a clear view of my subject, I shall

consider it under three aspects. Its absurdity, its inequality, its immorality. In remarking on the absurdity of this principle, it is necessary to recur to that part of the message of the President of the United States, at the opening of the present session of Congress, which introduced the objects proposed in this bill to the consideration of the House, and to observe the strange and left-handed conclusions it contains. The paragraph to which I allude is the following : —

"With a view to that vigorous prosecution of the war to which our national faculties are adequate, the attention of Congress will be particularly drawn to the insufficiency of existing provisions for filling up the military establishment. Such is the happy condition of our country arising from the facility of subsistence and the high wages for every species of occupation that, notwithstanding the augmented inducements provided at the last session, a partial success only has attended the recruiting service. The deficien y has been necessarily supplied during the campaign by other than regular troops, with all the inconveniences and expense incident to them. The remedy lies in establishing more favorably for the private soldier the proportion between his recompense and the term of enlistment. And it is a subject which cannot too soon, or too seriously, be taken into consideration."

Mr. Speaker, what a picture of felicity has the President of the United States here drawn in describing the situation of the yeomanry of this country? Their condition happy, subsistence easy, wages high, full employment, — to such favored beings, what would be the suggestions of love truly parental? Surely that so much happiness should not be put at hazard, that innocence should not be tempted to scenes of guilt, that the prospering ploughshare should not be exchanged for the sword. Such would be the lessons of parental love. And such will always be the lessons which a President of the United States will teach in such a state of things, whenever a father of his country is at the head of the nation. Alas, Mr. Speaker, how different is this message! The burden of the thought is, how to decoy the happy yeoman from home, from peace and prosperity, to scenes of blood, how to bait the man-trap; what inducements shall be held forth to avarice which neither virtue nor habit nor wise influences can resist. But this is not the whole. Our children are to be seduced from their parents. Apprentices are invited to abandon their masters. A legislative sanction is offered to perfidy and treachery. Bounty and wages to filial disobedience. Such are the moral means, by which a war, not of defence or of necessity, but of pride and ambition, should be prosecuted, — fit means to such end!

The absurdity of this bill consists in this, — in supposing these provisions to be the remedy for the evil of which the President complains. The difficulty is that men cannot be enlisted. The remedy proposed is, more money, and legislative liberty to corrupt our youth. And how is this proved to be a remedy? Why, it has been told us, on the other side of the House, that this is just the thing they do in France; that the age between eighteen and twenty-one is the best age to make soldiers; that it is the most favorite age in Bonaparte's conscription. Well, sir, what then? Are we in

France? Is Napoleon our King? or is he the President
of the United States? The style in which this example
has been urged on the House recalls to my recollection,
very strongly, a caricature print which was much circulated in the early period of our revolutionary war. The
picture represented America as a hale youth, about eighteen or twenty-one, with a huge purse in his pocket.
Lord North, with a pistol at his breast, was saying,
"Deliver your money." George III., pointing at the
young man and speaking to Lord North, said, "I give
you that man's money for my use." Behind the whole
group was a Frenchman capering, rubbing his hands for
joy, and exclaiming, "Begar, just so in France." Now,
Mr. Speaker, I have no manner of doubt that the day
that this act passes, and the whole class of our Northern
youth is made subject to the bribes of your recruiting
officers, that there will be thousands of Frenchmen in
these United States capering, rubbing their hands for
joy, and exclaiming, "Begar, just so in France." Sir,
the great mistake of this whole project lies in this, —
that French maxims are applied to American States.
Now, it ought never to be lost sight of by legislators in
this country that the people of it are not and never can
be Frenchmen; and, on the contrary; that they are,
and can never be any thing else than, Freemen.

The true source of the absurdity of this bill is a mistake in the nature of the evil. The President of the
United States tells us that the administration have not
sufficient men for their armies. The reason is, he adds,
the want of pecuniary motive. In this lies the error.
It is not pecuniary motive that is wanting to fill your
armies; it is moral motive in which you are deficient.

Sir, whatever difference of opinion may exist among the happy and wise yeomanry of New England in relation to the principle and necessity of this war, there is very little or at least much less diversity of sentiment concerning the invasion of Canada as a means of prosecuting it. They do not want Canada as an object of ambition. They do not want it as an object of plunder. They see no imaginable connection between the conquest of that province, and the attainment of those commercial rights which were the pretended objects of the war. On the contrary, they see, and very plainly too, that if our cabinet be gratified in the object of its ambition, and Canada become a conquered province, that an apology is immediately given for extending and maintaining in that country a large military force under pretence of preserving the conquered territories ; really, with a view to overawe the adjoining States. With this view of that project, the yeomanry of New England want that moral motive which will alone, in that country, fill your armies with men worthy enlisting. They have no desire to be the tools of the ambition of any man or any set of men. Schemes of conquest have no charms for them.

Abandon your projects of invasion ; throw your shield over the seaboard and the frontier ; awe into silence the Indians in your territory ; fortify your cities ; take the shackles from your commerce ; give us ships and seamen ; and show the people of this country a wise object of warfare, and there will be no want of men, money, or spirit.

I proceed to my second objection, which was to the inequality of the operation of the provisions of this bill. It is never to be forgotten, in the conduct of the govern-

ment of these United States, that it is a political association of independent sovereignties, greatly differing in
respect of wealth, resource, enterprise, extent of territory, and preparation of arms. It ought also never to
be forgotten that the proportion of physical force which
nature has given does not lie within precisely the same
line of division with the proportion of political influence
which the Constitution has provided. Now, sir, wise
men conducting a political association thus constructed,
ought always to have mainly in view not to disgust
any of the great sections of the country, either in regard
of their interests, their habits, or their prejudices.
Particularly ought they to be cautious not to burden
any of the great sections in a way peculiarly odious to
them, and in which the residue of the States cannot be
partakers, or at least only in a very small degree. I
think this principle of political action is incontrovertible.
Now, sir, of all the distinctions which exist in these
United States, that which results from the character of
the labor in different parts of the country is the most
obvious and critical. In the Southern States all the
laborious industry of the country is conducted by
slaves ; in the Northern States it is conducted by the
yeomanry, their apprentices or children. The truth is,
that the only real property in the labor of others which
exists in the Northern States is that which is possessed
in that of minors, the very class of which, at its most
valuable period, this law proposes to divest them. The
planter of the South can look round upon his fifty, his
hundred, and his thousand of human beings, and say,
" These are my property." The farmer of the North
has only one or two " ewe lambs," his children, of which

he can say, and say with pride, like the Roman matron, " These are my ornaments." Yet these this bill proposes to take from him, or what is the same thing, proposes to corrupt them, to bribe them out of his service, and that, too, at the very age when the desire of freedom is the most active, and the splendor of false glory the most enticing. Yet your slaves are safe ; there is no project for their manumission in the bill. The husbandman of the North, the mechanic, the manufacturer, shall have the property he holds in the minors subject to him put to hazard. Your property in the labor of others is safe. Where is the justice, — where the equality of such a provision ?

It is very well known in our country — indeed, it is obvious from the very nature of the thing — that the exact period of life at which the temptation of this law begins to operate upon the minor is the moment when his services begin to be the most useful to the parent or master. Until the age of eighteen the boy has hardly paid to the parent or master the cost of his clothing and education. Between the age of eighteen and twenty is just the period of profit to the father and master. It is also the period at which, from the approximation towards manhood, service begins to grow irksome and the desire of liberty powerful. The passions are then, also, in their most ungoverned sway ; and the judgment, not yet ripe, can easily be infatuated and corrupted by the vain dreams of military glory. At this period your law appears with its instruments of seduction. It offers freedom to the minor's desire of liberty, plunder to his avarice, glory to his weakness ; in short, it offers bounty and wages for disobedience to his natural or social obligations. This is a true view of this law. That it will have that full operation which its advocates hope and expect, that it will fill your armies with runaways from their masters and fathers, I do not believe. But that it will have a very great operation I know. The temptation to some of our youth will be irresistible. With my consent they shall never be exposed to it.

I offer another consideration. The Constitution of the United States declares, in its seventh amendment, — " Private property shall not be taken for public use, without just compensation." Now, of all the property which the laws of the Northern States secure to the people of that country, that which consists in the labor of the minor, and which by our laws is sacred to the guardian, master, or parent, is perhaps the most valued and most precious to our mechanics, manufacturers, and yeomen. Yet when the gentleman from New York (Mr. Stowe) proposed to secure the wages and bounty of the enlisting minor to those to whom his service belonged, it was rejected. What is this but a palpable violation of this provision of the Constitution ? What is it but taking private property for public use without compensation ?

But neither the pecuniary loss nor yet the violation of the Constitution is the evil which I most deprecate. It is the infringement of our moral rights, and the inroad which the bill makes in the moral habits of our quarter of the country. I know that gentlemen are very apt to sneer when they hear any thing said about our religious institutions or moral habits in the eastern country; but I will explain what I mean. It is not our religious institutions, our sabbaths, our fasts, our thanksgivings; nor yet our schools, colleges, and seminaries of education, — to which I refer when I speak of our moral habits. These are but means and precautions. It is certain established principles of life and conduct which, without being noticed in general laws, are often the foundation of them, and which always rule and control our positive institutions. I do not know, for instance, that the extent of the moral tie which binds the son to the father, or the apprentice to the master, is precisely assigned by any of our laws. Yet the principle upon which all our laws on this subject rest, is this, — that this tie is sacred and inviolate. The law regulates, but, except in case of misconduct, never severs it.

I know it is said that in our country minors are subjected to militia duty; and so they are. But this very service is a proof of the position which I maintain. Their obligation to serve in the militia is always subject to the paramount authority of the master and the parent.

The law says, it is true, that minors shall be subject to militia duty. But it also permits the father and the master to relieve them from that obligation at an established price. If either will pay the fine, he may retain the service of the minor, free from the militia duty. What is the consequence of all this? Why, that the minor always trains not free of the will, but subject to the will, of his natural or legal guardians. The moral tie is sacred. It is never broken. It is a principle that, cases of misconduct out of the question, the minor shall never conceive himself capable of escaping from the wholesome and wise control of his master or father.

The proposed law cuts athwart this wise principle. It preaches infidelity. It makes every recruiting officer in your country an apostle of perfidy. It says to every vain, thoughtless, discontented, or ambitious minor: "Come hither; here is an asylum from your bonds; here are wages and bounty for disobedience: only consent to go to Canada; forget what you owe to nature and your protectors; go to Canada, and you shall find freedom and glory." Such is the morality of this law.

Take a slave from his master, on any general and novel principle, and there would be an earthquake from the Potomac to the St. Mary's. Bribe an apprentice from his master; seduce a son, worth all the slaves Africa ever produced, from his father, — we are told it is only a common affair. It will be right when there is law for it. Such is now the law in France!

Mr. Speaker, I hope what I am now about to say will not be construed into a threat. It is not uttered in that spirit; but only to evince the strength of my convictions concerning the effect of the provisions of this law on the hopes of New England, particularly of Massachusetts. But pass it, and, if the legislatures of the injured States do not come down upon your recruiting officers with the old laws against kidnapping and manstealing, they are false to themselves, their posterity and their country.

SPEECH

IN RELATION TO MARITIME PROTECTION.

JAN. 25, 1812.

.

19

SPEECH

IN RELATION TO MARITIME PROTECTION.

JAN. 25, 1812.

[THIS speech had the singular good fortune, I believe unexampled in Mr. Quincy's congressional life, of being applauded
by both sides of the House. As the conflict with England,
which the war-party in Congress was bent upon bringing about,
became more and more imminent, the more intelligent of its
members could not shut their eyes to the necessity of some kind
of naval defence. Even the Southern democrats, who always
had resisted every attempt to strengthen the navy, as a protection only needed by the North, saw that a war with a great
maritime power must be waged on the ocean as well as on the
land. Accordingly, several of the principal Southern administration members, and Mr. Calhoun in particular, applied to Mr.
Quincy for his assistance in this matter. The speech gave
general satisfaction, in and out of Congress, the only exceptions
being some Federal extremists, who looked upon any measures
for the defence of the country in case of war as a strengthening of
the hands of the administration, and encouraging it to provoke
one. Ex-President John Adams, whose decided opinions in favor
of a powerful naval establishment are well known, expressed
his approbation of this speech in these strong terms: " I thank
you for your speech in relation to Maritime Protection, and much
more for making it. It is the speech of a man, a citizen, and a
statesman. It is neither hyperbole nor flattery in me to say, it
is the most important speech ever uttered in that House since
1789. — ED.]

Mr. Speaker, — I rise to address you on this occasion with no affected diffidence, and with many doubts concerning the expediency of taking any part in this debate. On the one hand, the subject has been discussed with a zeal, industry, and talent, which leave but little scope for novelty either in topic or illustration. On the other hand, arguments from this side of the House in favor of this question are received with so natural a jealousy that I know not whether more may not be lost than gained by so unpropitious a support. Indeed, sir, if this subject had been discussed on narrow or temporary or party principles, I should have been silent. On such ground I could not condescend to debate ; I could not hope to influence. But the scale of discussion has been enlarged and liberal, relative rather to the general system than to the particular exigency ; in almost every respect it has been honorable to the House and auspicious to the prospects of the nation. In such a state of feeling and sentiment, I could not refrain from indulging the hope that suggestions, even from no favorite quarter, would be received with candor, perhaps with attention. And, when I consider the deep interest which the State from which I have the honor to be a Representative has, according to my apprehension, in the event, I cannot permit the opportunity entirely to pass without bringing my small tribute of reflection into the general stock of the House.

The object I shall chiefly attempt to enforce is the necessity and duty of a systematic protection of our maritime rights by maritime means. I would call the thoughtful and intelligent men of this House and nation to the contemplation of the essential connection between a naval force proportionate to the circumstances of our sea-coast, the extent of our commerce, and the inherent enterprise of our people ; — I say, sir, I would call them to the contemplation of the essential connection between such a naval force and the safety, prosperity, and existence of our Union.   In the course of my observations, and as a subsidiary argument, I shall also attempt to show the connection between the adoption of the principle of a systematic maintenance of our maritime rights by maritime means, and relief from our present national embarrassments.

I confess to you, Mr. Speaker, I never can look — indeed, in my opinion, no American statesman ought ever to look — on any question touching the vital interests of this nation, or of any of its component parts, without keeping at all times in distinct view the nature of our political association, and the character of the independent sovereignties which compose it. Among States, the only sure and permanent bond of union is interest; and the vital interests of States, although they may be sometimes obscured, can never, for a very long time, be misapprehended.   The natural protection which the essential interests of the great component parts of our political association require will be, sooner or later, understood by the States concerned in those interests. If a protection, upon system, be not provided, it is impossible that discontent should not result.   And need I tell statesmen that, when great local discontent is combined in those sections with great physical power and with acknowledged portions of sovereignty, the inbred ties of nature will be too strong for the artificial ties of a parchment compact ?

Hence it results that the essential interests of the great component parts of our association ought to be the polar lights of all our statesmen; by them they should guide their course. According to the bearings and variations of those lights should the statesmen of such a country adjust their policy; always bearing in mind two assurances, as fundamental principles of action, which the nature of things teaches, — that although temporary circumstances, party spirit, local rivalries, personal jealousies, suggestions of subordinate interests, may weaken or even destroy for a time the influence of the leading and permanent interests of any great section of the country, yet those interests must ultimately and necessarily predominate and swallow up all these local, and temporary, and personal, and subordinate considerations: in other words, the minor interests will soon begin to realize the essential connection which exists between their prosperity and the prosperity of those great interests which, in such sections of the country, nature has made predominant, and that no political connection among free States can be lasting, or ought to be, which systematically oppresses or systematically refuses to protect the vital interests of any of the sovereignties which compose it.

I have recurred to these general considerations to introduce and elucidate this principle, which is the basis of my argument, that, as it is the incumbent duty of every nation to protect its essential interests, so it is the most impressive and critical duty of a nation, composed of a voluntary association of vast, powerful, and independent States, to protect the essential interests of all its great component parts. And I add that this protection must not be formal or fictitious, but that it must be proportionate to the greatness of those interests, and of a nature to give content to the States concerned in their protection.

In reference to this principle, the course of my reflections will be guided by two general inquiries, — the nature of the interest to be protected, the nature of the protection to be extended. In pursuing these inquiries, I shall touch very slightly, if at all, on the abstract duty of protection, which is the very end of all political associations, and without the attainment of which they are burdens and no blessings. But I shall keep it mainly in my purpose to establish the connection between a naval force and commercial prosperity; and to show the nature of the necessity, and the degree of our capacity, to give to our maritime rights a maritime protection.

In contemplating the nature of the interest to be protected, three prominent features strike the eye and direct the course of reflection, — its locality, its greatness, and its permanency.

The locality of any great interest, in an association of States such as compose this Union, will be a circumstance of primary importance in the estimation of every wise statesman. When a great interest is equally diffused over the whole mass, it may be neglected or oppressed, or even abandoned, with less hazard of internal dissension. The equality of the pressure lightens the burden. The common nature of the interest removes the causes of jealousy. A concern equally affecting the happiness of every part of the nation, it is natural to suppose is equally dear to all, and equally understood

by all. Hence results acquiescence in any artificial or
political embarrassment of it. Sectional fears and suspicions, in such case, have no food for support and no
stimulant for activity. But it is far otherwise when a
great interest is, from its nature, either wholly, or in
a very great proportion, local. In relation to such a
local interest, it is impossible that jealousies and suspicions should not arise whenever it is obstructed by any
artificial or political embarrassment. And it is also
impossible that they should not be, in a greater or less
degree, just. It is true of the wisest, and the best, and
the most thoughtful of our species that they are so constituted as not deeply to realize the importance of
interests which affect them not at all or very remotely.
Every local circle of States, as well as of individuals,
has a set of interests, in the prosperity of which the
happiness of the section to which they belong is identified ; in relation to which interests the hopes and the
fears, the reasonings and the schemes, of the inhabitants
of such sections are necessarily fashioned and conducted.
It is morally impossible that those concerned in such
sectional interests should not look with some degree of
jealousy on schemes adopted in relation to those interests, and prosecuted by men a majority of which have
a very remote or very small stake in them. And this
jealousy must rise to an extreme height when the course
of measures adopted, whether they have relation to the
management or the protection of such interests, wholly
contravene the opinions and the practical experience
of the persons immediately concerned in them. This
course of reflection has a tendency to illustrate this
idea, that as, in every political association, it is of

primary importance that the great interests of each local section should be skilfully and honestly managed and protected, so, in selecting the mode and means of management and protection, an especial regard should be had to the content and rational satisfaction of those most deeply concerned in such sectional interests. Theories and speculations of the closet, however abundant in a show of wisdom, are never to be admitted to take the place of those principles of conduct in which experience has shown the prosperity and safety of such interests to consist. Practical knowledge, and that sagacity which results from long attention to great interests, never fail to inspire a just self-confidence in relation to those interests, — a confidence not to be browbeaten by authority, nor circumvented by any abstract reasoning. And, in a national point of view, it is scarcely of more importance that the course adopted should be wise than that content and rational satisfaction should be given.

On this topic of locality, I shall confine myself to one or two very plain statements. It seems sufficient to observe that commerce is, from the nature of things, the leading interest of more than one-half, and that it is the predominating interest of more than one-third, of the people of these United States. The States north of the Potomac contain nearly four millions of souls ; and surely it needs no proof to convince the most casual observer that the proportion which the commercial interest bears to the other interests of that great section of the Union is such as entitles it to the denomination of a leading interest. The States north of the Hudson contain nearly two and a half millions of souls ; and surely there is as little need of proof to show that the proportion the commercial interest bears to the other interests of that northern section of the Union is such as entitles it there to the denomination of a predominating interest. In all the country between the Potomac and the Hudson, the interest of commerce is so great in proportion to the other interests that its embarrassment clogs and weakens the energy of every other description of industry. Yet the agricultural and manufacturing interests of this section are of a nature and a magnitude, both in respect of the staples of the one and the objects of the other, as render them in a very considerable degree independent of the commercial. And although they feel the effect of the obstruction of commerce, the feeling may be borne for a long time without much individual suffering, or any general distress. But in the country north of the Hudson, the proportion and connections of these great interests are different. Both agriculture and manufactures have there grown up in more intimate relation to commerce. The industry of that section has its shape and energy from commercial prosperity. To the construction, the supply, and the support of navigation, its manufactures have a direct or indirect reference. And it is not very different with its agriculture. A country divided into small farms, among a population great compared with its extent, requires quick circulation and easy processes in the exchange of its commodities. This can only be obtained by an active and prosperous commerce.

In order more clearly to apprehend the locality of the commercial interest, cast your eyes upon the abstract of tonnage lately laid upon our tables, according to annual custom, by the Secretary of our Treasury. It will be found that

	TONS.
The aggregate tonnage of the United States is . .	1,424,000
Of this there is owned between the Mississippi and the Potomac	221,000
Between the Potomac and the Hudson, ...	321,000
And north of the Hudson, ...	882,000
	1,424,000

If this tonnage be estimated, new and old, as it may without extravagance, at an average value of fifty dollars the ton : —

The total aggregate value of the tonnage of the United States may be stated, in round numbers, at	$70,000,000
Of which four-sevenths are owned north of the Hudson, equal to	40,000,000
Two-sevenths are owned between the Hudson and the Potomac, equal to	20,000,000
One-seventh is owned south of the Potomac, equal to	10,000,000
	$70,000,000

To place the locality of this interest in a light still more striking and impressive, I state that it appears by that abstract that the single State of Massachusetts alone, possesses nearly half a million of tonnage. Precisely, in round numbers, four hundred and ninety-six thousand tons; an amount of tonnage equal, within fifty thousand tons, to the whole tonnage owned by all the States south of the Hudson.

I refer to this excessive disproportion between the tonnage owned in different States and sections of the

United States rather as a type than as an estimate of the greatness of the comparative disproportion of the whole commercial interest in those respective States and sections. The truth is, this is much greater than the proportion of tonnage indicates, inasmuch as the capital and the industry occupied in finding employment for this great amount of tonnage are almost wholly possessed by the sections of the country to which that tonnage belongs. A satisfactory estimate of the value of that capital and industry would require a minuteness of detail little reconcilable either with your patience or with the necessity of the present argument. Enough has been said to convince any one who will take the trouble to reflect upon the subject that the interest is, in its nature, eminently local; that it is impossible it can be systematically abandoned without convulsing that whole section of country; and that the States interested in this commerce, so vital to their prosperity, have a right to claim and ought not to be content with less than efficient protection.

The imperious nature of this duty will be still farther enforced by considering the greatness of this interest. In doing this, I prefer to present a single view of it, lest, by distracting the attention to a great variety of particulars, the effect of the whole should be lost in the multitude of details. Let us inquire into the amount of property annually exposed to maritime depredation and what the protection of it is worth to the nation which is its proprietor. An estimate of this kind must necessarily be very loose and general. But it will be sufficiently accurate to answer all the purposes of the argument. For the subject is of that massive character that a mistake of many millions makes no material alteration in the conclusion to be drawn from the statement.

The total export of the United States, in the treasury year, ending on the first day of October, 1807, was $108,000,000. That of the year ending the first of October, 1811, was $61,000,000. The average value exceeds $80,000,000. But to avoid all cavil I state the annual average value of exports of the United States at $70,000,000

To this add the annual average value of the shipping of the United States, which, new and old, cannot be less than $50 the ton, and on one million four hundred thousand tons is also   70,000,000

To this add the average annual value of freight, out and home, which, calculated on voyages of all descriptions, may be fairly stated at $70 the ton, and is   98,000,000

For this estimate of the value of freight and tonnage, I am indebted to an honorable friend and colleague (Mr. Reed), whose information and general intelligence concerning commercial subjects are, perhaps, not exceeded by those of any gentleman in either branch of Congress.

To this add the total average value of property annually at risk in our coasting trade, which cannot be less than and probably far exceeds .   100,000,000

Our seamen are also the subjects of annual exposure. The value of this hardy, industrious, and generous race of men is not to be estimated in money. The pride, the hope, and, if you would permit, the bulwark of this commercial community, are not to be put into the scale against silver or gold in any moral or

Amount carried forward $338,000,000

Amount brought forward	$338,000,000

political estimate. Yet, for the present object,
I may be permitted to state the value of the
skill and industry of these freemen to their
country, at $500 each, which, on 120,000 sea-
men, the unquestionable number is   60,000,000

Making a gross aggregate of $398,000,000

Although I have no question of the entire correctness
of this calculation, yet, for the purpose of avoiding every
objection which might arise in relation to the value of
freight or tonnage, I put out of the question ninety-eight
millions of the above estimate, and state the amount of
annual maritime exposure at only three hundred millions
of dollars.

To this must be added the value of the property on
our seaboard, of all the lives of our citizens, and of all
the cities and habitations on the coast, exposed to
instant insult and violation from the most contemptible
maritime plunderer. No man can think that I am
extravagant if I add, on this account, an amount equal
to that annually exposed at sea, and state the whole
amount of maritime and sea-coast exposure in round
numbers at six hundred millions of dollars.

I am aware that this estimate falls short of the reality.
I know that the safety of our domestic hearths and our
altars, and the security of all the dear and tender objects
of affection and duty which surround them, are beyond
the reach of pecuniary estimates. But I lay those considerations out of the question, and simply inquire what
is the worth of a rational degree of security in time of
war for such an amount of property, considering it
merely as an interest to be insured at the market rate

of the worth of protection. Suppose an individual had
such a property at risk, which in time of peace was subject to so much plunder and insult, and in time of war
was liable to be swept away, would he not be deemed
unwise, or rather absolutely mad, if he neglected, at the
annual sacrifice of one or two or even three per cent, to
obtain for this property a very high degree of security, —
as high perhaps, as the divine will permits man to enjoy
in relation to the possessions of this life, which, according to the fixed dispensations of his Providence, are
necessarily uncertain and transitory? But suppose that
instead of one, two, or three per cent, he could, by the
regular annual application of two-thirds of one per cent
upon the whole amount of the property at risk, obtain a
security thus high and desirable, to what language of
wonder and contempt would such an individual subject
himself who, at so small a sacrifice, should refuse or
neglect to obtain so important a blessing? What, then,
shall be said of a nation thus neglecting and thus refusing, when to it attach not only all the considerations of
interest and preservation of property which belong to
the individual, but other, and far higher and more impressive, — such as the maintenance of its peace, of its
honor ; the safety of the lives of its citizens, of its seaboard from devastation, and even perhaps of its children
and females from massacre or brutal violence? Is there
any language of contempt and detestation too strong for
such blind infatuation, such palpable improvidence?
For let it be remembered that two-thirds of one per
cent, upon the amount of property thus annually exposed, is four millions of dollars, the annual systematic
appropriation of which amount would answer all the

purposes and hopes of commerce of your cities and seaboard.

But, perhaps, the greatness of this interest and our
pecuniary ability to protect it may be made more strikingly apparent by a comparison of our commerce with
that of Great Britain in the single particular of export.

I state, then, as a fact of which any man may satisfy
himself by a reference to M'Pherson's " Annals of Commerce," where the tables of British export may be found,
that, taking the nine years prior to the war of our Revolution, from 1766 to 1774 inclusive, the total average
export of Great Britain was sixteen million pounds sterling, equal to seventy-one million dollars, — an amount
less by ten million of dollars than the present total average export of the United States.

And again, taking the nine years beginning with 1789,
and ending with 1797 inclusive, the total average annual
export of Great Britain was twenty-four million pounds
sterling, equal to one hundred and six million dollars,
which is less by two millions of dollars than the total
export of the United States in 1807. It is true that
this is the official value of the British export, and that
the real value is somewhat higher, perhaps thirty per
cent. This circumstance, although it in a degree dimin-
ishes the approximation of the American to the British
commerce in point of amount, does not materially affect
the argument. Upon the basis of her commerce, Great
Britain maintains a maritime force of eight hundred or
a thousand vessels of war. And will it be seriously
contended that, upon the basis of a commerce, like ours,
thus treading upon the heels of British greatness, we are
absolutely without the ability of maintaining the security

of our sea-board, the safety of our cities and the unobstructed course of our coasting trade ?

By recurring to the permanency of this interest, the folly and madness of this negligence, and misplaced meanness, for it does not deserve the name of economy, will be still more distinctly exhibited. If this commerce were the mushroom growth of a night, if it had its vigor from the temporary excitement and the accumulated nutriment which warring elements in Europe had swept from the places of their natural deposit, then, indeed, there might be some excuse for a temporizing policy touching so transitory an interest. But commerce, in the Eastern States, is of no foreign growth, and of no adventitious seed. Its root is of a fibre which almost two centuries have nourished. And the perpetuity of its destiny is written, in legible characters, as well in the nature of the country as in the dispositions of its inhabitants. Indeed, sir, look along your whole coast, from Passamaquody to Capes Henry and Charles, and behold the deep and far-winding creeks and inlets, the noble basins, the projecting headlands, the majestic rivers, and those sounds and bays, which are more like inland seas than like any thing called by those names in other quarters of the globe. Can any man do this, and not realize that the destiny of the people inhabiting such a country is essentially maritime ? Can any man do this without being impressed by the conviction that, although the poor projects of politicians may embarrass for a time the dispositions growing out of the condition of such a country, yet that nature will be too strong for cobweb regulations, and will vindicate her rights with certain effect, perhaps with awful perils ? No nation

20

ever did, or ever ought to, resist such allurements and invitations to a particular mode of industry. The purposes of Providence, relative to the destination of men, are to be gathered from the circumstances in which his beneficence has placed them. And to refuse to make use of the means of prosperity which his goodness has put into our hands, what is it but spurning at his bounty, and rejecting the blessings which his infinite wisdom has designated for us by the very nature of his allotments? The employments of industry, connected with navigation and commercial enterprise, are precious to the people of that quarter of the country by ancient prejudice, not less than by recent profit. The occupation is rendered dear and venerable by all the cherished associations of our infancy and all the sage and prudential maxims of our ancestors. And, as to the lessons of encouragement derived from recent experience, what nation ever, within a similar period, received so many that were sweet and salutary? What nation, in so short a time, ever before ascended to such a height of commercial greatness?

It has been said, by some philosophers of the other hemisphere, that nature in this new world had worked by a sublime scale; that our mountains and rivers and lakes were, beyond all comparison, greater than any thing the old world could boast; that she had here made nothing diminutive *except its animals*. And ought we not to fear lest the bitterness of this sarcasm should be concentrated on our country by a course of policy wholly unworthy of the magnitude and nature of the interests committed to our guardianship? Have we not reason to fear that some future cynic, with an asperity which truth shall make piercing, will declare that all things in these United States are great *except its statesmen;* and that we are pigmies to whom Providence has intrusted, for some inscrutable purpose, gigantic labors? Can we deny the justice of such severity of remark, if, instead of adopting a scale of thought and a standard of action proportionate to the greatness of our trust and the multiplied necessities of the people, we bring to our task the mere measures of professional industry, and mete out contributions for national safety by our fee-tables, our yardsticks, and our gill-pots? Can we refrain from subscribing to the truth of such censure, if we do not rise, in some degree, to the height of our obligations; and teach ourselves to conceive, and with the people to realize, the vastness of those relations which are daily springing among States which are not so much one empire as a congregation of empires?

Having concluded what I intended to suggest in relation to the nature of the interest to be protected, I proceed to consider the nature of the protection which it is our duty to extend.

And here, Mr. Speaker, I am necessitated to make an observation which is so simple and so obvious that, were it not for the arguments urged against the principle of maritime protection, I should have deemed the mere mention of it to require an apology. The remark is this, that rights in their nature local can only be maintained where they exist, and not where they do not exist. If you had a field to defend in Georgia, it would be very strange to put up a fence in Massachusetts. And yet how does this differ from invading

Canada, for the purpose of defending our maritime
rights? I beg not to be understood, Mr. Speaker, by
this remark as intending to chill the ardor for the
Canada expedition. It is very true that, to possess
ourselves of the Canadas and Nova Scotia and their
dependencies, it would cost these United States, at the
least estimate, fifty millions of dollars ; and that Great
Britain — national pride, and her pledge of protection to
the people of that country, being put out of the question — would sell you the whole territory for half the
money. I make no objection, however, on this account.
On the contrary, for the purposes of the present argument, I may admit that pecuniary calculation ought to
be put out of the field when spirit is to be shown or
honor vindicated. I only design to inquire how our
maritime rights are protected by such invasion. Suppose that, in every land project, you are successful.
Suppose both the Canadas, Quebec, Halifax, every
thing to the North Pole yours by fair conquest. Are
your rights on the ocean therefore secure ? Does your
flag float afterwards in honor ? Are your seamen safe
from impressment ? Is your course along the highway
of nations unobstructed ? No one pretends it. No one
has or can show, by any logical deduction or any detail
of facts, that the loss of those countries would so depress Great Britain as to induce her to abandon for one
hour any of her maritime pretensions. What, then,
results ? Why, sir, what is palpable as the day, that
maritime rights are only to be maintained by maritime
means. This species of protection must be given, or
all clamor about maritime rights will be understood by
the people interested in them to be hollow or false, or,

what is worse, an intention to co-operate with the enemies of our commerce in a still farther embarrassment of it.

While I am on this point, I cannot refrain from noticing a strange solecism which seems to prevail touching the term " flag." It is talked about as though there was something mystical in its very nature ; as though a rag, with certain stripes and stars upon it, tied to a stick and called a flag was a wizard's wand, and entailed security on every thing under it or within its sphere. There is nothing like all this in the nature of the thing. A flag is the evidence of power. A land flag is the evidence of land power. A maritime flag is the evidence of maritime power. You may have a piece of bunting upon a staff, and call it a flag : but, if you have no maritime power to maintain it, you have a name and no reality ; you have the shadow without the substance ; you have the sign of a flag, but in truth *you have no flag.*

In considering this subject of maritime protection, I shall recur to the nature and degree of it and to our capacity to extend it. And here we are always met, at the very threshold, with this objection : " A naval force requires much time to get it into readiness, and the exigency will be past before the preparation can be completed." Thus want of foresight in times past is made an apology for want of foresight in the time present. We were unwise in the beginning, and unwise we resolve to continue until the end of the chapter. We refuse to do any thing until the moment of exigency, and then it is too late. Thus our improvidence is made sponsor for our disinclination. But what is the

law of nature and the dictates of wisdom on this subject? The casualties of life, the accidents to which
man is exposed, are the modes established by Providence
for his instruction. This is the law of our nature.
Hence it is that adversity is said to keep a school for
certain people who will learn in no other. Hence, too,
the poet likens it to " a toad ugly and venomous, which
bears a precious jewel in its head." And in another
place, but with the same general relation, "out of this
nettle danger, we pluck the flower safety." This law
is just as relative to nations as it is to individuals. For,
notwithstanding all the vaunting of statesmen, their
whole business is to apply an enlarged common-sense
to the affairs intrusted to their management. It is as
much the duty of the rulers of a State, as it is that of
an individual, to learn wisdom from misfortune, and to
draw, from every particular instance of adversity, those
maxims of conduct by the collection and application of
which our intellectual and moral natures are distinguished and elevated. In all cases of this kind, the
inquiry ought to be, Is this exigency peculiar, or is it
general? Is it one in which human effort is unavailing,
and therefore requires only the exercise of a resignation
and wise submission to the divine will? or is it one
which skill or power may limit or obviate? On the
result of this inquiry our obligations depend. For when
man conducts toward a general evil as though it were
peculiar; or when, through ignorance or pusillanimity,
he neglects to use the means of relief or prevention to
the extent in which he possesses them; if he stretches
himself out in a stupid languor, and refuses to do any
thing, because he finds he cannot do every thing, —

then, indeed, all his clamors against the course of nature, or the conduct of others, are but artifices by which he would conceal from the world, perhaps from himself, the texture of his own guilt. His misfortunes are, in such case, his crimes. Let them proceed from what source they will, he is himself, at least, a half-worker in the fabric of his own miseries.

Mr. Speaker, can any one contemplate the exigency which at this day depresses our country, and for one moment deem it peculiar? The degree of such commercial exigencies may vary, but they must always exist. It is absurd to suppose that such a population as is that of the Atlantic States can be either driven or decoyed from the ocean? It is just as absurd to imagine that wealth will not invite cupidity, and that weakness will not insure both insult and plunder. The circumstances of our age make this truth signally impressive. Who does not see in the conduct of Europe a general departure from those common principles which once constituted national morality? What is safe which power can seize or ingenuity can circumvent? or what truths more palpable than these, — that there is no safety for national rights but in the national arm; and that important interests systematically pursued must be systematically protected?

Touching the nature and degree of that maritime protection which it may be wise in this nation to extend to its maritime interests, it seems to me that our exertions should rather be excited than graduated by the present exigency; that our duty is to inquire, upon a general scale, what our commercial citizens have, in this respect, a right to claim; and what is the unquestionable obligation of a commercial nation to so great a class of its interests. For this purpose my observations will have reference rather to the principles of the system than to the provisions of the bill now under debate. Undoubtedly an appropriation for the building of ten or any other additional number of frigates would be so distinct a manifestation of the intention of the national legislature to extend to commerce its natural protection as in itself to outweigh any theoretic preference for a maritime force of a higher character. I cannot, there- fore, but cordially support an appropriation for a species of protection so important and desirable. Yet, in an argument having relation to the system rather than to the occasion, I trust I shall have the indulgence of the House if my course of reflections should take a wider range than the propositions on the table, and embrace within the scope of remark the general principles by which the nature and degree of systematic naval protection should in my judgment be regulated.

Here it seems hardly necessary to observe that a main object of all protection is satisfaction to the persons whose interests are intended to be protected ; and to this object a peculiar attention ought to be paid when it happens that the majority of the rulers of a nation are composed of persons not immediately concerned in those interests, and not generally suspected of having an overweening attachment to them. In such a state of things it is peculiarly important that the course of con-·duct adopted should be such as to indicate systematic intention as to the end, and wise adaptation as to the means. For in no other way can that satisfaction of which I speak result, and which is, in a national point of

view, at the same time one of the most important
objects of government, and one of the most certain
evidences of its wisdom ; for men interested in protection will always deem themselves the best judges of the
nature of that protection.   And as such men can never
be content with any thing short of efficient protection,
according to the nature of the object, so instinct not less
than reason will instruct them whether the means you
employ are in their nature real or illusory.   Now, in
order to know what will give this satisfaction to the
persons interested, so desirable both to them and to
the nation, it is necessary to know the nature and gradation in value of those interests, and to extend protection, not so much with a lavish as with a discriminating
and parental hand.   If it happen in respect of any
interest, as it is acknowledged on all sides it is at
present the case with the commercial, that it cannot be
protected against all the world, to the utmost of its
greatness and dispersion, then the inquiry occurs, what
branch of this interest is most precious to commercial
men, and what is the nature of that protection which
will give to it the highest degree of certainty of which
its nature is susceptible ?   It has been by the result of
these two inquiries, in my mind, that its opinion has
been determined concerning the objects and the degree
of protection.

Touching that branch of interest which is most
precious to commercial men, it is impossible that there
can be any mistake ; for however dear the interests of
property or of life exposed upon the ocean may be to
their owners or their friends, yet the safety of our
altars and of our firesides, of our cities and of our sea-

board, must, from the nature of things, be entwined into the affections by ties incomparably more strong and tender. And it happens that both national pride and honor are peculiarly identified with the support of these primary objects of commercial interest.

It is in this view I state that the first and most important object of the nation ought to be such a naval force as shall give such a degree of rational security as the nature of the subject admits to our cities, and seaboard, and coasting trade; that the system of maritime protection ought to rest upon this basis; and that it should not attempt to go further until these objects are secured. And I have no hesitation to declare, that until such a maritime force be systematically maintained by this nation, it shamefully neglects its most important duties and most critical interests.

With respect to the nature and extent of this naval force some difference of opinion may arise, according to the view taken of the primary objects of protection. For myself I consider that those objects are first to be protected in the safety of which the national character and happiness are most deeply interested; and these are chiefly concerned, beyond all question, in the preservation of our maritime settlements from pillage and our coast from violence. For this purpose it is requisite that there should be a ship of war for the harbor of every great city of the United States, equal, in point of force, to the usual grade of ships of the line of the maritime belligerents. These ships might be so instructed as to act singly or together as circumstances might require. My reason for the selection of this species of force is, that it puts every city and great harbor of the United States in a state of security from the insults, and the inhabitants of your sea-coasts from the depredation, of any single ship of war of any nation. To these should be added a number of frigates and smaller vessels of war. By such means our coasting trade might be protected, the mouths of our harbors secured, in particular that of the Mississippi, from the buccaneers of the West Indies, and hereafter, perhaps, from those of South America. A system of protection graduated upon a scale so conformable to the nature of the country and to the greatness of the commercial interest, would tend to quiet that spirit of jealousy which so naturally and so justly begins to spring among the States. Those interested in commerce would care little what local influences predominated, or how the ball of power vibrated among our factions, provided an efficient protection of their essential interests, upon systematic principles, was not only secured by the letter of the Constitution, but assured by a spirit pervading every description of their rulers.

But it is said that " we have not capacity to maintain such a naval force." Is it want of pecuniary, or want of physical capacity? In relation to our pecuniary capacity, I will not condescend to add any proof to that plain statement already exhibited, showing that we have an annual commercial exposure equal to six hundred millions of dollars, and that two-thirds of one per cent upon this amount of value, or four millions of dollars, is more than is necessary, if annually and systematically appropriated for this great object, so anxiously and rightfully desired by your seaboard, and so essential to the honor and obligations of the nation. I will only

make a single other statement by way of illustrating
the smallness of the annual appropriations necessary for
the attainment of this important purpose. The annual
appropriation of one-sixth of one per cent on the amount
of the value of the whole annual commercial exposure
(one million of dollars) is sufficient to build in two
years six seventy-four gun ships ; and taking the average
expense, in peace and war, the annual appropriation of
the same sum is sufficient to maintain them afterwards
in a condition for efficient service. This objection of
pecuniary inability may be believed in the interior country where the greatness of the commercial property and
all the tender obligations connected with its preservation are not realized. But in the cities and in the commercial States the extent of the national resources is
more truly estimated. They know the magnitude of
the interest at stake, and their essential claim to protection. Why, sir, were we seriously to urge this
objection of pecuniary incapacity to the commercial
men of Massachusetts they would laugh us to scorn.
Let me state a single fact. In the year 1745, the State,
then the colony of Massachusetts Bay, included a population of 220,000 souls ; and yet, in that infant state of
the country, it owned a fleet consisting of three ships, —
one of which carried twenty guns, — three snows, one
brig, and three sloops, being an aggregate of ten vessels
of war. These partook of the dangers and shared in
the glory of that expedition which terminated with the
surrender of Louisburgh. Comparing the population,
the extent of territory, the capital and all the other
resources of this great nation, with the narrow means
of the colony of Massachusetts at that period of its

history, it is not extravagant to assert that the fleet it
then possessed, in proportion to its pecuniary resources,
was greater than would be, in proportion to the resources
of the United States, a fleet of fifty sail of the line and
one hundred frigates.   With what language of wonder
and admiration does that great orator and prince of
moral statesmen, Edmund Burke, in his speech for con-
ciliation with America, speak of the commerce and enterprise of that people!   "When we speak of the
commerce with our colonies, fiction lags after truth;
invention is unfruitful, and imagination cold and barren."
" No sea but what is vexed by their fisheries ; no climate
that is not witness to their toils.   Neither the perseverance of Holland, nor the activity of France, nor the
dexterous and firm sagacity of English enterprise, ever
carried this most perilous mode of hard industry to the
extent to which it has been pushed by this recent people, — a people who are still, as it were, but in the
gristle, and not yet hardened into the bone of manhood."   And shall the descendants of such a people be
told that their commercial rights are not worth defending, that the national arm is not equal to their protection?   And this, too, after the lapse of almost
forty years has added an extent to their commerce
beyond all parallel in history, and after the strength and
resources associated to protect them exceed in point of
population seven millions of souls, possessing a real and
personal capital absolutely incalculable?

Our pecuniary capacity, then, is unquestionable ; but
it is said we are deficient in physical power.   It is
strange that those who urge this objection assert it only
as it respects Great Britain, and admit, either expressly

or by implication, — indeed, they cannot deny, — that it is within our physical capacity to maintain our maritime rights against every other nation. Now, let it be granted that we have such an utter incapacity in relation to the British naval power; grant that at the nod of that nation we must abandon the ocean to the very mouths of our harbors, nay, our harbors themselves. What then? Does it follow that a naval force is useless? Because we must submit to have our rights plundered by one power, does it follow that we must be tame and submissive to every other? Look at the fact. We have, within these ten years, lost more property by the plunder of the minor naval powers of Europe, France included, than would have been enough to have built and maintained twice the number of ships sufficient for our protection against their depredations. I cannot exceed the fact when I state the loss within that period by those powers at thirty millions of dollars. Our capacity to defend our commerce against every one of these powers is undeniable. Because we cannot maintain our rights against the strong, shall we bear insult and invite plunder from the weak? Because there is one leviathan in the ocean, shall every shark satiate his maw on our fatness with impunity?

But let us examine this doctrine of utter inability to maintain our maritime rights against Great Britain, so obtrusively and vehemently maintained by some who clamor the most violently against her insults and injuries. If the project were to maintain our maritime rights against that mistress of the sea by convoys spread over every ocean, there would indeed be something ludicrously fanciful and wild in the proposition.

But nothing like this is either proposed or desired. The humility of commercial hope in reference to that nation rises no higher than the protection of our harbors, the security of our coasts and coasting trade. Is it possible that such a power as this shall be denied to exist in this nation? If it exist, is it possible that its exercise shall be withheld?

Look at the present state of our harbors and sea-coast. See their exposure — I will not say to the fleets of Great Britain, but to any single ship of the line, to any single frigate, to any single sloop of war. It is true the policy of that nation induces her to regard your prohibitory laws, and her ships now seldom visit your ports. But suppose her policy should change; suppose any one of her ships of war should choose to burn any of the numerous settlements upon your sea-coast, or to plunder the inhabitants of it, — would there not be some security to those exposed citizens if a naval force were lying in every great harbor of the United States competent to protect or avenge the aggression of any single ship of war of whatever force? Would not the knowledge of its existence teach the naval commanders of that nation both caution and respect? It is worthy of this nation, and fully within its capacity, to maintain such a force. Not a single sea-bull should put his head over our acknowledged water-line without finding a power sufficient to take him by the horns.

But it is said that, "in case of actual war with Great Britain, our ships would be useless. She would come and take them." In reply to this objection, I shall not recur to those details of circumstances, already so frequently stated, which would give our ships of war, fighting on their own coasts and in the proximity of relief and supply, so many advantages over the ships of a nation obliged to come three thousand miles to the combat. But, allowing this argument from British naval superiority its full force, I ask, What is that temper on which a nation can most safely rely in the day of trial? Is it that which takes counsel of fear, or that which listens only to the suggestions of duty? Is it that which magnifies all the real dangers until hope and exertion are paralyzed in their first germinations? or is it that which dares to attempt noble ends by appropriate means; which, wisely weighing the nature of any anticipated exigency, prepares according to its powers, resolved that, whatever else it may want, to itself it will never be wanting? Grant all that is said concerning British naval superiority, in the events of war has comparative weakness nothing to hope from opportunity? Are not the circumstances in which this country and Great Britain would be placed, relative to naval combats upon our own coast, of a nature to strengthen the hope of such opportunity? Is it of no worth to a nation to be in a condition to avail itself of conjunctures and occurrences, Mr. Speaker? Preparation, in such cases, is every thing. All history is replete with the truth that " the battle is not always to the strong, but that time and chance happen to all." Suppose that Great Britain should send twelve seventy-fours to burn our cities or lay waste our coasts. Might not such a naval force be dispersed by storms, diminished by shipwrecks, or delayed and weakened by the events of the voyage? In such case, would it be nothing to have even half that number of line-of-battle ships, in a state of vigorous preparation, ready to take the advantage of so probable a circumstance, and so providential an interposition ? The adage of our school-books is as true in relation to States as to men in common life, — " Heaven helps those who help themselves." It is almost a law of nature. God grants every thing to wisdom and virtue. He denies every thing to folly and baseness. But suppose the worst. Grant that, in a battle such as our brave seamen would fight in defence of their country, our naval force be vanquished. What then ? Did enemies ever plunder or violate more fiercely when weakened and crippled by the effects of a hard-bought victory than when flushed, their veins full, they rush upon their prey, with cupidity stimulated by contempt? Did any foe ever grant to pusillanimity what it would have denied to prowess? To be conquered is not always to be disgraced. The heroes who shall perish in such combats shall not fall in vain for their country. Their blood will be the most precious, as well as the strongest cement of our Union. What is it that constitutes the moral tie of our nation ? Is it that paper contract called the Constitution ? Why is it that the man of Virginia, the man of Carolina, and the man of Massachusetts, are dearer to each other than is to either the man of South America or the West Indies? Locality has little to do with implanting this inherent feeling, and personal acquaintance less. Whence, then, does it result but from that moral sentiment which pervades all, and is precious to all, of having shared common dangers for the attainment of common blessings. The strong ties of every people are those which spring from the heart and twine through

21

the affections. The family compact of the States has
this for its basis, that their heroes have mingled their
blood in the same contests; that all have a common
right in their glory; that, if I may be allowed the
expression, in the temple of patriotism all have the
same worship.

But it is inquired, What effect will this policy have
upon the present exigency? I answer, The happiest
in every aspect. To exhibit a definitive intent to maintain maritime rights by maritime means, what is it but
to develop new stamina of national character? No
nation can or has a right to hope respect from others
which does not first learn to respect itself. And how
is this to be attained? By a course of conduct conformable to its duties and relative to its condition. If
it abandons what it ought to defend, if it flies from the
field it is bound to maintain, how can it hope for honor?
To what other inheritance is it entitled but disgrace?
Foreign nations, undoubtedly, look upon this union
with eyes long read in the history of man, and with
thoughts deeply versed in the effects of passion and
interest, upon independent States associated by ties so
apparently slight and novel. They understand well
that the rivalries among the great interests of such
States; the natural envyings which in all countries
spring between agriculture, commerce, and manufactures; the inevitable jealousies and fears of each other
of South and North, interior and seaboard; the incipient or progressive rancor of party animosity, — are the
essential weaknesses of sovereignties thus combined.
Whether these causes shall operate, or whether they
shall cease, foreign nations will gather from the features

of our policy. They cannot believe that such a nation is strong in the affections of its associated parts when they see the vital interests of whole States abandoned. But reverse this policy; show a definitive and stable intent to yield the natural protection to such essential interests: then they will respect you. And to powerful nations honor comes attended by safety.

Mr. Speaker, what is national disgrace? Of what stuff is it composed? Is a nation disgraced because its flag is insulted; because its seamen are impressed; because its course upon the highway of the ocean is obstructed? No, sir. Abstractedly considered, all this is not disgrace. Because all this may happen to a nation so weak as not to be able to maintain the dignity of its flag, or the freedom of its citizens, or the safety of its course. Natural weakness is never disgrace. But, sir, this is disgrace, — when we submit to insult and to injury which we have the power to prevent or redress. Its essential constituents are want of sense or want of spirit. When a nation, with ample means for its defence, is so thick in the brain as not to put them into a suitable state of preparation; or when, with sufficient muscular force, it is so tame in spirit as to seek safety not in manly effort, but in retirement, — then a nation is disgraced; then it shrinks from its high and sovereign character into that of the tribe of Issachar, crouching down between two burdens; the French burden, on the one side, and the British burden on the other, so dull, so lifeless, so stupid, that, were it not for its braying, it could not be distinguished from the clod of the valley.

It is impossible for European nations not to know

that we are the second commercial country in the world ; that we have more than seven millions of people, with less annual expenditure and more unpledged sources of revenue than any nation of the civilized world. Yet a nation thus distinguished — abounding in wealth, in enterprise, and in power — is seen flying away from " the unprofitable contest ; " abandoning the field of controversy ; taking refuge behind its own doors, and softening the rigors of oppression abroad by a comparison with worse torments at home. Ought such a nation to ask for respect? Is there any other mode of relief from this depth of disgrace than by a change of national conduct and character?

With respect to Great Britain, it seems impossible that such a change in our policy should not be auspicious. No nation ever did or ever can conduct towards one that is true in the same way as it conducts towards one that is false to all its obligations. Clear conceptions of interest and faithful fulfilment of duty as certainly insure, sooner or later, honor and safety, as blindness to interest and abandonment of duty do assuredly entail disgrace and embarrassment. In relation to the principle which regulates the commercial conduct of Great Britain towards the United States, there is much scope for diversity of opinion. Perhaps those judge most truly who do not attribute to her any very distinct or uniform system of action in relation to us, but who deem her course to result from views of temporary expediency, growing out of the circumstances of the time and the character of our administration. If this be the case, then whatever course of conduct has a tendency to show a change in the character of the

American policy must produce a proportionate change in that of the British.   And if tameness and systematic abandonment of our commercial rights have had the effect to bring upon us so many miseries, a contrary course of conduct, having for its basis a wise spirit and systematic naval support, it may well be hoped, will have the opposite effect, — of renewing our prosperity. But if it be true, as is so frequently and so confidently asserted, that Great Britain is jealous of our commercial greatness ; if it be true that she would depress us as rivals ; if she begins to regard us as a power which may soon curb, if not in aftertimes spurn, her proud control on her favorite element, — then, indeed, she may be disposed to quench the ardor of our naval enterprise ; then, indeed, it may be her care so to shape the course of her policy as to deprive our commerce of all hope of its natural protection, and to co-operate with and cherish such an administration in this country as hates a naval force and loves commercial restriction.   In this view of her policy, — and I am far from asserting it is not correct, — is it not obvious that she may be content with the present condition of our commerce ?   Except acknowledged colonial vassalage, what state of things would be more desirable to her ?   The whole sea is her own.   Her American rival tamely makes cession of it to her possession.   Our commercial capital is already seeking employment in her cities, and our seamen in her ships.   What then results ?   Is it not, on this view of her policy, undeniable that an administration in this country, for the purposes of Great Britain, is such as thinks commerce not worth having or not worth defend-

ing; such as, in every scheme of nominal protection,
meditates to it nothing but additional embarrassment
and eventual abandonment? Must not such an administration be convenient to British ministry if such be a
British policy? And if British ministers should ever
find such an administration in this country made to
their hands, may we not anticipate that they will take
care to manage with a view to its continuance in power?
Of all policy the most ominous to British ascendency is
that of a systematic maritime defence of our maritime
rights.

The general effect of the policy I advocate is to produce confidence at home and respect abroad. These
are twin shoots from the same stock, and never fail to
flourish or fade together. Confidence is a plant of no
mushroom growth and of no artificial texture. It
springs only from sage councils and generous endeavors.
The protection you extend must be efficient and suited
to the nature of the object you profess to maintain. If
it be neither adequate nor appropriate, your wisdom
may be doubted, your motives may be distrusted, but in
vain you expect confidence. The inhabitants of the
seaboard will inquire of their own senses and not of
your logic concerning the reality of their protection.

As to respect abroad, what course can be more certain
to insure it? What object more honorable, what more
dignified, than to behold a great nation pursuing wise
ends by appropriate means; rising to adopt a series of
systematic exertions suited to her power and adequate
to her purposes? What object more consolatory to the
friends, what more paralyzing to the enemies, of our

Union, than to behold the natural jealousies and rivalries, which are the acknowledged dangers of our political condition, subsiding or sacrificing? What sight more exhilarating than to see this great nation once more walking forth among the nations of the earth under the protection of no foreign shield? peaceful, because powerful; powerful, because united in interests, and amalgamated by concentration of those interests in the national affections.

But let the opposite policy prevail; let the essential interests of the great component parts of this Union find no protection under the national arm; instead of safety let them realize oppression, and the seeds of discord and dissolution are inevitably sown in a soil the best fitted for their root, and affording the richest nourishment for their expansion. It may be a long time before they ripen; but sooner or later they will assuredly burst forth in all their destructive energies. In the intermediate period, what aspect does an union thus destitute of cement present? Is it that of a nation keen to discern and strong to resist violations of its sovereignty? It has rather the appearance of a casual collection of semibarbarous clans, with the forms of civilization, and with the rude and rending passions of the savage state: in truth, powerful; yet, as to any foreign effect, imbecile: rich in the goods of fortune, yet wanting that inherent spirit without which a nation is poor indeed: their strength exhausted by struggles for local power; their moral sense debased by low intrigues for personal popularity or temporary pre-eminence; all their thoughts turned, not to the safety of the state, but to the elevation of a chieftain. A people presenting such an aspect, what have they to expect abroad? what but pillage, insult, and scorn?

The choice is before us. Persist in refusing efficient maritime protection; persist in the system of commercial restrictions: what now is, perhaps, prophecy will hereafter be history.

SPEECH

ON THE RELIEF OF SUNDRY MERCHANTS FROM PENALTIES INNOCENTLY INCURRED.

Dec. 14, 1812.

SPEECH

ON THE RELIEF OF SUNDRY MERCHANTS FROM PENALTIES INNOCENTLY INCURRED.

DEC. 14, 1812.

[IN the remarks preliminary to the speech of February 25, 1811, I have related how England refused to comply with the conditions of the act repealing non-intercourse with her and France, and of the consequent re-enactment of that measure as far as she was concerned. After somewhat more than a year, just about the time of our declaration of war, June 18, 1812, she had thought better of the matter and revoked her Orders in Council, which, if done eighteen months earlier, would have saved the two countries from a conflict from which neither reaped much credit or any advantage. After the revocation, and before our declaration of war had reached England, American merchants residing there, taking it for granted that the non-intercourse would be repealed, if it did not cease, *ipso facto*, by the action of the British ministry, openly and in entire good faith, loaded their ships with the prohibited articles and despatched them to the United States. But the act was still in force; war had been declared; the goods were forfeited, and, by the letter of the law, three times their value besides. To exact these penalties was more than even Mr. Madison's government ventured to propose. But, as it was in the most pressing need of money, Mr. Gallatin, the Secretary of the Treasury, devised this plan for extracting about nine millions of dollars from the honest

error of the importers. The invoice value of the merchandise
was about eighteen millions. By the law, the entire importation
was forfeited, one half to go to the government and the other to
the informer. Mr. Gallatin proposed to relinquish the informer's
moiety to the importers, and to put that of the government into
the Treasury. How he justified to himself this cavalier treatment of the informers we are not told; it would certainly not
have been submitted to without an outcry by that valuable class
of citizens in our day : but this modified proposition was regarded
by the sufferers and the impartial part of the public as only a
mitigated form of spoliation of innocent parties. The resistance
to its infliction upon them which is expressed in this speech had
the effect of causing the project to fail and the entire forfeitures
to be remitted. — Ed.]

MR. QUINCY (of Massachusetts) said that, in listening
to the debate, what had impressed his mind the most
forcibly was the simplicity of the question. He was
less surprised at the arguments which were urged than
that any argument was necessary. A mere statement
of the case, he should have thought, would have settled
the question. Twenty millions of dollars were said to
be forfeited to the United States, — an amount equal
to one-third of the whole national debt. This sum was
alleged to be due from comparatively a small class of
men, in particular sections of the country, in the cities
and on the seaboard. It was distributed among the
individuals of that class in various proportions. To
every one of them, the amount demanded is material.
The greater part of the fortunes of some is at stake.
To others it is a simple question of prosperity or ruin.
The principles arising out of the case and connected
with the decision are, in their nature, so complicated
and delicate that scarcely two men can be found on the

floor of Congress who can agree by what scale remission shall be graduated, if remitted at all. A case of this magnitude, — so important to the public, so critical to the individuals, so dubious in point of principle, and so consequential in sectional alarm and interest, — it is seriously contended, should be referred to the decision of a single individual ; that one man should be invested with the power to decide the fates of multitudes of his fellow-citizens, and decree riches or poverty, not by any known rule or standard, but according to his absolute will and discretion ! Such is the power seriously contended for, in a country calling itself free, by men who pretend to understand the nature of civil liberty and to venerate its principles ! !

Mr. Quincy said that the nature of the proposition was not more astonishing than the main reason urged in its support. And this was, that the Secretary of the Treasury possessed this power already ; that the law now placed it in its hands. As if the greatness of a power, and its exceeding the trust which any man ought to possess, and its irreconcilableness with the settled principles on which public safety in a free country depends, were not conclusive either that no such power ever was invested, or that the possessor ought to be deprived of it.

Mr. Quincy then proceeded to investigate the general powers vested in the Secretary of the Treasury for the mitigation or remission of fines, penalties, and forfeitures. He contended that no such power was invested in the head of that department as the Secretary had asserted in his letter to the Committee of Ways and Means. In this letter, the Secretary asserts that " the power to remit the share of the United States, and of all other persons, in whole or in part, and on such terms and conditions as may be deemed reasonable and just, is by law vested in the Secretary of the Treasury." Mr. Quincy said that this was nothing less than the assertion of an absolute discretion in relation to the subject-matter, — a discretion without limit, or principle, or measure of control, or rule of decision, except the sovereign will and pleasure of the individual possessing it. For he who can do in relation to any matter or thing, in the whole or in the part, and fix such terms and conditions, as he may deem reasonable and just, has as absolute an authority in that matter or thing as heart can desire. And if, by any general law, such power be invested in any person whatsoever, we have not much to boast, in this respect, either of the wisdom or of the freedom of our laws.

The question, then, is, whether this power, thus asserted to exist in himself by the Secretary of the Treasury, be vested in him by law. Mr. Quincy said that he confessed that, on the first reading of the statute, being under the influence of the opinion thus unequivocally expressed by the Secretary, and not at once perceiving how the terms of law had been wrested to the purposes of official construction, he yielded a momentary, and reluctant assent to the claim of the Secretary. Recollecting, however, what a fascinating thing absolute power is, and how little implicit faith any man has a right to claim in a case where the degree of his power is dependent upon his own construction; recollecting also the character of the men who, in the year 1797, when the law in question was passed, had

the reins of power, he began to doubt of the construction, and set himself carefully to investigate on what
grounds this arbitrary discretion, thus obtrusively asserted by the Secretary as existing in himself, was
founded. He said that the men who, at the time when
the law in question was passed, presided over the construction of our laws were not only learned and able
men and true lovers of their country, but they were
men, also, deeply versed in the principles of civil liberty; they were natives of the soil, and had not been
educated in the arbitrary doctrines of the civil law, but
had drank in the essential principles of the ancient
Saxon common law, as it were, with their mother's
milk. Such men were not likely to grant so enormous
a power, by any general terms, even in an unguarded
moment. For, had reason failed them in a case of this
nature, instinct would have come to their aid. He
determined, therefore, to investigate this question, aloof
from the prejudices which the assertion of the Secretary
of the Treasury, and the corroborative opinion of the
Committee of Ways and Means, had created, and set
himself to examine what were those essential principles
of civil liberty which lay, as it were, at the base of all
statutes of this kind, and which were, in their nature,
so predominant and inherent that no friend of freedom
could possibly forget them when framing such a statute.

Mr. Quincy said that, on turning this subject in his
mind, he had found two principles of the nature which
he sought. The first was, that the innocent should
never be confounded with the guilty: of consequence,
that the law must have been intended to be so constructed as that, as far as possible, the former should

always escape, and the latter should always be punished. The second was, that the object of the penalty was only the enforcement of the provisions of the law ; of consequence, that, when this object was attained, there ought to be an end of the penalty, which was ever to be considered as the sanction or vindicatory branch of the law, and never be perverted to the purposes of the ways and means of the Treasury. When the terms of the statute under consideration were considered in reference to these principles, all doubt as to its true construction vanished. The character of the framers of the law was vindicated. No such power as that asserted by the Secretary of the Treasury, in relation to the subject of the penalties, was vested in him. On the contrary, the real grant of power was precise, limited, and perfectly consistent with the principles of civil liberty.

The law contained two clauses, which comprehended all the powers relative to this subject vested in the Secretary of the Treasury. The words are these. After prescribing the modes by which testimony concerning the circumstances of the case shall be collected and transmitted to the Secretary of the Treasury, the statute proceeds: " Who shall, thereupon, have power to mitigate or remit such fine, forfeiture, or penalty, or remove such disability, or any part thereof, if, in his opinion, the same shall have been incurred without wilful negligence or any intention of fraud in the person or persons incurring the same ; and to direct the prosecution, if any shall have been instituted for the recovery thereof, to cease and be discontinued, upon such terms or conditions as he may deem reasonable and just."

From these clauses in the statute, if from any, the

Secretary of the Treasury derives that unlimited discretion, which he asserts in his letter to the Committee of Ways and Means to be vested in his department. Now these clauses are distinct and substantive, having relation to two objects, also distinct and substantive. The first clause relates to the penalty incurred; the second, to the prosecution commenced.

As to the first clause relative to the penalty, fine, or forfeiture incurred, so far from vesting an unlimited discretionary power, it vests, strictly speaking, no discretion whatever. It is in truth a power to mitigate, remit, or remove, according to a stated and specified statute standard. This authority is to exercise his judgment, upon the circumstances of the case, touching the existence or non-existence of either of two particulars stated in the statute, wilful negligence or fraud. If neither exist, he has the power to remit. If either exist but in a partial degree, he has the power to graduate the penalty, fine, or forfeiture to the degree of guilt. And this is his whole power resulting from this clause. The head of the Treasury is a mere tribunal to decide, whether the statute guilt has been incurred, or any part of it, and according to that judgment to graduate the fine, penalty, or forfeiture. If there be no guilt, his power of mitigation, that is of graduation, is at an end. In such case it cannot be exercised. The single authority he has is to remit altogether. He has no more right to talk of " profits " or " extra profits," or " equivalents," or to intimate boons or " loans," as the grounds of remission, than he has to decree the whole penalty into his own pocket for his private use. The plain purpose of the law is, that guilt should suffer

22

and that innocence should escape. And by guilt and innocence is only meant statute guilt or statute innocence. Whatever is either wilful negligence or fraud is statute guilt. Whatever is neither one nor the other is innocence. It is easy to see how perfectly reconcilable this is to the established principles of civil liberty. Instead of a sharp-scented statesman, invested with powers to hunt among fines, penalties, and forfeitures, for the ways and means of the Treasury, we find only a benignant and wisely constituted tribunal, with power to judge, upon the circumstances of the case, how far any statute guilt has been incurred, and to graduate suffering according to the degree which shall appear.

As to the second clause, relative to the prosecution commenced, there is, indeed a discretion invested in the head of the Treasury. But it is a discretion extremely limited in its nature, arising out of the necessity of the case, extending only to very subordinate considerations, and in the exercise of which there is little or no temptation to abuse. It relates only to the terms and conditions on which he may direct the prosecution to cease. These he is permitted to fix " as he may deem reasonable and just." That such a power is necessary is obvious, because, although the innocent has a right to be free from the imputation and penalty of guilt, yet the costs and expenses which have been incurred is a loss which must fall somewhere. The nature of things has thrown it upon him, and no principle of justice can transfer it to another. But the discretionary power here given is, in the nature of things, extremely limited, and extends only to those particulars which are incident to the prosecution, to costs, expenses and sometimes compensation to custom-house officers for services rendered, either in their seizure or in the care of the property. It is obvious, also, that in exercising such a discretion the danger of abuse is limited, not only from the circumscribed nature of the sphere, but from the circumstances in which it is exercised. He has no official inducement to abuse his power. The particulars which are incident to a prosecution are distinct, notorious, and easily to be ascertained ; and, as to compensation due to the custom-house officer, the Secretary having, by no possibility, any interest, personal or official, in the decision, may safely be intrusted with it ; and ought to be, out of regard to the indemnification of the officer. Here, again, there is no interference with the established principles of civil liberty. The question relative to causing the prosecution to cease has no connection with guilt or innocence. It is merely ascertaining the inevitable loss which he must bear on whom the bolt of heaven has fallen. If a compensation is decreed, it is for the custom-house officer and not the Treasury. It is decreed not as a part of the penalty, for that is incurred only in consequence of guilt, which is in this case out of the question ; but is decreed only as a part of that inevitable loss which some one must bear, and of course he on whom the lot is cast.

When the statute is considered, it will easily be seen what are the means by which the Secretary of the Treasury grasps at this unlimited and arbitrary discretion which he asserts in his letter to the committee. It is by confounding what is distinct, and associating what are separate. By a sort of Treasury amalgam, he consolidates both clauses of the statute into one, and attaches the power of annexing "terms and conditions which he shall deem reasonable and just" to the clause which has relation to the penalty, instead of restricting it to the clause which has relation to the prosecution. This may be a very happy construction for the Treasury, but it is a very ruinous one for the citizen: at least, so it is likely to prove, judging by the proposition now under consideration.

If any one asks why these powers are to be construed as though distinct and substantive, instead of amalgamated and consolidated, I answer on four plain and solid grounds : the terms of the law ; the policy of the law ; the nature of the thing ; and the established principles of civil liberty.

The terms of the law are select and appropriate. Those connected with the remission or mitigation, in whole or in part, not only give the power, but limit the exercise of it by an express statute standard, — he is to do the one or the other, according to the non-existence or the degree of existence of " wilful negligence or intention of fraud." Those connected with the causing the prosecution to cease are equally precise. The power of annexing terms and conditions, such as he may deem reasonable and just, relates to that object, — the causing of the prosecution to cease, — and nothing else.

The policy of the law is not less corroborative of this construction. It is a remedial statute ; as such it must be construed liberally. Its policy is to suffer all the innocent and none of the guilty to escape. For this purpose it has set up a statute standard by which the Secretary is to decide who is innocent and the degree of innocence, and graduate the penalty accordingly.

Therefore it is that the power of affixing conditions is not annexed by the terms of the law to the power of mitigating and remitting. To the degree of statute guilt which a man has incurred, the Secretary is morally bound to punish. But when of this degree there is none, he is then morally bound to acquit. Of " terms and conditions " here there is no use ; for guilt must be punished according to its degree, and innocence must escape. Now the law permits no "terms or conditions " to be made with the innocent; no " equivalent " is asked for not confounding them with the guilty. It is the policy, it is the delight, of the law that they should go free and unspotted, according to their innate purity. ·

The nature of the thing shows also that the power of annexing such " terms and conditions as he may deem reasonable and just " exclusively belongs to the power of causing the prosecution to cease. For, from the nature of the thing, the question concerning causing the prosecution to cease is subordinate in point of importance and secondary in point of time to the question concerning mitigating or remitting the penalty. For whether the decision of the Secretary be guilty of a part or not guilty at all, the Secretary's power is in the same state. It has thus far done its work. The degree of guilt or innocence is ascertained ; the penalty is remitted or graduated. The only remaining prerogative of the Secretary relates to the prosecution. Here he possesses the discretion before noticed. But it is a power which, from the nature of the thing, cannot retroact, and bring again innocence or guilt into view. That is already settled, at least in principle, and must be before the question concerning the prosecution can be agitated.

But there is a stronger argument than all these, resulting from the established principles of civil liberty.
What is the nature of that proud consciousness which
freemen feel and delight to acknowledge? and of what
stuff is it composed? What is it but the certainty with
which each individual is inspired that he holds life, liberty, and property, subject only to known laws and
aloof from the will of any individual? So long as he is
innocent, he has no compromise to make, no equivalent
to offer, no truckling to assume. He on whom any fine,
penalty. or forfeiture of the collection law has fallen by
any mischance or by the act of God, has as much right
to possess this consciousness as the proudest mortal of
us all. He stands before the tribunal of the Secretary
not to chaffer for a pardon. He is innocent. If there
be any portion of the statute guilt, graduate the punishment; but if there be none, cruel, wicked, despotic is
that construction which obliges him to compound for his
escape from a statute framed only to punish guilt; to
pay " profits ; " to make " forced loans ; " to promise
" equivalents." For what? Why, truly that, though
innocent, he should not partake the fate of guilt.

When I speak of innocence and guilt, I mean always
statute innocence or statute guilt. I have nothing to
do with the money dreams of the Secretary of the
Treasury, nor with the day dreams of the gentleman
from Tennessee (Mr. Grundy). He did not pretend,
no man has pretended, no man can pretend, that there
was any intention of fraud or any wilful negligence in
the merchants whose case is now before the House.
But he told us at one time that their crime consisted
" in purchasing in Great Britain ; " at another, that it

consisted " in not co-operating with the policy of the American government." Grant, for argument's sake, all the guilt these charges include. Is that wilful negligence or intention of fraud? Free of this, are they not innocent? Innocent, are they not entitled to entire remission?

This construction for which I contend, I think I can safely state, is conformable to the practice of the Treasury, antecedent to the accession of the present Secretary. At least so it appears, from the book of abstracts of the Treasury, entirely to my satisfaction. Yet, upon this point, I would not be considered as expressing myself with absolute certainty, as I have not had an opportunity to examine the original records of the cases, nor yet to converse with the Secretary of the Treasury, although I have been twice at his office for that purpose. The abstracts of the Treasury, antecedent to that period, do not indicate any thing like a compromise with innocence for the sake of profit to the Treasury. The judgments stated are " remission " or " mitigation " on payment of fees or duties or costs, and sometimes of a sum certain; fifty or a hundred dollars to the revenue officers, or to parties other than the United States. Although I do not conceive the former practice of the Treasury very material on the point, yet it is some satisfaction to state that the early decisions to which I allude seem to be guided by this principle, that the Treasury should never gain any thing from fine, penalty, or forfeiture, except in case of guilt. The first case I could find, although there may have been others antecedent, was that of Robert Gillespie in June, 1802. It was the case of an importation of porter in casks, of less capacity than those required by law. The judgment of the Secretary of the Treasury was: No wilful negligence or fraud; claim of the United States released on payment of costs and one-fourth net proceeds.

Another case was that of Theodoric Armistead, decided in February, 1812. Brandy had been imported in casks of less capacity than required by law. The judgment of the Secretary of the Treasury was: No wilful negligence or fraud; claim of the United States released on payment of costs and charges, and two cents per gallon for the use of the United States. And this levy is expressly stated to be in addition to the duty established by law. Why, Mr. Speaker, what a principle is this? A Secretary of the Treasury declares, in so many words, that the guilt specified in the statute to which the penalty is annexed does not exist, yet mulcts the individual at his discretion as the condition on which innocence is not made subject to the penalty! If the Secretary of the Treasury can lay a tax of "two cents per gallon," why not of twenty; if he can take "one-fourth of the proceeds," according to his arbitrary will, why not the half or the whole? In these cases what has become of that essential principle of civil liberty, that innocence and guilt shall never be confounded? Both Gillespie and Armistead, though clear by the statute, have gone away from the legal tribunal taxed by the Secretary. I dare say it will be said, they were both satisfied. Doubtless, sir. The Secretary had resolved himself into an arbitrary tribunal, and what private individual dare question the opinion of the Secretary? But it is the business of the legislature to consider subjects in their principles and consequences, and not by the convenience of this or that individual. The importance of withstanding the beginnings of oppressive encroachments could never be better illustrated than by the instances before us. These, and cases like these, were the nest-eggs of the Treasury; and now we see what a monstrous brood is likely to be produced. The Secretary has gone on, year after year, exercising an arbitrary discretion in cases of small amount and affecting individuals only, till at last he starts up a gigantic power, authorized to carve what he pleases out of twenty millions of dollars, and to settle the destinies of a whole class of citizens! If doctrines and constructions like these are to receive the sanction of this legislature, come, Bonaparte, as soon as thou wilt, and thou shalt find cabinet principles suited to all thy purposes!

I have hitherto considered the case of the merchants' bonds as though it were strictly within the principle of the collection laws. And the bearing of my argument has been this, — that if no such power as is asserted by the Secretary is truly vested in him, in the cases of the ordinary revenue, that much less ought he to be permitted to exercise this most dangerous power in cases of so much magnitude, and in all aspects so critical, as are those under consideration. But is it true that the fines, penalties, and forfeitures, accruing under the restrictive system, have no other claims for relief than those general ones which arise under the collection laws? Alas, sir! the nature of these laws are such as to make those claims far higher and more impressive.

I shall touch this subject of the restrictive system with as much delicacy as possible. I wish not to offend any prejudices. I know that the zeal and ardent affection which some gentlemen show for this restrictive system very much resemble the loves of those who, according to ancient legends, had taken philtres and love-powders. The ecstasy of desire is just in proportion to the deformity of the object. I shall not, however, meddle with that topic any further than it is connected with the subject before the House.

A great deal is said about the policy of the restrictive system, and the necessity of a rigorous enforcement of it. Now it appears to me that the desire to make this system effectual ought to induce the release of these bonds, and not their enforcement. The object of the restrictive system is averred to be to produce a change in the measures of the British cabinet by the suffering which the loss of our commerce occasions to her citizens. If this be the policy, then those measures are beyond all question the best calculated to insure its success whose tendency is to diminish the suffering as far as possible of the citizens of your own country. The best chance for success must necessarily be by convincing the thinking part of the community in Great Britain that, while they suffer much, we suffer little or nothing. Were such the case, then indeed the system might have some hope of a prosperous result. But, when suffering there is found to be attended with suffering here, then the whole potency of the restrictive system results in this question, — which can suffer the most, or which can bear suffering the best. And what judgment will the people of that country be likely to form, in relation to the degree this people suffer or their capacity to endure, when a sweep of twenty millions of dollars is seriously advocated by some ; and when a majority seem inclined

to turn the penalties of the restrictive system, not into
a mean of punishment of fraudulent or wilful violations,
but into an instrument of ways and means of the Treasury? Does it need any ghost from the dead, or seer
from the skies, to tell the people of Great Britain that,
in a free country, such a system of oppression must be
short-lived, and that its supporters must soon become
detested? So that, if the policy of the system be con-
sulted, it requires that its rigor should be softened as it
respects your own citizens.

But are there not other considerations materially dis-
tinguishing the character of the restrictive system from
that of your collection laws, and requiring a correspondent mildness in the construction of the laws relative to
the former which the latter cannot claim? Concerning
the constitutional power of the national legislature to
pass the laws of collection, there never was any question.
But concerning its power, under the Constitution, to
pass such a body of laws as those which compose the
restrictive system, there always has been, there is, and
ever will be, a question. A very great majority in all
the commercial States always have denied that the
power of regulating commerce included the power of
annihilating it altogether. They believe nothing in the
project; and they believe as little in your right to con-
vert their only means of prosperity to the purposes of
hostility. They ever will deny that any power is vested
in this or any other body of men to bring down direct
and certain ruin on the whole commercial section of the
country under pretence of producing an indirect and
uncertain pressure upon a foreign nation. Surely this
is a reason for a mild exercise of the power arising under

these restrictive laws. If a right be dubious, the exercise of it ought not to be made more obnoxious by oppression.

Not only the authority is dubious, but the provisions of the law outrage every received notion of legislative prudence and foresight. They " outherod Herod." In six years Congress have passed twenty laws creating at least one hundred new offences. These offences are constituted of acts, previously not only innocent, but laudable ; not only laudable, but they were the most common and necessary acts of whole sections of country and whole classes of men. These new offences subject the offenders to the most grievous penalties, fines, and forfeitures, known to the revenue laws ; and are involved in such a complexity of enactments, re-enactments, pro- visions, proclamations, whole revocations and half revo- cations, that no man under heaven can tell when he is safe, or how or where to steer his course, without being meshed in the web spread for him by your statutes. Some idea may be had of the degree of oppression added to these penal laws, by the restrictive system, from comparing the applications for remission antecedent to the commencement of that system with those subse- quent to it. Antecedent to the 19th of April, 1806, when your restrictive system commenced, all the appli- cations for remission in the fifteen previous years amounted to somewhat short of thirteen hundred. In the six years the restrictive system has been in opera- tion, there have been nine hundred and fifty-four, and, if to these be added those known at the department and not yet acted upon, the whole number exceeds one thousand. So that the annual average of applications for remission, since the restrictive system, is double the annual average of applications antecedent to that period. In other words, you have doubled the number of the snares of the law, and the cries of its victims are heard in a double proportion. Do you think that, when the web of the law is thus extended beyond all reason and precedent, you can strain its penalties to the extremest rigor of the statute without public sentiment revolting against you? Is it in human nature to see its fellow struggling innocently in the toils of unnatural laws, without coming to its aid and taking vengeance on its persecutors?

I know it will be said that it is not proposed to confiscate the whole, but only a part. In other words, you will take not all that you want, but all that you dare. To this I reply, You have no right to a single dollar, not to a cent. The merchants are free of all legal taint. They are free from all statute guilt. There is in the case neither " wilful negligence nor fraud." The Secretary of the Treasury does not pretend either. But this is his situation, and this is the secret of his application to Congress for their sanction to his exercise of this great discretionary power. Confiscate the whole of this immense amount, ruin hundreds and thousands on account of the breach of the letter of a penal statute, he dare not. Mitigate, upon any principle which would aid the Treasury in its necessities, he could not. He therefore transfers the whole matter to the broad shoulders of the legislature ; talks about " the magnitude and unforeseen nature of the case ; " asserts roundly an unlimited discretion existing in his department; tells of " profits and extra profits " made by the merchants ; of the " tax levied " by them on the community ; and sums up the whole matter with a hint that " it was thought proper not to exercise his authority until Congress had taken the subject into consideration, and prescribed, if they thought proper, the course to be pursued." Well, sir, and what do we witness now that the subject is before Congress ? Why, we see every friend of the Secretary, every man who is supposed to be in his particular confidence, advocating that Congress " should think proper to prescribe no course whatever to be pursued," but refer the whole to the absolute discretion of the Secretary. Can any man witness all this and not understand the meaning ? To my ear it is as plain as though he uttered it in so many words on this floor : " The poverty of the Treasury and not my will consents. If Congress will take the odium and the risk, I will take the knife and the flesh, and I will cut where and just as much as you shall authorize."

I shall not be able to speak upon this subject, I fear, without offending the nice sensibilities of some gentlemen in the House. Of late an opinion seems to be gaining ground upon this floor that a member cannot denominate a doctrine or principle to be base or wicked without attributing those qualities to those who may have happened to advocate such doctrine or principle ; and this, too, notwithstanding he expressly declares that he has no intention of applying attributes to such persons, nor even intimating that their view is the same with his own upon the subject. I protest, sir, against such a restriction of the rights of debate as totally inconsistent with the necessary freedom of public investigation. It is not only the right but it is the duty of every man to whose moral perception any thing proposed or asserted seems base or wicked to brand such proposition or assertion with its appropriate epithet. He owes this duty not only to the public, but to the individual who has been unfortunate or mistaken enough to advocate such an opinion or make such assertion. And provided he does this as the state of his own perception on the subject, and without attributing motives or similar perceptions of the thing to others, not only there is no reasonable ground of offence, but, on the contrary, such a course is the only one reconcilable with duty. How else shall the misguided or mistaken be roused from their moral lethargy or blindness to a sense of the real condition or nature of things? What mortal has an intellect so clear as not sometimes to have his view of things doubtful or obscure? Whose moral standard is so fixed and perfect as that it never fails him at the moment of need? If, after these explanations, any person takes an exception at the statement of my perceptions on this subject, and any hot humor should fly out into vapor upon the occasion, — it has its liberty, — I shall regard it no more than " the snapping of a chestnut in a farmer's fire."

I say, then, Mr. Speaker, that to my view, — let it be understood, sir, I do not assert that it is even the true view, much less that it is the view of any gentleman who advocates an opposite doctrine, — I say that to my view, and for my single self, I would as soon be concerned in a highway robbery as in this Treasury attempt. Sir, I think a highway robbery a little higher in point of courage, and a little less in point of iniquity. In point of courage there is obviously no comparison. In point of the quality of the moral purpose, the robber who puts his pistol to your breast only uses his power to get your property. He attacks nothing but your person. But in this Treasury attempt the reputation of the victim is to be attacked to make an apology for confiscating his property. Guilt is alleged, — guilt, of which he is clear by the terms of the law, — for the purpose of making him, though innocent, compound for escaping the penalty. What is this but making calumny the basis of plunder?

This is not the view of a solitary individual. I have letters on this subject from men not merchants, nor, as I am apprised, particularly connected with the mercantile class, whose language is perfectly similar to that I have expressed. Indeed, sir, some exceed even these expressions in bitterness and indignation. Men look very differently at a question of this kind when they are removed a thousand miles from the sufferers, and see the principle through the fascinating medium of Treasury relief, than when they stand by the side of the victims, and see distress and ruin entailed upon innocence, or, what in a moral view is worse, witness innocence compelled to compound for mercy as though it were guilt!

I have been told, sir, that this state of opinion ought to be concealed; that it was calculated to offend. I have been also told that we on this side of the House ought not to take any part in this debate; that a party current would be made to set upon the question, and this to the merchants was inevitable ruin. To all this I have but one answer. My sense of duty allows no compromise on this occasion nor any concealment. I stand not on this floor as a commercial agent, huckstering for a bargain. As one of the representatives of the people of Massachusetts, I maintain the rights of these men, not because they are merchants, but because they are citizens. The standard by which their rights are proposed to be measured may be made the common standard for us all. There will soon be no safety for any man, if fines, penalties, and forfeitures be once established as the ways and means of the Treasury.

If I could wish that evil might be done that good might result, I should hope that you would confiscate the property of these merchants. If such a disposition really prevails in the national legislature towards this class of men, it is desirable that it should be known. Act out your whole character. Show the temper which is in you. The sooner will the people of the commercial States understand what they owe to themselves and to their section of country when there is no longer any veil over the purposes of the cabinet and its supporters.

But, it will be asked, what will become in the mean time of the individuals whose whole fortunes are at stake ? Trembling for the prospects of themselves and their families, they stand, like thrice-knouted Russians, before the Treasury czar and autocrat. I say, sir, let them be true to themselves and true to their class and true to their country, and they have nothing to fear. Let them remember that it is under the pretexts of law that all tyranny makes its advances. It bribes the avarice of the many to permit it to oppress the few. It talks of necessity, — necessity, the beggar's cloak, the tyrant's plea. Let the merchants refuse all compromise,

23

whether in the shape of loans or of equivalents or of com-
mutation for extra profits.   Let them scorn, while innocent, to pay any part of a penalty which is due only in
case of guilt; fly to the States, and claim their constitutional interposition ;   interest their humanity to
afford a shield against so grievous a tyranny; above
all, let them throw themselves upon the moral sentiment of the community, which will never countenance,
when once made to realize the nature of, the oppression.
And let this be their consolation that, as in the natural
so it is often in the moral and political world, the dark-
est hour of the night is that which precedes the first
dawning of the day.

SPEECH

ON THE INVASION OF CANADA.

JAN. 5, 1813.

SPEECH

ON THE INVASION OF CANADA.

Jan. 5, 1813.

[This speech, with which I shall conclude this collection, was one of the most effective — the most so, probably, unless with the exception of the one on the Admission of Louisiana — that Mr. Quincy ever delivered. It came at the moment when party spirit raged the most furiously ; and it certainly did not have, nor did it propose to have, any tendency to calm its violence. In his old age he declared that he stood by it in its substance and in its form, and that " he shrunk not from the judgment of after-times." And he had no reason to do so. Keen as is its invective, bitter as is its sarcasm, and severe and heavy as are its denunciations, the facts on which all these rest are clearly stated and fully sustained. It was this, indeed, which gave them their force and their sting and aroused the rage of the friends of the administration to the height of fury. For three or four days Mr. Quincy and his speech formed the object of the attack and denunciation of the democratic speakers, with Mr. Clay, who left the Speaker's chair for the purpose, at their head. But these things moved him not, or were accepted as unwilling testimonies to the strength of the position he had taken up. Though most sensitive to any thing that could affect his true honor and real reputation, Mr. Quincy was singularly indifferent to all attacks made upon him in Congress or by the press, which he knew were not deserved. No one was ever more scrupulously careful to make sure that his words and actions, as a public man, were exactly true and just, and none more unaffectedly indifferent as to what was thought or said of the one or the other by friend or foe. — ED.]

MR. SPEAKER, — I fear that the state of my health may prevent my doing justice to my sentiments concerning this bill. I will, however, make the attempt, though I should fail in it.

The bill proposes that twenty thousand men should be added to the existing military establishment. This, at present, consists of thirty-five thousand men. So that the effect of this bill is to place at the disposal of the executive an army of fifty-five thousand. It is not pretended that this addition is wanted either for defence or for the relief of the Indian frontier. On the contrary, it is expressly acknowledged that the present establishment is sufficient for both of those objects. But the purpose for which these twenty thousand men are demanded is the invasion of Canada. This is unequivocally avowed by the Chairman of the Committee of Foreign Relations (Mr. D. R. Williams), the organ, as is admitted, of the will and the wishes of the American cabinet.

The bill brings necessarily into deliberation the conquest of Canada, either as an object in itself desirable, or inferentially advantageous by its effect in producing an early and honorable peace.

Before I enter upon the discussion of those topics which naturally arise from this state of the subject, I will ask your indulgence for one moment, while I make a few remarks upon this intention of the American cabinet, thus unequivocally avowed. I am induced to this from the knowledge which I have that this design is not deemed to be serious by some men of both political parties, as well within this House as out of it. I know that some of the friends of the present administration do consider the proposition as a mere feint, made for the purpose of putting a good face upon things, and of strengthening the hope of a successful negotiation by exciting the apprehensions of the British cabinet for the fate of their colonies. I know, also, that some of those who are opposed in political sentiment to the men who are now at the head of affairs laugh at these schemes of invasion, and deem them hardly worth controversy, on account of their opinion of the imbecility of the American cabinet and the embarrassment of its resources.

I am anxious that no doubt should exist upon this subject, either in the House or in the nation. Whoever considers the object of this bill to be any other than that which has been avowed is mistaken. Whoever believes this bill to be a means of peace, or any thing else than an instrument of vigorous and long-protracted war, is grievously deceived. And whoever acts under such mistake or such deception will have to lament one of the grossest, and perhaps one of the most critical, errors of his political life. I warn, therefore, my political opponents — those honest men, of which I know there are some who, paying only a general attention to the course of public affairs, submit the guidance of their opinions to the men who stand at the helm — not to vote for this bill under any belief that its object is to aid negotiation for peace. Let such gentlemen recur to their past experience on similar occasions. They will find that it has been always the case, whenever any obnoxious measure is about to be passed, that its passage is assisted by the aid of some such collateral suggestions. No sooner do the cabinet perceive that any potion which they intend to administer is loathed by a considerable part of the majority, and that their apprehensions are alive lest it should have a scouring effect upon their popularity, than certain under-operators are set to work, whose business it is to amuse the minds and beguile the attention of the patients while the dose is swallowing. The language always is, " Trust the cabinet doctors. The medicine will not operate as you imagine, but quite another way." After this manner the fears of men are allayed, and the purposes of the administration are attained under suggestions very different from the true motives. Thus the embargo, which has since been unequivocally acknowledged to have been intended to coerce Great Britain, was adopted, as the executive asserted, " to save our essential resources." So also, when the present war was declared against Great Britain, members of the House were known to state that they voted for it under the suggestion that it would not be a war of ten days; that it was known that Mr. Foster had instructions to make definitive arrangements in his pocket; and that the United States had only to advance to the point of war, and the whole business would be settled. And now an army which in point of numbers Cromwell might envy, greater than that with which Cæsar passed the Rubicon, is to be helped through a reluctant Congress, under the suggestion of its being only a parade force, to make negotiation successful; that it is the incipient state of a project for a grand pacification!

I warn also my political friends. These gentlemen
are apt to place great reliance on their own intelligence
and sagacity. Some of these will tell you that the
invasion of Canada is impossible. They ask where are
the men, where is the money, to be obtained? And
they talk very wisely concerning common-sense and
common prudence, and will show with much learning
how this attempt is an offence against both the one and
the other. But, sir, it has been my lot to be an observer
of the character and conduct of the men now in power,
for these eight years past. And I state without hesitation that no scheme ever was, or ever will be, rejected
by them merely on account of its running counter to
the ordinary dictates of common-sense and common
prudence. On the contrary, on that very account, I
believe, it more likely to be both suggested and adopted
by them. And — what may appear a paradox — for
that very reason the chance is rather increased that
it will be successful.

I could illustrate this position twenty ways. I shall
content myself with remarking only upon two instances,
and those recent, — the present war, and the late invasion of Canada. When war against Great Britain was
proposed at the last session, there were thousands in
these United States — and, I confess to you, I was myself
among the number — who believed not one word of the
matter. I put my trust in the old-fashioned notions of
common-sense and common prudence. That a people
which has been more than twenty years at peace should
enter upon hostilities against a people which had been
twenty years at war; that a nation whose army and
navy were little more than nominal should engage in

war with a nation possessing one of the best appointed
armies and the most powerful marine on the globe; that
a country to which neutrality had been a perpetual harvest should throw that great blessing away for a controversy in which nothing was to be gained and every
thing valuable put in jeopardy, — from these and innumerable like considerations the idea seemed so absurd
that I never once entertained it as possible. And now,
after war has been declared, the whole affair seems so
extraordinary, and so utterly irreconcilable to any previous suggestions of wisdom and duty, that I know not
what to make of it or how to believe it. Even at this
moment my mind is very much in the state of certain
Pennsylvanian Germans, of whom I have heard it
asserted that they are taught to believe by their political leaders, and do at this moment consider, the allegation that war is at present existing between the United
States and Great Britain to be a "federal falsehood."

It was just so with respect to the invasion of Canada.
I heard of it last June. I laughed at the idea, as did
multitudes of others, as an attempt too absurd for
serious examination. I was in this case, again, beset
by common-sense and common prudence. That the
United States should precipitate itself upon the unoffending people of that neighboring colony, unmindful
of all previously subsisting amities, because the parent
state, three thousand miles distant, had violated some
of our commercial rights; that we should march inland
to defend our ships and seamen; that, with raw troops,
hastily collected, miserably appointed, and destitute of
discipline, we should invade a country defended by
veteran forces, at least equal in point of numbers to the

invading army; that bounty should be offered, and
proclamations issued, inviting the subjects of a foreign
power to treason and rebellion under the influences of a
quarter of the country upon which a retort of the same
nature was so obvious, so easy, and in its consequences
so awful, — in every aspect, the design seemed so
fraught with danger and disgrace that it appeared
absolutely impossible that it should be seriously entertained. Those, however, who reasoned after this manner
were, as the event proved, mistaken. The war was
declared. Canada was invaded. We were in haste to
plunge into these great difficulties, and we have now
reason, as well as leisure enough, for regret and re-
pentance.

The great mistake of all those who reasoned concerning the war and the invasion of Canada, and concluded
that it was impossible that either should be seriously
intended, resulted from this, that they never took into
consideration the connection of both those events with
the great election for the chief magistracy which was
then pending. It never was sufficiently considered by
them that plunging into war with Great Britain was
among the conditions on which support for the presidency was made dependent. They did not understand
that an invasion of Canada was to be, in truth, only a
mode of carrying on an electioneering campaign. But,
since events have explained political purposes, there is
no difficulty in seeing the connections between projects
and interests. It is now apparent to the most mole-
sighted how a nation may be disgraced, and yet a cabinet attain its desired honors. All is clear. A country
may be ruined in making an administration happy.

I said, Mr. Speaker, that such strange schemes, apparently irreconcilable to common-sense and common prudence, were on that very account, more likely to be successful. Sir, there is an audacity which sometimes stands men instead both of genius and strength. And most assuredly he is most likely to perform that which no man ever did before, and will never be likely to do again, who has the boldness to undertake that which no man ever thought of attempting in time past, and no man will ever think of attempting in time future. I would not, however, be understood as intimating that this cabinet project of invasion is impracticable, either as it respects the 'collection of means and instruments or in the ultimate result. On the contrary, sir, I deem both very feasible. Men may be obtained. For if forty dollars bounty cannot obtain them, a hundred dollars bounty may, and the intention is explicitly avowed not to suffer the attainment of the desired army to be prevented by any vulgar notions of economy. Money may be obtained. What by means of the increased popularity derived from the augmentation of the navy, what by opening subscription offices in the interior of the country, what by large premiums, the cupidity of the moneyed interest may be tempted beyond the point of patriotic resistance, and all the attained means being diverted to the use of the army, pecuniary resources may be obtained, ample at least for the first year. And, sir, let an army of thirty thousand men be collected, let them be put under the command of a popular leader, let them be officered to suit his purposes, let them be flushed with victories and see the fascinating career of military glory opening upon them, and they will not thereafter ever be deficient in resources. If they cannot obtain their pay by your votes, they will collect it by their own bayonets; and they will not rigidly observe any air-lines or water-lines in enforcing their necessary levies, nor be stayed by abstract speculations concerning right, or learned constitutional difficulties.

I desire, therefore, that it may be distinctly understood, both by this House and this nation, that it is my unequivocal belief that the invasion of Canada, which is avowed by the cabinet to be its purpose, is intended by it, — that continuance of the war and not peace is its project. Yes, sir, as the French Emperor said concerning ships and colonies, so our cabinet, the friends of the French Emperor, may say, with respect to Canada and Halifax, — "They enter into the scope of its policy."

[Mr. Quincy was here called to order by Mr. Hall, of Georgia, for intimating that the members of the cabinet were friends of the French Emperor.

MR. QUINCY said that he understood that the relations of amity did subsist between this country and France, and that in such a state of things he had a right to speak of the American cabinet as the friends of France, in the same manner as he had now a right to call them the enemies of Great Britain.

The SPEAKER said that the relations of amity certainly did subsist between this country and France, and that he did not conceive the gentleman from Massachusetts to be out of order in his expressions; that it was impossible to prevent gentlemen from expressing themselves so as to convey an innuendo.]

Mr. Quincy proceeded : If, Mr. Speaker, the gentleman from Georgia and his political friends would take
one thing into consideration, he and they will have no
reason to complain in case the cabinet be of that im-
maculate nature he supposes. No administration, no
man, was ever materially injured by any mere "innuendo." The strength of satire is the justness of the
remark, and the only sting of invective is the truth of
the observation.

I will now proceed to discuss those topics which
naturally arise out of the bill under consideration and
examine the proposed invasion of Canada at three different points of view.

1. As a means of carrying on the existing war.

2. As a means of obtaining an early and honorable
peace.

3. As a means of advancing the personal and local
projects of ambition of the members of the American
cabinet.

Concerning the invasion of Canada as a means of
carrying on the subsisting war, it is my duty to speak
plainly and decidedly, not only because I herein express
my own opinions upon the subject, but, as I conscien-
tiously believe, the sentiments also of a very great
majority of that whole section of country in which I
have the happiness to reside. I say, then, sir, that I
consider the invasion of Canada as a means of carrying
on this war as cruel, wanton, senseless, and wicked.

You will easily understand, Mr. Speaker, by this very
statement of opinion, that I am not one of that class of
politicians which has for so many years predominated in
the world, on both sides of the Atlantic. You will

readily believe that I am not one of those who worship
in that temple where Condorcet is the high priest, and
Machiavel the God.   With such politicians the end
always sanctifies the means; the least possible good to
themselves perfectly justifies, according to their creed,
the inflicting the greatest possible evil upon others.   In
the judgment of such men, if a corrupt ministry, at
three thousand miles distance, shall have done them an
injury, it is an ample cause to visit with desolation a
peaceable and unoffending race of men, their neighbors, who happen to be associated with that ministry by
ties of mere political dependence.   What though these
colonies be so remote from the sphere of the questions
in controversy that their ruin or prosperity could have
no possible influence upon the result?   What though
their cities offer no plunder?   What though their conquest can yield no glory?   In their ruin there is revenge;
and revenge to such politicians is the sweetest of all
morsels.   With such men neither I, nor the people
of that section of country in which I reside, hold any
communion.   There is, between us and them, no one
principle of sympathy, either in motive or action.

That wise, moral, reflecting people which constitute
the great mass of the population of Massachusetts,
indeed of all New England, look for the sources of their
political duties nowhere else than in those fountains
from which spring their moral duties.   According to
their estimate of human life and its obligations, both
political and moral duties emanate from the nature of
things, and from the essential and eternal relations
which subsist among them.   True it is that a state of
war gives the right to seize and appropriate the property

and territories of an enemy. True it is that the colonies of a foreign power are viewed, according to the law of nations, in the light of its property. But in estimating the propriety of carrying desolation into the peaceful abodes of their neighbors, the people of New England will not limit their contemplation to the mere circumstance of abstract right, nor ask what lawyers and jurisprudists have written or said, as if this was conclusive upon the subject. That people are much addicted to think for themselves, and, in canvassing the propriety of such an invasion, they will consider the actual condition of those colonies, their natural relations to us, and the effect which their conquest and ruin will have, not only upon the people of those colonies, but upon themselves, and their own liberties and constitution. And, above all, what I know will seem strange to some of those who hear me, they will not forget to apply to a case occurring between nations, as far as is practicable, that heaven-descended rule which the great Author and Founder of their religion has given them for the regulation of their conduct towards each other. They will consider it the duty of these United States to act towards those colonies as they would wish those colonies to act in exchange of circumstances towards these United States.

The actual condition of those colonies, and the relation in which they stood to the United States antecedent to the declaration of war, were of this nature. Those colonies had no connection with the questions in dispute between us and their parent state. They had done us no injury. They meditated none to us. Between the inhabitants of those colonies and the citizens of the United States the most friendly and mutually useful intercourse subsisted.   The borderers on this and those on the other side of the St. Lawrence and of the boundary line scarcely realized that they were subjects of different governments.   They interchanged expressions and acts of civility.   Intermarriages took place among them.   The Canadians sometimes settled in the United States.   Sometimes our citizens emigrated to Canada.   After the declaration of war, had they any disposition to assail us ?   We have the reverse expressly in evidence.   They desired nothing so much as to keep perfect the then subsisting relations of amity.   Would the conquest of those colonies shake the policy of the British Cabinet ?   No man has shown it.   Unqualified assertions, it is true, have been made, but totally unsupported by any evidence or even the pretence of argument.   On the contrary, nothing was more obvious than that an invasion of Canada must strengthen the ministry of Great Britain by the excitement and sympathy which would be occasioned in the people of that country, in consequence of the sufferings of the innocent inhabitants of those colonies on account of a dispute in which they had no concern and of which they had scarcely a knowledge.   All this was anticipated.   All this was frequently urged to this House, at the last and preceding sessions, as the necessary effect of such a measure.   The event has justified those predictions.   The late elections in Great Britain have terminated in the complete triumph of the friends of the British ministry.   In effecting this change, the conduct of these United States in relation to Canada has had undeniably a mighty influence by the disgust and indignation felt by the British people at a step so apparently wanton and cruel.

24

As there was no direct advantage to be hoped from the conquest of Canada, so also there was none incidental. Plunder there was none; at least none which would pay the cost of the conquest. Glory there was none. Could seven millions of people obtain glory by precipitating themselves upon half a million and trampling them into the dust? a giant obtain glory by crushing a pigmy! That giant must have a pigmy's spirit who could reap or hope glory from such an achievement.

Surely a people with whom we were connected by so many natural and adventitious ties had some claims upon our humanity. Surely, if our duty required that they and theirs should be sacrificed to our interests or our passions, some regret mingled in the execution of the purpose. We postponed the decree of ruin until the last moment. We hesitated, we delayed, until longer delay was dangerous. Alas, sir! there was nothing of this kind or character in the conduct of the cabinet. The war had not yet been declared when General Hull had his instructions to put in train the work of destruction. There was an eagerness for the blood of the Canadians, a headlong precipitation for their ruin, which indicated any thing else rather than feelings of humanity or visitings of nature on account of their condition. Our armies were on their march for their frontier, while yet peace existed between this country and the parent State; and the invasion was obstinately pursued after a knowledge that the chief ground of controversy was settled by the abandonment of the British Orders in Council, and after nothing remained but a stale ground of dispute, which, however important in itself,

was of a nature for which no man has ever yet pretended
that for it alone war would have been declared. Did
ever one government exhibit towards any people a more
bloody and relentless spirit of rancor? Tell not me of
petty advantages, of remote and possibly useful contingencies, which might arise from the devastation of those
colonies. Show any advantage which justifies that
dreadful vial of wrath, which, if the intention of the
American cabinet had been fulfilled, would at this day
have been poured out upon the heads of the Canadians.
It is not owing to the tender mercies of the American
administration if the bones of the Canadians are not at
this hour mingled with the ashes of their habitations.
It is easy enough to make an excuse for any purpose.
When a victim is destined to be immolated, every hedge
presents sticks for the sacrifice. The lamb who stands
at the mouth of the stream will always trouble the
water, if you take the account of the wolf who stands
at the source of it. But show a good to us bearing
any proportion to the multiplied evils proposed to be
visited upon them. There is none. Never was there
an invasion of any country worse than this, in point of
moral principle, since the invasion of the West Indies
by the buccaneers, or that of these United States by
Captain Kidd. Indeed, both Kidd and the buccaneers
had more apology for their deed than the American
cabinet. They had at least the hope of plunder. But
in this case there is not even the poor refuge of cupidity.
We have heard great lamentations about the disgrace of
our arms on the frontier. Why, sir, the disgrace of our
arms on the frontier is terrestrial glory in comparison
with the disgrace of the attempt. The whole atmos-

phere rings with the utterance, from the other side of
the House, of this word, " Glory, glory," in connection
with this invasion.   What glory? Is it the glory of the
tiger, which lifts his jaws, all foul and bloody, from the
bowels of his victim, and roars for his companions of
the wood to come and witness his prowess and his
spoils?   Such is the glory of Genghis Khan and of
Bonaparte.   Be such glory far, very far, from my country.   Never, never may it be accursed with such fame.

> " Fame is no plant that grows on mortal soil,
>   Nor in the glistering foil
>   Set off to the world, nor in broad rumor lies;
>   But lives and spreads aloft by those pure eyes
>   And perfect witness of all-judging Jove,
>   As he pronounces lastly on each deed."
> May such fame as this be my country's meed!

But the wise and thoughtful people of our northern
section will not confine their reflections to the duties
which result from the actual condition of those colonies
and their general relations to the United States.   They
will weigh the duties the people of the United States
owe to themselves, and contemplate the effect which the
subjugation of those Canadians will have upon our own
liberties and Constitution.   Sir, it requires but little
experience in the nature of the human character, and
but a very limited acquaintance with the history of
man, to be satisfied that with the conquest of the
Canadas the liberties and Constitution of this country
perish.

Of all nations in the world this nation is the last
which ought to admit among its purposes the design of
foreign conquests.   States such as are these, connected

by ties so peculiar, into whose combination there enters necessarily numerous jealousies and fears, whose interests are not always reconcilable, and the passions, education, and character of whose people on many accounts are repugnant to each other, with a Constitution made merely for defence, it is impossible that an association of independent sovereignties, standing in such relations to each other, should not have the principles of its Union and the hopes of its Constitution materially affected by the collection of a large military force, and its employment in the subjugation of neighboring territories.   It is easy to see that an army collected in such a state of society as that which exists in this country, where wages are high and subsistence easily to be obtained, must be composed, so far as respects the soldiery, for the most part of the refuse of the country; and, as it respects the officers, — with some honorable exceptions, indeed, — must consist in a considerable degree of men desperate sometimes in fortune, at others in reputation, "choice spirits," men "tired of the dull pursuits of civil life," who have not virtue or talents to rise in a calm and settled state of things, and who, all other means of advancement or support wanting or failing, take to the sword. A body of thirty or fifty thousand such men combined, armed and under a popular leader, is a very formidable force.   They want only discipline and service to make them veterans.   Opportunity to acquire these Canada will afford.   The army which advances to the walls of Quebec, in the present condition of Canadian preparation, must be veteran.   And a veteran army under a popular leader, flushed with victory, each individual realizing that while the body remains combined he may be something, and possibly very great, that if dissolved he sinks into insignificance, will not be disbanded by vote. They will consult with one another, and with their beloved chieftain upon this subject, and not trouble themselves about the advice of the old people who are knitting and weaving in the chimney-corners at Washington. Let the American people receive this as an undoubted truth which experience will verify : whoever plants the American standard on the walls of Quebec conquers it for himself, and not for the people of these United States. Whoever lives to see that event — may my head be low in the dust before it happen ! — will witness a dynasty established in that country by the sword. He will see a king or an emperor, dukedoms and earldoms and baronies distributed to the officers, and knights' fees bestowed on the soldiery. And such an army will not trouble itself about geographical lines in portioning out the divisions of its new empire, and will run the parallels of its power by other steel than that of the compass. When that event happens, the people of New England, if they mean to be free, must have a force equal to defend themselves against such an army. And a military force equal to this object will itself be able to enslave the country.

Mr. Speaker, when I contemplate the character and consequences of this invasion of Canada, when I reflect upon its criminality and its danger to the peace and liberty of this once happy country, I thank the great Author and Source of all virtue that, through his grace, that section of country in which I have the happiness to reside is in so great a degree free from the iniquity of this transgression. I speak it with pride : the people of that section have done what they could to vindicate themselves and their children from the burden of this sin.   That whole section has risen, almost as one man, for the purpose of driving from power by one great constitutional effort the guilty authors of this war.   If they have failed, it has been, not through the want of will or of exertion, but in consequence of the weakness of their political power.   When in the usual course of divine providence, who punishes nations as well as individuals, his destroying angel shall on this account pass over this country, — and, sooner or later, pass it will, — I may be permitted to hope that over New England his hand will be stayed.   Our souls are not steeped in the blood which has been shed in this war.   The spirits of the unhappy men who have been sent to an untimely audit have borne to the bar of divine justice no accusations against us.

This opinion concerning the principle of this invasion of Canada is not peculiar to me.   Multitudes who approve the war detest it.   I believe this sentiment is entertained, without distinction of parties, by almost all the moral sense and nine-tenths of the intelligence of the whole northern section of the United States.   I know that men from that quarter of the country will tell you differently.   Stories of a very different kind are brought by all those who come trooping to Washington for place, appointments, and emoluments ; men who will say any thing to please the ear, or do any thing to please the eye, of Majesty, for the sake of those fat contracts and gifts which it scatters ; men whose fathers, brothers, and cousins are provided for by the departments ; whose full-grown children are at suck at the money-distilling breasts of the Treasury; the little men who sigh after great offices; those who have judgeships in hand or judgeships in promise; toads that live upon the vapor of the palace; that stare and wonder at all the fine sights which they see there, and most of all wonder at themselves, — how they got there to see them. These men will tell you that New England applauds this invasion.

But, Mr. Speaker, look at the elections. What is the language they speak? The present tenant of the chief magistracy rejected by that whole section of country, with the exception of a single State, unanimously. And for whom? In favor of a man, out of the circle of his own State, without much influence and personally almost unknown: in favor of a man against whom the prevailing influences in New England had previously strong political prejudices; and with whom, at the time of giving him their support, they had no political understanding: in favor of a man whose merits, whatever in other respects they might be, were brought into notice in the first instance, chiefly, so far as that election was concerned, by their opinion of the utter want of merit of the man whose re-election they opposed.

Among the causes of that universal disgust which pervaded all New England at the administration and its supporters was the general dislike and contempt of this invasion of Canada. I have taken some pains to learn the sentiments which prevail on this subject in New England, and particularly among its yeomanry, the pride and the hope of that country. I have conversed with men, resting on their spades and leaning on the handles of their ploughs, while they relaxed for a moment from the labor by which they support their families, and which gives such a hardihood and character to their virtues. They asked, "What do we want of Canada? We have land enough. Do we want plunder? There is not enough of that to pay the cost of getting it. Are our ocean rights there? or is it there our seamen are held in captivity? Are new States desired? We have plenty of those already? Are they to be held as conquered territories? This will require an army there: then, to be safe, we must have an army here; and, with a standing army, what security for our liberties?"

These are no fictitious reasonings. They are the suggestions, I doubt not, of thousands and tens of thousands of our hardy New England yeomanry, — men who when their country calls, at any wise and real exigency, will start from their native soils and throw their shields over their liberties, like the soldiers of Cadmus, "armed in complete steel;" yet men who have heard the winding of your horn to the Canada campaign with the same apathy and indifference with which they would hear in the streets the trilling of a jews-harp or the tinkling of a banjo.

The plain truth is, that the people of New England have no desire for Canada. Their moral sentiment does not justify, and they will not countenance, its invasion. I have thus stated the grounds on which they deem, and I have felt myself bound to maintain, that this contemplated invasion of that territory is, as it respects the Canadians, wanton and cruel; because it inflicts the greatest imaginable evils on them without any imaginable benefit to us; that, as it respects the

United States, such an invasion is senseless, because ultimately ruinous to our own political safety; and wicked, because it is an abuse of the blessings of Divine Providence, and a manifest perversion of his multiplied bounties to the purpose of desolating an innocent and unoffending people.

I shall now proceed to the next view I proposed to take of this project of invading Canada, and consider it in the light of a means to obtain an early and honorable peace. It is said, and this is the whole argument in favor of this invasion in this aspect, that the only way to negotiate successfully with Great Britain is to appeal to her fears, and raise her terrors for the fate of her colonies. I shall here say nothing concerning the difficulties of executing this scheme, nor about the possibility of a deficiency both in men and money. I will not dwell on the disgust of all New England, nor on the influence of this disgust with respect to your efforts. I will admit for the present that an army may be raised, and that during the first years it may be supported by loans, and that afterwards it will support itself by bayonets. I will admit farther, for the sake of argument, that success is possible, and that Great Britain realizes the practicability of it. Now, all this being admitted, I maintain that the surest of all possible ways to defeat any hope from negotiation is the threat of such an invasion, and an active preparation to execute it. Those must be very young politicians — their pin-feathers not yet grown, and, however they may flutter on this floor, they are not yet fledged for any high or distant flight — who think that threats and appealing to fear are the ways of producing a disposition to negotiate in Great Britain, or in any other nation which understands what it owes to its own safety and honor. No nation can yield to threat what it might yield to a sense of interest; because, in that case, it has no credit for what it grants, and, what is more, loses something in point of reputation from the imbecility which concessions made under such circumstances indicate. Of all nations in the world, Great Britain is the last to yield to considerations of fear and terror. The whole history of the British nation is one tissue of facts tending to show the spirit with which she meets all attempts to bully and browbeat her into measures inconsistent with her interests or her policy. No nation ever before made such sacrifices of the present to the future. No nation ever built her greatness more systematically on the principle of a haughty self-respect, which yields nothing to suggestions of danger, and which never permits either her ability or inclination to maintain her rights to be suspected. In all negotiations, therefore, with that power, it may be taken as a certain truth that your chance of failure is just in proportion to the publicity and obtrusiveness of threats and appeals to fear.

The American cabinet understand all this very well, although this House may not. Their policy is founded upon it. The project of this bill is to put at a still further distance the chance of amicable arrangement, in consequence of the dispositions which the threat of invasion of their colonies and attempt to execute it will excite in the British nation and ministry. I have some claim to speak concerning the policy of the men who constitute the American cabinet. For eight years I have studied their history, characters, and interests. I know no reasons why I should judge them severely, except such as arise from those inevitable conclusions which avowed principles and distinct conduct have impressed upon the mind. I say then, sir, without hesitation, that in my judgment the embarrassment of our relations with Great Britain, and keeping alive between this country and that a root of bitterness, has been, is, and will continue to be, a main principle of the policy of this American cabinet. They want not a solid settlement of our differences. If the nation will support them in it, they will persevere in the present war. If it will not, some general arrangements will be the resort, which will leave open opportunities for discord, which, on proper occasions, will be improved by them. I shall give my reasons for this opinion. I wish no sentiments of mine to have influence any farther than the reasons upon which they are founded justify. They are public reasons, arising from undeniable facts: the nation will judge for itself.

The men who now, and who for these twelve years past have, to the misfortune of this country, guided its councils and directed its destinies, came into power on a tide which was raised and supported by elements constituted of British prejudices and British antipathies. The parties which grew up in this nation took their origin and form at the time of the adoption of the treaty negotiated by Mr. Jay in 1794. The opposition of that day, of which the men now in power were the leaders, availed themselves very dexterously of the relics of that hatred towards the British name which remained after the revolutionary war. By perpetually blowing upon the embers of the ancient passions they excited a flame in the nation; and, by systematically directing it against the honorable men who at that time conducted its affairs, the strength and influence of those men were impaired. The embarrassments with France, which succeeded in 1798 and 1799, were turned to the same account. Unfortunately those who then conducted public affairs attended less to the appearances of things than to their natures, and considered more what was due to their country than was prudent in the state of the prejudices and jealousies of the people, thus artfully excited against them. They went on in the course they deemed right, regardless of personal consequences, and blind to the evidences of discontent which surrounded them. The consequences are well known. The supreme power in these United States passed into the hands which now possess it, in which it has been continued down to the present time. This transfer of power was effected undeniably principally on the very ground of these prejudices and antipathies which existed in the nation against Great Britain, and which had been artfully fomented by the men now in power and their adherents, and directed against their predecessors. These prejudices and passions constitute the main pillar of the power of these men. In my opinion they never will permit it to be wholly taken away from them. They never will permit the people of this country to look at them and their political opponents free of that jaundice with which they have carefully imbued the vision of their own partisans. They never will consent to be weighed in a balance of mere merits, but will always take care to keep in reserve some portion of these British antipathies to throw as a make-weight into the opposite scale whenever they find their own sinking. To continue, multiply, strengthen, and extend these props of their power has been and still is the object of the daily study and the nightly vigils of our American cabinet. For this the British treaty was permitted to expire by its own limitation ; notwithstanding the state of things which the treaty of Amiens had produced in Europe was so little like permanent peace that the occurrence of the fact on which the force of that limitation depended might easily have been questioned with but little violence to the terms and in perfect conformity with its spirit; for this a renewal of the treaty of 1794 was refused by our cabinet, although proffered by the British government; for this the treaty of 1807, negotiated by Messrs. Monroe and Pinkney, was rejected; for this, in 1811, fifty thousand dollars were paid out of the public Treasury to John Henry for the obvious purpose of enabling the American cabinet to calumniate their political opponents on this very point of British influence upon the eve of elections occurring in Massachusetts, on the event of which the perpetuation of their own power was materially dependent. Mr. Speaker, such men as these never will permit a state of things to pass away so essential to their influence. Be it peace or war, arrangement or hostility, the association of these British antipathies in the minds of the mass of the community with the characters of their political opponents constitutes the great magazine of their power. This composes their whole political larder. It is, like Lord Peter's brown loaf, their " beef, mutton, veal, venison, partridge, plum-pudding, and custard."

From the time of the expiration of the British treaty of 1794, and the refusal to renew it, the American cabinet have been careful to precede negotiation with some circumstance or other calculated to make it fail, or at least to make a successful result less certain. Thus, in 1806, when, from the plunder of our commerce by British cruisers, a negotiation, notwithstanding the obvious reluctance of the cabinet, was forced upon them by the clamors of the merchants, the non-importation law of April in that year was obtruded between the two countries. In the course of the debate upon that law, it was opposed upon this very ground, that it was an obstacle to a successful negotiation. It was advocated, like the bill now under discussion, as an aid to successful negotiation. It was also said, by the opponents of that law of 1806, that Great Britain would not negotiate under its operation, and that arrangement, attempted under proper auspices, could not be difficult, from the known interests and inclinations of that nation. What was the consequence? Precisely that which was anticipated. The then President of the United States was necessitated to come to this House and recommend a suspension of the operation of that law, upon the openly avowed ground of its being expedient to give that evidence of a conciliatory disposition, really because, if permitted to continue in operation, negotiation was found to be impracticable. After the suspension of that law a treaty was formed. The merits of that treaty it is not within the scope of my present argument to discuss. It is sufficient to say it was deemed good enough to receive the sanction of Messrs. Monroe and Pinkney. It arrived in America, and was rejected by

the authority of a single individual,[1] apparently because
of the insufficiency of the arrangement about impressment, really because a settlement with Great Britain at
that time did not " enter into the scope of the policy "
of the American cabinet.   The negotiation was, indeed,
renewed ; but it was followed up with the enforcement
of the non-importation law and the enactment of the
embargo ; both which steps were stated at the time, as
they proved afterwards, to be of a nature to make hopeless successful negotiation.

In this state, the executive power of this nation formally passed into new hands, but substantially remained
under the old principles of action and subject to the
former influences.   It was desirable that a fund of popularity should be acquired for the new administration.
Accordingly an arrangement was made with Mr. Erskine,
and no questions asked concerning the adequacy of his
powers.   But, lest this circumstance should not defeat
the proposed arrangement, a clause was inserted in the
correspondence, containing an insult to the British government, offered in the face of the world, such as no
man ever gave to a private individual whom he did not
mean to offend.   The President of the United States
said in so many words to the person at the head of
that government that he did not understand what belonged to his own honor as well as it was understood
by the President himself.   The effect of such language
was natural ; it was necessary ; it could not but render the
British government averse to sanction Erskine's arrangement.   The effect was anticipated by Mr. Robert Smith,

---

[1] President Jefferson, who rejected the treaty, without submitting it to
the Senate, as he was constitutionally bound to do, or even consulting his
own cabinet.

then acting as Secretary of State. He objected to its
being inserted; but it was done in the President's own
handwriting. As Mr. Erskine's authority was denied
by the British government, it is well known that in fact
on the point of this indignity the fate of that arrangement
turned. Can, any one doubt that our cabinet meant
that it should have this effect? I send you word, Mr.
Speaker, " that I have agreed with your messenger, and
wish you to ratify it. I think you, however, no gentleman notwithstanding, and that you do not understand
as well as I what is due to your own honor." What
think you, sir? Would you ratify such an arrangement
if you could help it? Does a proffer of settlement, connected with such language, look like a disposition or an
intention to conciliate? I appeal to the common-sense
of mankind on the point.

The whole state of the relations induced between this
country and Great Britain, in consequence of our embargo and restrictive systems, was in fact a standing
appeal to the fears of the British Cabinet; for, notwithstanding those systems were equal in their terms so far
as they affected foreign powers, yet their operation was
notoriously almost wholly upon Great Britain. To yield
to that pressure, or do any thing which should foster in
this country the idea that it was an effectual weapon of
hostility, was nothing more than conceding that she was
dependent upon us, — a concession which when once
made by her was certain to encourage a resort to it by
us on every occasion of difficulty between the two nations. Reasoning, therefore, upon the known nature of
things, and the plain interests of Great Britain, it was
foretold that during its continuance she would concede

25

nothing, and the event has justified those predictions. But the circumstance the most striking, and that furnishing the most conclusive evidence of the indisposition of the American cabinet to peace and their determination to carry on the war, is that connected with the pretended repeal of the French decrees, in November, 1810, and the consequent revival, in 1811, of our restrictive system against Great Britain.

If ever a body of men were pledged to any thing, the American cabinet, its friends and supporters, were pledged for the truth of this fact, that the French decrees of Berlin and Milan were definitively repealed, as it respects the United States, on the 1st of November, 1810. If ever any body of men staked their whole stock of reputation upon any point, our cabinet did it on this. They and their partisans asserted and raved. They denounced every man as a British partisan who denied it. They declared the restrictive system was revived by the mere effect of the proclamation. But, lest the courts of law should not be as subservient to their policy as might be wished, they passed the law of the 2d March, 1811, upon the basis of this repeal, and of its being definitive. The British government refused, however, to recognize the validity of this repeal, and denied that the Berlin and Milan decrees were repealed on the 1st November, 1810, as our cabinet asserted. Thus, then, stood the argument between the British ministry and our cabinet. The British ministry admitted that, if the Berlin and Milan decrees were repealed on the 1st November, 1810, they were bound to revoke their Orders in Council. But they denied that repeal to exist. Our cabinet, on the other hand, admitted that, if the Berlin and Milan decrees were not repealed on the 1st November, 1810, the restrictive system ought not to have been revived against Great Britain. But they asserted that repeal to exist. This was virtually the state of the question between the two countries on this point. And it is agreed, on all hands, that this refusal of the British government to repeal their Orders in Council, after the existence of the repeal of the Berlin and Milan decrees, as asserted by the American cabinet, was the cause of the declaration of war between the two countries. So that, in truth, the question of the right of war depended upon the existence of that fact; for if that fact did not exist, even the American cabinet did not pretend that, in the position in which things then stood, they had a right to declare war on account of the continuance of the British Orders in Council.

Now, what is the truth, in relation to this all-important fact, the definitive repeal of the Berlin and Milan decrees on the 1st November, 1810, — the pivot upon which turned the revival of the restrictive system and our declaration of war? Why, sir, the event has proved that, in relation to that fact, the American cabinet was, to say the least, in an error. Bonaparte himself, in a decree dated the 28th of April, 1811, but not promulgated till a year afterwards, distinctly declares that the Berlin and Milan decrees were not definitively repealed, as relates to the United States, on the 1st November, 1810. He also declares that they are then, on that 28th of April, for the first time repealed. And he founds the issuing of this decree on the act of the American Congress of the 2d of March, 1811, — that

very act which was passed upon the ground of the
definitive repeal of the Berlin and Milan decrees on the
1st November, 1810; and which, it is agreed on all
sides, the American government were bound in honor
not to pass, except in case of such antecedent repeal!!

Were ever a body of men so abandoned in the hour
of need as the American cabinet, in this instance, by
Bonaparte? Was ever any body of men so cruelly
wounded in the house of their friend? This — this
was "the unkindest cut of all." But how was it received by the American cabinet? Surely, they were
indignant at this treatment. Surely, the air rings with
reproaches upon a man who has thus made them stake
their reputation upon a falsehood, and then gives little
less than the lie direct to their assertions. No, sir,
nothing of all this is heard from our cabinet. There is
a philosophic tameness that would be remarkable if it
were not in all cases affecting Bonaparte characteristic.
All the executive of the United States has found it in
his heart to say in relation to this last decree of Bonaparte, which contradicts his previous allegations and
asseverations, is that "this proceeding is rendered,
by the time and manner of it, liable to many objections"!!!

I have referred to this subject as being, connected
with future conduct, strikingly illustrative of the disposition of the American cabinet to carry on the war, and
of their intention, if possible, not to make peace.
Surely, if any nation had a claim for liberal treatment
from another, it was the British nation from the American, after the discovery of the error of the American
government in relation to the repeal of the Berlin and

Milan decrees in November, 1810. In consequence of that error, the American cabinet had ruined numbers of our own citizens who had been caught by the revival of the non-intercourse law : they had revived that law against Great Britain under circumstances which now appeared to have been fallacious ; and they had declared war against her on the supposition that she had refused to repeal her Orders in Council, after the French decrees were in fact revoked ; whereas, it now appears that they were in fact not revoked. Surely the knowledge of this error was followed by an instant and anxious desire to redress the resulting injury. As the British Orders in Council were in fact revoked, on the knowledge of the existence of the French decree of repeal, surely the American cabinet at once extended the hand of friendship, met the British government half way, stopped all further irritation, and strove to place every thing on a basis best suited to promote an amicable adjustment. No, sir, nothing of all this occurred. On the contrary, the question of impressments is made the basis of continuing the war. On this subject, a studied fairness of proposition is preserved, accompanied with systematic perseverance in measures of hostility. An armistice was proposed by them. It was refused by us. It was acceded to by the American general on the frontiers. It was rejected by the cabinet. No consideration of the false allegation on which the war in fact was founded, no consideration of the critical and extremely essential nature to both nations of the subject of impressment, no considerations of humanity, interposed their influence. They renewed hostilities. They rushed upon Canada. Nothing would satisfy them

but blood.   The language of their conduct is that of the
giant, in the legends of infancy, —

Fee, Faw, Fum,
I smell the blood of an Englishman,
Dead or alive, I will have some.

Can such men pretend that peace is their object?
Whatever may result, the perfect conviction of my mind
is that they have no such intention, and that, if it come,
it is contrary both to their hope and expectation.

I would not judge these men severely.   But it is my
duty to endeavor to judge them truly, and to express
fearlessly the result of that judgment, whatever it may
be.   My opinion results from the application of the well-
known principle of judging concerning men's purposes
and motives, — to consider rather what men do than what
they say ; and to examine their deeds in connection with
predominating passions and interests, and on this basis
decide.   In making an estimate of the intentions of
these or any other politicians, I make little or no account of pacific pretensions.   There is a general reluctance at war and desire of peace which pervades the
great mass of every people ; and artful rulers could
never keep any nation at war, any length of time
beyond their true interests, without some sacrifice to
that general love of peace which exists in civilized men.
Bonaparte himself will tell you that he is the most pacific creature in the world.   He has already declared, by
his proclamation to Frenchmen, that he has gone to
Moscow for no other end than to cultivate peace and
counteract the Emperor of Russia's desire of war.   In
this country, where the popular sentiment has so strong

an impulse on its affairs, the same obtrusive pretension
must inevitably be preserved. No man, or set of men,
ever can or will get this country at war, or continue it
long in war, without keeping on hand a stout, round
stock of gulling matter. Fair propositions will always .
be made to go hand in hand with offensive acts. And
when something is offered so reasonable that no man
can doubt but it will be accepted, at the same moment
something will be done of a nature to embarrass the
project, and if not to defeat at least to render its acceptance dubious. How this has been in past time I have
shown. I will now illustrate what is doing and intended
at present.

As, from the uniform tenor of the conduct of the
American cabinet in relation to the British government,
I have no belief that their intention has been to make a
solid arrangement with that nation, so, from the evidence of their disposition and intention existing abroad
and on the table, I have no belief that such is at present
their purpose. I cannot possibly think otherwise than
that such is not their intention. Let us take the case
into common life. I have demands, Mr. Speaker,
against you, very just in their nature, but different.
Some of recent, others of very old, date. The former
depending upon principles very clearly in my favor;
the latter critical, difficult, and dubious, both in principle and settlement. In this state of things, and during your absence, I watch my opportunity, declare
enmity; throw myself upon your children and servants
and property which happen to be in my neighborhood,
and do them all the injury I can. While I am doing
this, I receive a messenger from you, stating that the

grounds of the recent injury are settled, that you comply fully with my terms.   Your servants and children,
whom I am plundering and killing, invite me to stay
my hand until you return, or until some accommodation
can take place between us.   But, deaf to any such
suggestions, I prosecute my intention of injury to the
utmost.   When there is reason to expect your return, I
multiply my means of injury and offence.   And no
sooner do I hear of your arrival than I thrust my fist
into your face, and say to you, " Well, sir, here are fair
propositions of settlement.   Come to my terms, which
are very just.   Settle the old demand in my way, and
we will be as good friends as ever."   Mr. Speaker, what
would be your conduct on such an occasion ?   Would
you be apt to look as much at the nature of the propositions as at the temper of the assailant ?   If you did not
at once return blow for blow and injury for injury, would
you not at least take a little time to consider ?   Would
you not tell such an assailant that you were not to be
bullied nor beaten into any concession ?   If you settled
at all, might you not consider it your duty in some way
to make him feel the consequences of his strange intemperance of passion ?   For myself, I have no question how
a man of spirit ought to act under such circumstances.
I have as little, how a great nation, like Great Britain,
will act.   Now, I have no doubt, sir, that the American
cabinet view this subject in the same light.   They understand well that — by the declaration of war, the
invasion of Canada, the refusal of an armistice, and perseverance in hostilities, after the principal ground of
war had been removed — they have wrought the minds
of the British cabinet and people to a very high state of

irritation. Now is the very moment to get up some grand scheme of pacification, such as may persuade the American people of the inveterate love of our cabinet for peace, and make them acquiescent in their perseverance in hostilities. Accordingly, before the end of the session, a great tub will be thrown out to the whale. Probably, a little while before the spring elections, terms of very fair import will be proffered to Great Britain: such as, perhaps, six months ago, our cabinet would not have granted, had she solicited them on her knees; such as, probably, in the opinion of the people of this country, Great Britain ought to accept; such, perhaps, as, in any other state of things, she would have accepted: but such, as I fear, under the irritation produced by the strange course pursued by the American cabinet, that nation will not accept. Sir, I do not believe that our cabinet expect that they will be accepted. They think the present state of induced passion is sufficient to prevent arrangement. But, to make assurance doubly sure, to take a bond of fate that arrangement shall not happen, they prepare this bill, — a bill which proposes an augmentation of the army for the express purpose of conquering the Canadas, — a bill which — connected with the recent disposition evinced by our cabinet in relation to those provinces, and with the avowed intent of making their subjugation the means of peace through the fear to be inspired into Great Britain — is as offensive to the pride of that nation as can well be imagined; and is, in my apprehension, as sure a guarantee of continued war as could be given. On these grounds, my mind cannot force itself to any other conclusion than this, that the avowed object of this bill is the true one;

that the Canadas are to be invaded the next season ; that the war is to be protracted; and that this is the real policy of the American cabinet.

I will now reply to those invitations to "union" which have been so obtrusively urged upon us. If by this call to union is meant an union in a project for the invasion of Canada, or for the invasion of East Florida, or for the conquest of any foreign country whatever, either as a means of carrying on this war or for any other purpose, I answer distinctly, I will unite with no man, nor any body of men, for any such purposes. I think such projects criminal in the highest degree and ruinous to the prosperity of these States. But if by this invitation is meant union in preparation for defence, strictly so called; union in fortifying our sea-board; union in putting our cities into a state of safety ; union in raising such a military force as shall be sufficient, with the local militia in the hands of the constitutional leaders, the executives of the States, to give a rational degree of security against any invasion, sufficient to defend our frontiers, sufficient to awe into silence the Indian tribes within our territories; union in creating such a maritime force as shall command the seas on the American coasts, and keep open the intercourse at least between the States, — if this is meant I have no hesitation ; union on such principles you shall have from me cordially and faithfully ; and this, too, sir, without any reference to the state of my opinion in relation to the justice or the necessity of this war; because I well understand such to be the condition of man in a social compact that he must partake of the fate of the society to which he belongs, and must submit to the privations and sacrifices its defence requires, notwithstanding these may be the result of the vices or crimes of its immediate rulers. But there is a great difference between support- ing such rulers in plans of necessary self-defence, on which the safety of our altars and firesides essentially depends, and supporting them in projects of foreign invasion, and encouraging them in schemes of conquest and ambition which are not only unjust in themselves, but dreadful in their consequences; inasmuch as, let the particular project result as it may, the general effect must be, according to human view, destructive to our own domestic liberties and Constitution.   I speak as an individual, sir, for my single self; did I support such projects as are avowed to be the objects of this bill, I should deem myself a traitor to my country.   Were I even to aid them by loan or in any other way, I should consider myself a partaker in the guilt of the purpose. But when these projects of invasion shall be abandoned; when men yield up schemes, which not only openly con- template the raising of a great military force, but also the concentrating them at one point and placing them in one hand; schemes obviously ruinous to the fates of a free republic, as they comprehend the means by which such have ever heretofore been destroyed, — when, I say, such schemes shall be abandoned, and the wishes of the cabinet limited to mere defence, and frontier and mari- time protection, there will be no need of calls to union. For such objects there is not, there cannot be, but one heart and soul in this people.

I know, Mr. Speaker, that while I utter these things a thousand tongues and a thousand pens are preparing without doors to overwhelm me, if possible, by their pestiferous gall. Already I hear in the air the sound of "traitor," "British agent," "British gold," and all those changes of vulgar calumny by which the imaginations of the mass of men are affected, and by which they are prevented from listening to what is true and receiving what is reasonable.

Mr. Speaker, it well becomes any man standing in the presence of such a nation as this to speak of himself seldom ; and such a man as I am it becomes to speak of himself not at all, except, indeed, when the relations in which he stands to his country are little known, and when the assertion of those relations has some connection and may have some influence on interests which it is peculiarly incumbent upon him to support.

Under this sanction, I say, it is not for a man whose ancestors have been planted in this country now for almost two centuries ; it is not for a man who has a family, and friends, and character, and children, and a deep stake in the soil ; it is not for a man who is self-conscious of being rooted in that soil, as deeply and as exclusively as the oak which shoots among its rocks : it is not for such a man to hesitate or swerve a hair's breadth from his country's purpose and true interests, because of the yelpings, the howlings, and snarlings of that hungry pack which corrupt men keep directly or indirectly in pay, with the view of hunting down every man who dare develop their purposes, — a pack composed, it is true, of some native curs, but for the most part of hounds and spaniels of very recent importation, whose backs are seared by the lash, and whose necks are sore with the collars of their former masters. In fulfilling his duty, the lover of his country must often be obliged to breast the shock of calumny. If called to that service, he will meet the exigency with the same firmness as, should another occasion call, he would breast the shock of battle. No, sir, I am not to be deterred by such apprehensions. May heaven so deal with me and mine, as I am true or faithless to the best interests of this people! May it deal with me according to its just judgments when I fail to bring men and measures to the bar of public opinion, and to expose projects and systems of policy which I know to be ruinous to the peace, prosperity, and liberties of my country!

This leads me naturally to the third and last point of view at which I proposed to consider this bill, — as a means for the advancement of the objects of the personal or local ambition of the members of the American cabinet. With respect to the members of that cabinet, I may almost literally say I know nothing of them except as public men. Against them I have no personal animosity. I know little of them in private life, and that little never made me ambitious to know more. I look at them as public men, wielding powers and putting in operation means and instruments materially affecting the interests and prospects of the United States.

It is a curious fact, but no less true than curious, that for these twelve years past the whole affairs of this country have been managed, and its fortunes reversed, under the influence of a cabinet little less than despotic, composed, to all efficient purposes, of two Virginians and a foreigner. When I speak of these men as Virginians, I mean to cast no odium upon that State, as

though it were not entitled to its full share of influence
in the national councils ; nor, when I referred to one of
them as being a foreigner, do I intend thereby to suggest any connections of a nature unworthy or suspicious.
I refer to these circumstances as general and undoubted
facts which belong to the characters of the cabinet, and
which cannot fail to be taken into view in all estimates
of plans and projects, so long as man is constituted as
he is, and so long as the prejudices and principles of
childhood never fail to influence in different degrees in
even the best men the course of thinking and action of
their riper years.

I might have said, perhaps, with more strict propriety, that it was a cabinet composed of three Virginians and a foreigner,[1] because once in the course of the
twelve years there has been a change of one of the
characters. But, sir, that change was notoriously matter of form rather than substance. As it respects the
cabinet, the principles continued the same ; the interests
the same ; the objects at which it aimed the same.

I said that this cabinet had been, during these twelve
years, little less than despotic. This fact also is notorious. During this whole period the measures distinctly
recommended have been adopted by the two Houses of
Congress with as much uniformity and with as little
modification, too, as the measures of the British ministry
have been adopted during the same period by the British
Parliament. The connection between cabinet councils
and parliamentary acts is just as intimate in the one
country as in the other.

---

[1] Mr. Jefferson, Mr. Madison, Mr. Monroe, and Mr. Gallatin.

I said that these three men constituted, to all efficient purposes, the whole cabinet. This also is notorious. It is true that during this period other individuals have been called into the cabinet. But they were all of them comparatively minor men, such as had no great weight either of personal talents or of personal influence to support them. They were kept as instruments of the master spirits; and when they failed to answer the purpose, or became restive, they were sacrificed or provided for. The shades were made to play upon the curtain; they entered; they bowed to the audience; they did what they were bidden; they said what was set down for them. When those who pulled the wires saw fit, they passed away. No man knew why they entered; no man knew why they departed; no man could tell whence they came; no man asked whither they were gone.

From this uniform composition of the cabinet it is obvious that the project of the master spirits was that of essential influence within the cabinet; for in such a country as ours, so extended, and its interests so complicated, it is impossible but those who would conduct its affairs wisely and with a single eye to the public good should strive to call around themselves the highest and most independent talents in the nation, at least of their own political friends. When this is not the case, it must be apparent that the leading influences want not associates but instruments. The same principle applies to the distribution of office out of the cabinet as to filling places within it. Some mistakes may be expected to happen in selections among candidates for appointments at a distance; but if at any time a cabinet shall be systematically guided in such selection by a regard, not to merit or qualifications, but to electioneering services; if the obvious design be to reward partisans, and encourage defection to its party standard, then the people may rest assured that the project such cabinet has in view is not to serve the public interest, but to secure their personal influence, and that they want not competency for the employment but subserviency in it. How this matter is I shall not assert, not because I have not very distinct opinions upon the subject, but because the sphere of appointment is too extensive to be comprehended in the grasp of a single individual; and I mean to make no assertion concerning motive or conduct of which there does not exist in my mind evidence as well complete as conclusive. I refer to this subject, therefore, only as a collateral and corroborative proof of the purposes of the cabinet. Every man can decide for himself in his own circle or neighborhood concerning the apparent principle upon which the cabinet have proceeded in making appointments, remembering always that the section of country against whose prosperity the policy of the cabinet is most systematically levelled will be that in which subserviency to all its purposes will be most studiously inculcated among its adherents. It will be in that quarter that the flames of party animosity will be enkindled with the most sedulous assiduity, as the means of making men forgetful of their true interests, and obedient to their employers, in spite of their natural prejudices and inclinations.

It is natural to inquire what are the projects connected with the cabinet thus composed, and to what ends it is advancing. To answer this question it is necessary to look into the nature and relations of things. Here the true criterions of judgment are to be found. Professions are always plausible. Why, sir, Bonaparte himself is the very milk of human kindness; he is the greatest lover of his species in the world; he would not hurt a sparrow if you take his own account of the matter. What, then, do nature and the relations of things teach? They teach this, that the great hazard in a government where the chief magistracy is elective is from the local ambition of States and the personal ambition of individuals. It is no reflection upon any State to say that it is ambitious. According to their opportunities and temptations all States are ambitious. This quality is as much predicable of States as of individuals. Indeed, State ambition has its root in the same passions of human nature, and derives its strength from the same nutriment as personal ambition. All history shows that such passions always exist among States combined in confederacies. To deny it is to deceive ourselves. It has existed, it does exist, and always must exist. In our political relations, as in our personal, we then walk most safely when we walk with reference to the actual existence of things, admit the weaknesses, and do not hide from ourselves the dangers, to which our nature is exposed. Whatever is true let us confess. Nations, as well as individuals, are only safe in proportion as they attain self-knowledge, and regulate their conduct by it.

What fact upon this point does our own experience present? It presents this striking one, — that, taking the years for which the presidential chair is already filled into the account, out of twenty-eight years since

our Constitution was established, the single State of
Virginia has furnished the President for twenty-four
years. And, farther, it is now as distinctly known and
familiarly talked about in this city and vicinity who is
the destined successor of the present President after the
expiration of his ensuing term, and known that he, too,
is to be a Virginian, as it was known and familiarly
talked about during the presidency of Mr. Jefferson,
that the present President was to be his successor.
And the former was, and the latter is, a subject of as
much notoriety, and, to human appearance, of as much
certainty too, as who will be the successor to the British crown is a matter of notoriety in that country. To
secure this succession and keep it in the destined line
has been, is, and will continue to be, the main object of
the policy of these men. This is the point on which
the projects of the cabinet for the three years past have
been brought to bear, that James the First should be
made to continue four years longer. And this is the
point on which the projects of the cabinet will be
brought to bear for the three years to come, that James
the Second shall be made to succeed, according to the
fundamental rescripts of the Monticellian dynasty.

[Mr. Quincy was here again called to order. The
Speaker said that really the gentleman laid his premises
so remote from his conclusions that he could not see
how his observations applied to the bill.]

Mr. Quincy proceeded: On the contrary, sir, I maintain that both my premises and conclusions are very
proximate to each other, and intimately connected with
the bill on the table, and with the welfare of this people.

Is it not within the scope of just debate to show that the general policy of the cabinet, and that also this particular project, have for their object the aggrandizement of the cabinet themselves, or some member of it? If this be the object of the bill, is it not proper to be exhibited? The topic may be of a nature high and critical, but no man can deny that it is both important and relevant. To secure the power they at present possess, to perpetuate it in their own hands, and to transfer it to their selected favorites, is the great project of the policy of the members of our cabinet. It would be easy to trace to this master passion the declaration of war at the time and under the circumstances in which it occurred. Antecedent to the declaration of war, it was distinctly stated by individuals from that quarter of the country under the influences of which this war was adopted, that the support of the present President of the United States, by their quarter of the country, depended upon the fact of the cabinet's coming up to the point of war with Great Britain. This state of things, and the knowledge of it by the members of the cabinet, was repeatedly urged in conversation by members of this and the other branch of the legislature to shake the incredulity in a declaration of war which at that time existed in some of our minds. Without placing any reliance on the reports of that day, this I assert, unequivocally and without fear of contradiction, that such were the passions which existed in the Southern and Western States, and such the avowed determination to war, that, had not the cabinet come up to that point, its influence in those quarters was at an end. Without their support, the re-election of the present Chief Magistrate was hopeless.   Now, sir, when continuance of power is put into the scale, as in this instance it was unquestionably, it is not for human nature to deny that it had not a material influence in determining the balance.   For myself, I have never had but one opinion on this matter, — I have never doubted that we should not have had war declared at the last session if the presidential election had not been depending.

Just so with respect to the invasion of Canada.   It was, in my judgment, a test required by the state of opinion in the Southern and Western States of the sincerity of the cabinet, and of its heartiness in the prosecution of this war.   This accounts for the strange and headlong haste, and the want of sufficient prepara- tion, with which the invasion was expedited.   This accounts for the neglect to meet the proposition for an armistice when made by the Governor of Canada, after a knowledge of the revocation of the Orders in Council. This accounts for the obtrusive attempts to gain a foot- ing in Canada, and the obstinate perseverance in the show of invasion until the members of the electoral colleges had been definitively selected.   Since which event our armies have been quiet enough.   When I see a direct dependence between the perpetuation of power in any hand, and the adoption of, and the perseverance in, any particular course of measures, I cannot refrain from believing that such a course has been suggested and regulated by so obvious and weighty an interest.   This subject is capable of much greater elucidation.   But according to your suggestion, sir, I shall confine myself to trace the connection of this master passion of the cabinet with the bill now under consideration.

The projects of the cabinet for the present year are loans, to the amount, at least, of twenty millions; an army of fifty-five thousand men; a grand scheme of pacification, founded on some legislative acts or resolves; and a perpetuation of the war. The loans are expected to be filled partly from the popularity derived in the commercial cities by the vote for building seventy-fours, partly by opening offices for receiving subscriptions in the interior. Whatever is received will be diverted to the army service. The grand scheme of pacification will be made to appear very fair in terms; but in the state of irritation which has been produced in Great Britain by the continuance of the war after the repeal of the Orders in Council, and by the pertinacious perseverance in the threats and preparation to invade Canada, it will, it is expected, be rejected by her. This, it is supposed, will give popularity to the war in this country. The forty dollars bounty will, it is hoped, fill the ranks. The army for the conquest of Canada will be raised: to be commanded by whom? this is the critical question. The answer is in every man's mouth. By a member of the American cabinet; by one of the three; by one of that " trio" who at this moment constitute in fact, and who efficiently have always constituted, the whole cabinet. And the man who is thus ntended for the command of the greatest army this new world ever contained, an army nearly twice as great as was at any time the regular army of our Revolution, I say the man who is intended for this great trust is the individual who is notoriously the selected candidate for the next presidency !

Mr. Speaker, when I assert that the present Secretary

of State, who is now the acting Secretary of War, is destined, by a cabinet of which he himself constitutes one-third, for the command of this army, I know that I assert intentions to exist which have not yet developed themselves by an official avowal. The truth is, the moment for an official avowal has not yet come. The cabinet must work along by degrees, and only show their cards as they play them. The army must first be authorized. The bill for the new majors-general must be passed. Then, upon their plan, it will be found necessary to constitute a lieutenant-general. "And who so proper," the cabinet will exclaim, "as one of ourselves?" "And who so proper as one of the cabinet?" all its retainers will respond, from one end of the continent to the other. I would willingly have postponed any animadversion upon this intention of the cabinet until it should have been avowed. But then it would have been too late. Then the fifty-five thousand men would have been authorized, and the necessity for a lieutenant-general inevitable. Sir, I know very well that this public animadversion may possibly stagger the cabinet in its purpose. They may not like to proceed in the design after the public eye has been directed distinctly upon it. And the existence of it will be denied, and its partisans will assert that this suggestion was mere surmise. Be it so. It is, comparatively, of little importance what happens to my person or character, provided this great evil can be averted from my country. I consider the raising such an army as this, and the putting it under the command of that individual, taking into view his connection with the present cabinet, so ominous to the liberties of this country that I am not anxious what happens to me, if, by any constitutional responsibility, I can prevent it.

However, to the end that it may not be thought I have made this assertion lightly, I will briefly state the evidence upon which it is founded, and which to my mind has given perfect conviction as to the intentions of the cabinet.

First. As long ago as last June, it was, to my knowledge, asserted by individuals connected with the administration, in this and the other branch of the legislature, that it was the intention of the American cabinet to place the Secretary of State at the head of the army.

Second. This intention was, early in the present session, distinctly avowed by members in this and the other branch of the legislature, to be the intention of the cabinet. And these members were persons intimate with the cabinet, and connected with them in politics ; and, of all men, the most likely to know their intentions. This can be proved, if denied. But it will not be. I do not believe there is a man on this floor who is not acquainted with the fact as well as myself.

Third. As soon as the session opened, the old Secretary at War was hunted down.

Fourth. The burden of the whole department of war is now transferred to the shoulders of the Secretary of State. This great and oppressive trust which, at the last session, it was seriously urged no single living wight could bear, but that it required three persons to support its pressure, is now cast solely upon this individual, who, it seems, is able to uphold the mighty mountain of that department in one hand, while he balances the department of state in the other.

Fifth. The Secretary of State has not merely entered into a still-life possession of the department of war. He is actively employed in arranging its details, and putting it into a state of preparation. This work of drudgery it can hardly be expected that any man would undertake, for the sake of an unknown successor, unless he had himself some prospect of interest in it.

Sixth. The Secretary of State is no sooner in possession of the department of war, than the plan of a great army, an efficient pecuniary bounty, and a brilliant campaign against Canada, is promulgated: of all which he is the known author; having communicated to the Committee on Military Affairs the whole project, not only in general, but in its details. Above all, that no doubt concerning the ultimate purpose may exist, —

Seventh. Immediately after the Secretary of State enters upon the duties of Secretary at War, he puts to Adjutant-General Cushing this question: "How many majors-general and brigadiers are necessary for an army of thirty-five thousand men?" Now, as this question was put by authority, and was intended to be communicated to Congress, and was in its nature very simple, one would have supposed that it would have been enough, in all conscience, to have given to it a direct answer. Besides, it is not always thought proper, for those who are in the under grades of departments, when one question is proposed, to enter into the discussion of another. However, notwithstanding these obvious suggestions, one-half of the whole reply of General Cushing is taken up in investigating, not the question which was asked, but the question on which the honest adjutant, in the simplicity of his soul, tells the Secretary, " You have not required my opinion." The whole of this part of the letter runs thus : —

" In this country we have never had a grade between the commander-in-chief and that of major-general; hence it was found necessary, in the ' continental army,' to give to the senior major-general the command of the right wing, and to the next in rank that of the left; which, from the limited number of general officers, often left a division to a brigadier, a brigade to a colonel, and a regiment to a subordinate field officer; but in Europe this difficulty is obviated by the appointment of general officers of higher grades.

" From the best information I have been able to obtain on this subject, I have no hesitation in saying that eight majors-general and sixteen brigadiers to command the divisions and brigades of an army of thirty-five thousand men is the lowest estimate which the uniform practice of France, Russia, and England, will warrant; and that this is much below the proportion of officers of these grades actually employed in the army of the Revolution.

" As you have not required my opinion, whether it be necessary to have a higher grade than that of major-general, I have not deemed it proper to touch this subject, and have confined myself to the number of majors-general and brigadiers deemed necessary to command the divisions and brigades of an army of thirty-five thousand men. It may not, however, be improper to remark that, if it is intended to have no higher grade than that of major-general, their number should be increased to eleven; so as to give one for the chief com-

27

mand, one for each wing, and one for each division of four thousand men."

It is entertaining to see how much trouble the worthy adjutant takes to impress upon the mind that the Secretary of State "had not required his opinion" on the subject of a grade higher than that of a major-general. He even goes so far as to say that he has "not deemed it proper to touch this subject."

Now, sir, I think he has touched the subject, and treated it pretty thoroughly too. For he has shown, not only that it is "difficult" to do without, but that it is more economical to have, a grade higher than a major-general. And this, too, in an army of only thirty-five thousand men. But when this bill passes, the army will consist of fifty-five thousand. The result is then inevitable: you must have, in such case, a grade higher than a major-general; in other words, a lieutenant-general. Such, it cannot be denied, is the intention of the cabinet. As little can it be denied that the Secretary of State, the acting Secretary of War, is the cabinet candidate for that office. So it has been distinctly avowed by the friends and confidants of that cabinet; and as such, I have no question, is known by every individual in this House.

Mr. Speaker, what an astonishing and alarming state of things is this! Three men, who efficiently have had the command of this nation for many years, have so managed its concerns as to reduce it, from an unexampled height of prosperity, to a state of great depression, — not to say ruin. They have annihilated its commerce, and involved it in war. And now the result of the whole matter is, that they are about to raise an

army of fifty-five thousand men, invest one of their own
body with this most solemn command, and he the man
who is the destined candidate for the President's chair!
What a grasp at power is this! What is there in history
equal to it? Can any man doubt what will be the result
of this project? No man can believe that the conquest
of Canada will be effected in one campaign. It cost the
British six years to acquire it when it was far weaker
than at present. It cannot be hoped that we can acquire it under three or four years. And what then
will be the situation of this army and our country?
Why then the army will be veteran; and the leader a
candidate for the presidency! And, whoever is a candidate for the presidency, with an army of thirty thousand veterans at his heels, will not be likely to be
troubled with rivals or to concern himself about votes.
A President elected under such auspices may be nomi-
nally a President for years; but really, if he pleases, a
President for life.

I know that all this will seem wild and fantastical to
very many, perhaps to all, who hear me. To my mind,
it is neither the one nor the other. History is full of
events less probable, and effected by armies far inferior
to that which is proposed to be raised. So far from
deeming it mere fancy, I consider it absolutely certain,
if this army be once raised, organized, and enter upon
a successful career of conquest. The result of such a
power as this, intrusted to a single individual, in the
present state of parties and passions in this country, no
man can anticipate. There is no other means of absolute safety but denying it altogether.

I cannot forget, Mr. Speaker, that the sphere in

which this great army is destined to operate is in the
neighborhood of that section of country where it is probable, in case the present destructive measures be continued in operation, the most unanimous opposition will
exist to a perpetuation of power in the present hands, or
to its transfer to its destined successor. I cannot forget
that it has been distinctly avowed by a member on this
floor, a gentleman from Virginia too (Mr. Clay), and
one very likely to know the view of the cabinet, that
" one object of this army was to put down opposition."

Sir, the greatness of this project and its consequences
overwhelm my mind. I know very well to what oblo-
quy I expose myself by this development. I know
that it is always an unpardonable sin to pull the veil
from the party deities of the day, and that it is of a
nature not to be forgiven either by them or their wor-
shippers. I have not willingly, nor without long reflection, taken upon myself this responsibility. But it has
been forced upon me by an imperious sense of duty. If
the people of the Northern and Eastern States are destined to be hewers of wood and drawers of water to
men who know nothing about their interests, and care
nothing about them, I am clear of the great transgression. If, in common with their countrymen, my children
are destined to be slaves, and to yoke in with negroes,
chained to the car of a Southern master, they, at least,
shall have this sweet consciousness as the consolation of
their condition, — they shall be able to say, " Our father
was guiltless of these chains."

www.ingramcontent.com/pod-product-compliance
Lightning Source LLC
Chambersburg PA
CBHW032307280326
41932CB00009B/736